Aham Sphurana

A Glimpse of Self Realisation

Aham Sphurana

A Glimpse of Self Realisation

A Selection of Teachings from Bhagavan Sri Ramana Maharshi

OPEN SKY PRESS
www.openskypress.com

Bhagavan Sri Ramana Maharshi

30.12.1879 – 14.04.1950

There is a Destiny guiding the course of events. One need not fret about anything, imagining oneself to be personally responsible for It.

Aham Sphurana – A Glimpse of Self Realisation

A Selection of Teachings from Sri Bhagavan Ramana Maharshi

Published by Open Sky Press GbR
office@openskypress.com
www.openskypress.com

First Edition 2022
Second Edition 2024

ISBN: 978-1-9163211-7-5

Cover design by Om
Photographs from Bhagavan's Ashram Archives
All other photographs from Open Sky House archive

Printed in Poland

OPEN SKY PRESS
www.openskypress.com

Acknowledgements

Suddenly in October 2021 a friend sent me news of a huge manuscript, *Aham Sphurana,* a diary of Sri Ramana Maharshi's meetings and the day-to-day life of the Ashram in 1936.

When I shared the *Aham Sphurana* texts with my students and in particular the residents of Open Sky House, they gave me the needed response and encouragement to choose and edit around fifty texts.

Rajen in particular introduced me to texts written about the daily ashram life, and how Bhagavan used the different situations to show a practical teaching. Also, Indira pointed out the insights that different visitors painted of Bhagavan and the ashram. She was one of several proof readers.

I wish to thank the members of Open Sky Press (OSP) who have, over the years, published some thirty spiritual books and films, my own but also Papaji's own books and several Ramana Maharshi books, notably a superb Art Quality version of *Nan Yar (Who am I?)*. These were published in three Indian languages and four European languages.

As a small spiritual publisher, Open Sky Press has been supported financially by the residents of the Open Sky House Community for eighteen years. They donate their time, seeing it as their way to thank Existence for all the benedictions received whilst living in community. Now the whole Community wished to support the publication of *Aham Sphurana* and so we contacted those responsible for putting the manuscript out in the world.

At a moment of personal doubt, I met Swami Hamsananda of Athithi Ashram at Arunachala who talked with me about the material and convinced me to publish the whole manuscript in several volumes. He continued to act as a valuable adviser through the editing process.

As Bhagavan spoke Tamil and naturally used India's spiritual language, Sanskrit, we had great need of translation help. In January 2022 OSP had just published our Art Quality book *Nan Yar* in Tamil, Hindi and Telugu and S Nagarajan, a Tamil scholar, devotee of Bhagavan and a writer, gave hours of his time to help us translate Tamil and Sanskrit. He has generously continued his wonderful contribution to *Aham Sphurana.*

My ex-wife and friend, Sally, has diligently proofed all my edited texts and given invaluable help in the preparation of this book in so many different ways.

The whole OSP team has worked intensely together over six weeks in a retreat house in Sri Lanka. Over six months a team of ten people have freely given days of their time to bring Bhagavan's valuable teachings into the public realm.

Special mention to Om for his brilliant cover designs and his constant computer help to the whole team. He has formatted the book and readied it as an e-book and a print book for publishing.

I would also like to thank Pravin Anand from the Indian law firm Anand & Anand who is an expert in copyright issues and provided us top quality legal advice.

A big thank you to Blutkeim, Athreya and Nalini for all their devotion in being the midwives of this important manuscript. Athreya's mother, Nalini, typed up the whole manuscript some years ago before her passing. As she is so lovely, I decided to publish this photo of Nalini and allow that the rest of the family are also wonderful people. They requested the following acknowledgement:

This work is dedicated to Bhagavan Sri Ramana Maharshi, the peerless Master of Non-duality, who, for more than half a century, silently poured out his Grace on all sentient beings that came to him and who uninterruptedly shines forever as 'I'-'I' in the Heart-lotus of all, as the One Perfect Reality.

In conclusion I would like to thank the Ashram management for their tireless efforts to maintain the ashram as a service to the thousands of devotees who feel a deeper connection to Bhagavan while spending some time inside this hallowed place.

I would particularly like to thank the amazingly strong, divine, beautiful energy which has surrounded me, and in fact the whole team, in the last months. I have become so intimate with Bhagavan and the daily life around him that often I felt I was in the Ashram Hall basking in his light. So, to him a huge thank you for touching my life so deeply.

John David, Director, Open Sky Press, June 2022

Disclaimer

We discovered the manuscript known as *Aham Sphurana* in October 2021, through a friend who told us of the manuscript's availability on Amazon. News of the manuscript brought great excitement and it was immediately downloaded, only to discover that it was an unformatted continuous stream of text which was painstakingly difficult to read.

In the process of preparing this formatted and edited book *Aham Sphurana – A Glimpse of Self Realisation*, it has felt as if destiny has worked to make this treasure available to a wider public. We have felt surrounded by an energy which has brought us closer to Bhagavan, sometimes as if we were sitting in the Hall. We hope this will be the case for all readers of the book.

It soon became clear that *Aham Sphurana* is a controversial manuscript. Due to its old age, it has proven impossible to authenticate directly. We are in possession of a few original notebooks which purportedly formed part of the original manuscript. The Cologne Institute of Conservation Sciences investigated the paper and stated that the original notebook and the paper were likely to be from the 1930s (see p. 230). The antiquated English (some we modernised) is reminiscent of something that would have been written 100 years ago.

We have consulted Bhagavan experts about the authenticity of the manuscript. A majority of the experts agree that especially the teaching dialogues carry the unmistakable spiritual clarity typical of Bhagavan. These texts form the majority of this current book. Several find that at least some parts of the manuscript might not be trustworthy, or are exaggerated.

So, even if the question of authenticity remains unclear, we feel confident that this selection of teachings, *Aham Sphurana – A Glimpse of Self Realisation*, will bring tremendous value to those who are open to receiving Bhagavan's grace and guidance. We invite you to explore this book with an open mind, and to treat it as a great and surprising mystery.

Open Sky Press Team
Cologne, June 2022

Foreword

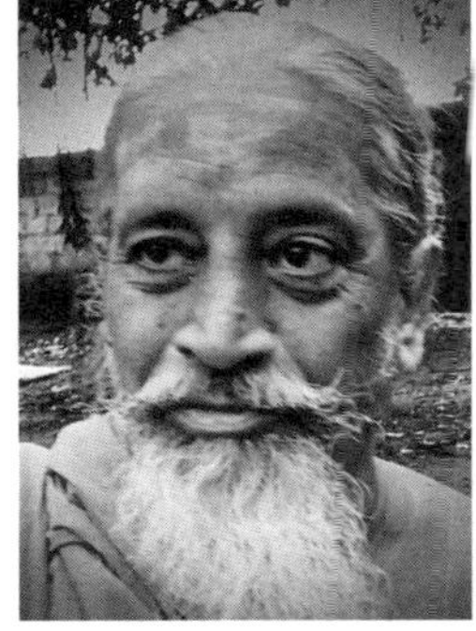

Swami Hamsananda is the Founder President of Athithi Ashram in Tiruvannamalai. The ashram provides care to the sadhus passing through in the form of daily free food and some accommodation. They specialise in providing medical care. In the Ashram's puja *room, there is a fabulous Statue of Bhagavan that came to Swami in a miraculous way.*

Swami himself is available for personal Satsangs *for sincere seekers. As a young man he lived with Annamalai Swami and later was a resident of Ramana Ashram where he cared for many elder devotees. An accomplished scholar, he was also part of the publication department.*

Sri Gajapathi Aiyyer, a young devotee of Bhagavan Sri Ramana Maharshi, stayed at Ramana Ashram from July to December 1936, and recorded the devotees' meetings with Bhagavan in the Hall and the day-to-day ashram life. This present volume, *Aham Sphurana – A Glimpse of Self Realisation* is a selection of teachings based on Gajapathi's 1936 diary.

In my opinion *Aham Sphurana – A Glimpse of Self Realisation* is a Treasure Trove of Wisdom to the Seekers of Truth in general, and particularly to the devotees of Bhagavan. It is based on the voluminous recordings of Sri Gajapathi Aiyyer who painstakingly recorded almost all interactions between his master and the ashram visitors.

The uniqueness of this book is very significant and deals in elaborate detail with the teachings of Bhagavan – importantly, in the words of Bhagavan Himself. It gives the necessary clarifications, removes the cobweb of the illusion of doubts, ignorance, and mistaken knowledge of the illusory mind and paves the way to Self realisation.

The book's title, *Aham Sphurana,* indicates a glimpse of Self-realisation. *Sphurana* was revealed to Bhagavan during his Death experience at the age of sixteen at Madurai. In his case, *Sphurana* had become continuous, and the ego sense died. The body became a tool in the hands of the Almighty and ecstasy filled the Soul.

Bhagavan says, **"Bhagavan did not decide, 'Let me go to Arunachala'. Rather, I came here, that is all" (p. 22).**

Bhagavan himself asserts that the *jnani's* mind is not operated by a *jnani* [the Self-realised sage], as he has no mind, but by the Divine. Similarly, we too surrender our mind to the Self and are acted by the Self and not by the thinking mind. Bhagavan says, **"The mind is actually owned by the Self, and we are the thieves who stole the mind and think it belongs to us and get identified with it, and thus illusion is created.**

Give back the stolen mind to its rightful owner by surrender and be governed by it. By this you would realise that 'you are not the doer' and everything is done by God."

I invite the attention of the readers to the account narrated by Sri GV Subbaramayya in his book, *Ramana Reminiscences* (p. 20-21). His daughter, Indira, became mortally ill and he sought urgent help from Bhagavan.

Later he asked, "Sri Bhagavan, did you not think that you must do something to save the child?" Straight came Bhagavan's reply, **"Even the thought to save the child is a *sankalpa* [will], and one who has any *sankalpa* is no *jnani*. In fact, such thinking is unnecessary. The moment the *jnani's* eye falls upon a thing, there starts a 'divine automatic action' which itself leads to the highest good."**

This selection of teachings will likely cause some debate as it presents previously unknown material about Bhagavan's life and teachings. Also, this book is derived from a 1936 manuscript, which, due to the time elapsed, is impossible to verify as fully authentic.

However, to me there is no doubt about the authenticity of the selections included here and, in fact, it touches the core teachings of Bhagavan like no other book. Let me guide you through some beautiful, unmistakable examples.

In the entry from 6th July 1936 – *Who am I?* – Bhagavan privately explained the practice of Self-enquiry to Major Chadwick and it is in itself proof enough for the authenticity of the book.

Bhagavan approved the summary of *Who am I?* prepared by Major Chadwick for memorising and repeating but insisted on actual practice. **"Asking 'Who am I?' should return the mind to its primordial nature of Naked Beingness. That is the purpose and the goal" (p. 45).**

Bhagavan clarifies that all our actions are born out of illusion due to our identification with the body, while truly all the actions are happening due to a Higher Power that is inherent in us. On 11th July 1936, in answer to Samuel Cohen asking questions about renunciation, Bhagavan says: **"Giving up worldly duties will lead to more complications than you might be able to presently imagine. You will be jumping from the frying pan, straight into the fire" (p. 60).**

Extensive comments on the topic of *Samadhi* can be found in the 13th July 1936 entry from *Major Chadwick's Notebook.* In a very detailed way, it sheds more light on the different states of *Samadhi.*

In particular Bhagavan warns of the dangers of *Kevala Nirvikalpa Samadhi:* **"Many pour souls when asked to remain without thinking go to this state because this is the only thought-free state they know. They think this is the goal of Self-enquiry – think this is liberation – but this is a dead end – worst thing that could happen to a *sadhaka* [seeker]" (p. 66).**

In many chapters Bhagavan clarifies the path of Self-enquiry, *Vichara.* The chapter *Vichara, Self-Enquiry* on 16th July 1936, illuminates and clarifies this direct path to Self Realisation.

An easy to grasp example given by Bhagavan: **"The best preparation for *Vichara* is *Vichara.* The tongue knows that the splinter is a foreign body and must go. It will go on fighting until the alien appendage comes loose. Likewise, the mind must be able naturally to discern the ego, to which it owes its apparent existence, as being an unnatural and alien entity" (p. 86).**

In the 12th August entry, *Guru's Grace,* Bhagavan elaborates on the essential quality of surrender to the teacher: **"If you will have Realisation you must be prepared to irrevocably relinquish everything you think you have, including yourself first and foremost" (p. 113).**

And at the end of the same chapter: **"Please carry on with your *Sadhana* [practice] and keep quiet. Know that if the *Satguru***

[true guru] has decided to grant Liberation to a devotee even *Brahma* [The Creator] is powerless to raise any objection. The one fail-proof way to attain liberation, therefore, is to win the grace of the *Satguru*" (p. 115).

This carefully selected book deals in details of the Heart and will definitely touch earnest seekers with core teachings of Bhagavan like no other book: **"When you are asked to merge back into the Heart, from where you have come, it does not mean 'doing'. To 'do' is to use the mind" (p. 223).**

What you have in hand is only a first volume of selected teachings. More volumes will come as this book contains only a small selection of the complete manuscript. I beseech you to take this work out to all sincere seekers.

I pray to Bhagavan to rescue the earnest Seekers from the illusion of the world and redeem them with His bountiful Grace.

Swami Hamsananda
Founder President, Athithi Ashram, Tiruvannamalai

Contents

Unpublished Notebook Fragments - Winter 1936

Sri Gajapathi Aiyyer

Informative Chapters

Introduction

This book is a selection from a huge manuscript recorded from Bhagavan's meetings in July, August and September of 1936 – apparently by a young Indian man, Sri Gajapathi Aiyyer, who had consumed English literature when growing up and so had fine spoken English and a superior writing ability.

The essence of this book is a phenomenon called *Aham Sphurana* or 'I'-pulsation. It indicates that a state of incomplete or partial absorption in the Heart was prevailing at the time when such scintillation/pulsation took place. Complete absorption is the desirable state, which can be called Self-realisation.

The huge manuscript, unformatted and unedited, is available from Amazon as an e-book and from Pothi as a print-on-demand book. Patience is needed to get a relaxed benefit from the manuscript. There is also lots of unnecessary history about the manuscript. Also, Blutkeim's disappointment that Ramana Ashram hasn't published it. The ashram was sent the manuscript in 2019, along with seventeen pages of the original notebooks.

Since I came in contact with this manuscript in October 2021, I have been filled with an unstoppable energy to edit this jewel into a readable book. It has been a miraculous journey seemingly orchestrated by Bhagavan himself. From the beginning I was deeply touched by the detailed quality of how Bhagavan's teachings are reported, for example the importance of a Master and of Surrender as the direct path, which is confronting and difficult for most people. Many new details of his central teaching of Self-enquiry are revealed.

During my first months, many selections were made spontaneously from throughout the manuscript. These are posted on the blog on my website where you will also find a special Bhagavan Sri Ramana Maharshi page. Over the months these where edited and became the basis for the selection found in this book.

In the beginning only one-on-one teaching dialogues were chosen.

Gradually the quality of the reporting of daily life around Bhagavan was seen to throw new understanding onto him and we saw that teachings were included in these glimpses. They gave a more practical insight, in contrast to the intense meetings Bhagavan had with his visitors in the hall.

Following the publication of Paul Brunton's *A Search in Secret India* in 1934, many seekers arrived inspired by the complimentary portrait of Bhagavan painted in that book. Major Chadwick (Sadhu Arunachala) had arrived in 1935 and continued to live in the ashram until his death in 1962. Chadwick had invited Annamalai Swami (Bhagavan's former close attendant) to share his room. As it turned out, 1936 was the year when many Westerners arrived to meet Bhagavan, giving this record increased value.

There were many Theosophical Society members staying in Madras (now Chennai) and visitors to Sri Aurobindo's ashram in Pondicherry who heard about Bhagavan and came to meet him. Hence the high quality of many dialogues that occurred with mature Western spiritual seekers.

In 1936 Bhagavan was fifty-six years old, a healthy and active middle-aged man. The Jungle Hermitage described by Paul Brunton was making way for the stone buildings that can be experienced today. The developing ashram had its own kitchen where Bhagavan was the chief cook and Annamalai Swami was busy arranging the daily construction work, which was supervised by Bhagavan.

In January 2022, when I visited Tiruvannamalai for my annual Bhagavan Homage Retreat (the 21st year), I approached the Ramana Ashram authorities about the manuscript. Previously I had written three times to the President, Dr Venkata S Ramanan, offering our publishing team to support any project they had for publishing the manuscript. I never received any reply and it soon became clear that having been given the manuscript two years previously the ashram authorities had no plan to publish it.

The situation with the ashram's lack of interest caused me some doubts as to the value in publishing, but then a miracle happened. A visitor to one of my meetings introduced me to Swami Hamsananda, Founder President of the Athithi Ashram. It is well known as an ashram that provides medical care, as well as some accommodation and food, to sadhus.

Swami Hamsananda showed me an astounding statue of Bhagavan in the ashram's *Puja* room that had come to him in a miraculous way some years earlier. I took a small number of edited texts to him asking for his opinion on their value.

He shared stories from his life. He had slept on the floor of Annamalai Swami's tiny bedroom for some three years when he was in his twenties. Annamalai regaled him with wonderful stories of his life with Bhagavan. Later he became an ashram resident where he looked after the older residents from Bhagavan's time.

He also worked some years in the publication department of Ramana Ashram. Our meetings continued for a week, and he encouraged me to continue with our plans to publish the manuscript, finally offering his total support and help with the editing. He has kindly agreed to write the foreword to this book.

On our last meeting he told me the quality of the manuscript was of such value we should plan to publish the whole manuscript in several volumes. He compared the manuscript's teachings with *Talks*, a book covering talks given by Bhagavan over the same period as the manuscript. However, in *Talks* only thirty pages are devoted to July to September 1936, while in this selection there are three hundred pages of detailed teachings for the same period. Hardly any of the dialogues with Westerners appear in *Talks*.

Talks was recorded by Munagala Venkataramiah for four years, from 1935 to 1939. He was also Bhagavan's main translator of English and Tamil. It's noticeable that most of the dialogues that Gajapathi Aiyyer recorded with Western visitors are absent from *Talks*. It would be likely that while actively translating, Munagala would be unable to make detailed notes. One might wonder if Gajapathi therefore took up that task.

From the recorded narrative interspersed around the teachings it is clear Gajapathi Aiyyer had a close connection to Chadwick. His record contains several notes copied from Chadwick's notebook. There had been a period when Bhagavan would visit Chadwick's room and answer his questions. Gajapathi Aiyyer had access to those notebooks. Hence, Bhagavan's detailed answers to Chadwick are also included in this manuscript. Gajapathi Aiyyer was a young well-educated man who also translated occasionally for Bhagavan when Munagala Venkataramiah wasn't available. He appears to have had a close bond with Bhagavan and was invited to be part of some of Bhagavan's adventures.

As I was receiving encouragement from Swami Hamsananda, I had requested Mr S Nagarajan, a well-known Tamil spiritual writer who publishes in Tamil, to help on the project. I had met him while publishing our recent edition of *Nan Yar* in Tamil. He had given important advice to us.

In the original manuscript, parts of Bhagavan's answers remained in the original Tamil, which was Bhagavan's native language. Bhagavan also had a good knowledge of English. With Mr S Nagarajan's involvement, we translated the Tamil.

Over the last months I have come into a deep empathy with Bhagavan himself, which is very touching. Often it felt almost like being in his meetings. Gajapathi writes beautifully with profound insight and particular sensitivity. His connection with Bhagavan was deeply felt and personal. I have now spent six months involved with this manuscript on a daily basis. The team working on polishing this book swelled to ten, everyone donating their time. I have come to feel totally convinced that Sri Gajapathi Aiyyer's part of the manuscript is authentic.

It may well be that Gajapathi's original notebooks have been added to, and these added texts may then not be an authentic record of Bhagavan's spoken words. Swami Rajeshwarananda, a close friend of Gajapathi, who had been an ashram resident, had rescued the original notebooks, which later became the manuscript. He brought them, with Gajapathi, to Bhagavan in 1948 and recorded Bhagavan's approval (p. 7).

He had been keen for the ashram to publish them in the 1950s. Later he published a spiritual magazine, *Call Divine,* based in Bombay, so he would have been in contact with possible additional writings that were added when the notebooks became the manuscript.

The manuscript has appeared through the huge efforts of a Bhagavan devotee, Blutkeim (an alias), an older Indian man living in Chennai. Open Sky Press became involved after we made contact with him. He is pleased that we have taken on the publishing of the manuscript. He is supported by Athreya, a younger man whose mother, Nalini had typed up the manuscript.

As a sign of his affection and trust he has given us four pages of the original notebooks as described by Gajapathi, (p. 231) as well as four notebooks which are from the 1930s but have perhaps been copied from the original writing. These four gifted notebooks have been scanned then transcribed and published in this book. They haven't been published before.

We have been encouraged to have the paper from the notebooks analysed. The report from CICS, Cologne Institute of Conservation Sciences, Germany, says it can be assumed that it originates from the 1930s. In one place there is a date entry from 1936. The paper is from after 1929 as at that time the technique of paper production changed.

If there would be a Bhagavan devotee who would like to support the publication of this whole edited manuscript with some financial donation, that would certainly speed things along.

The Open Sky Press team and advisers have donated many hours to prepare these teachings as we are passionate devotees of Bhagavan. The cost of printing more volumes urgently is not within our possibility. We will certainly slowly publish more of the manuscript as the income from one book can finance the printing of the next.

John David, Director, Open Sky Press, June 2022

Book Formatting Using these Fonts and Symbols

The following Fonts are used throughout the Book

The Diarist's font.............................. Normal
The questioner's font.......................... *Italic*
Bhagavan's font.................................. **Bold**
Stories from Bhagavan......................... ***Bold Italic Indented***
Stories from others............................. Normal Indented
Sanskrit words.................................... *Italic*

The following Symbols are used throughout the Book

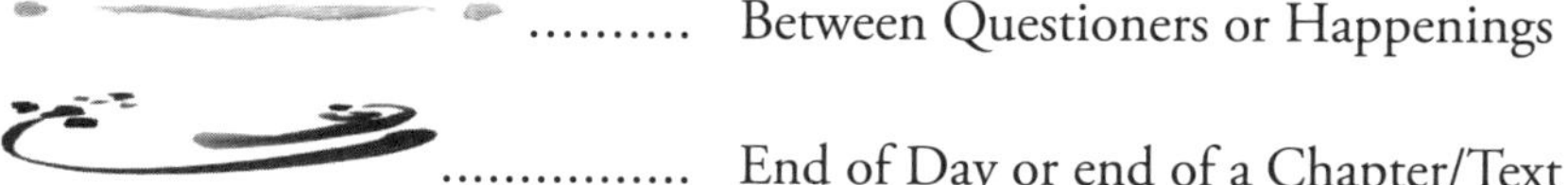

.... Between Questioners or Happenings
.... End of Day or end of a Chapter/Text

Q–Questioner, B–Bhagavan, G–Gajapathi, C–Chadwick, Co–Cohen, K–Kunja Swami, CP–Cycle-Pillai

Further Notes

Ed.................................... Editor's Note
Sanskrit word [meaning]......... In the text and a detailed Glossary
Antiquated English............... Replaced by modern English
August 10th......................... Meetings are set out in Date Order

Dec 1948

Sri Gajapathi Visiting Bhagavan with his Diaries

Sri Gajapathi Aiyyer was a distinguished lawyer and a devotee par excellence of the Maharshi. He came to Ramana Ashram in 1936. He stayed for perhaps six months and kept meticulous diaries of the meetings in Bhagavan's Hall.

These diaries are the core of the manuscript known as *Aham Sphurana* ['I'-Pulsation]. It seems that in the 1950s his friend, Swami Rajeshwarananda, wanted to publish these notebooks. At that time the ashram didn't have the necessary resources.

Now some seventy years later a manuscript has appeared, ***Aham Sphurana,*** which appears to contain the material from *Sri Gajapathi Aiyyer's Red Notebooks.* It may well be that other material has been added. It is a huge text of more than 1000 pages.

In December 1948 Sri Gajapathi Aiyyer and his friend Swami Rajeshwarananda took a trunk containing half a dozen notebooks to Ramana Ashram and it was unpacked in front of Bhagavan.

Gajapathi Aiyyer ran through the books patiently. They are hardbound notebooks, all of the same variety, done in beautiful red rexine. The pages are serially numbered from one to three-hundred, in black ink. The pages opening on to the left-hand side have their number inscribed at the top left corner and those on the right-hand side at the top right corner. The pages are lined with bluish lines in narrow spacing, and filled with young Gajapathi's meticulous note-making competencies, all written in pencil.

(See back of book p. 231 for four of these original pages – Ed)

Bhagavan smiled and said: See, how nicely the child has written everything!
Swami Rajeshwarananda: Gajapathi feels that he has committed an offence by chronicling your words without having sought out your permission.
B: Does not matter.

Gajapathi: I only wrote for my own recollection; if shown to others, will it not lead to confusion? Bhagavan gives specific advice to individual persons on spiritual matters; if shown to an unrelated person will that person not erroneously think that the advice is also applicable to his own case, and so mislead himself, with unwarranted consequences? Yet Swami Rajeshwarananda wants to make it available for all in the ashram to inspect.

Swami Rajeshwarananda: Bhagavan's words are more solemn and sacred than the Upanishads *[sacred Hindu scriptures] even. Why opine they could mislead anyone?*
B: Somebody may have the same doubts as that of the entries in these books.

Gajapathi: But Bhagavan gives different responses to the same question to different persons, depending upon individual temperament!
B: If the reply found is not satisfactory, the search continues! The earnest seeker does not make himself content with the receipt of a response felt by him to be unsuitable, or only partially satisfactory. An intellect made subtler and subtler by repeated and prolonged submergence in Being, will automatically reject advice that directs it away from the Heart.

Practising firm Permanence in the Shining of the Heart strengthens the faculty of intuition to the extent that it seeks out, time and again, only those words that redirect its course toward the self-resplendent Heart; such discrimination is not a function of the fictitious sense of individual free will; rather, it is automatic and comes by God's Grace to the sincere seeker.

Gajapathi was about to say something, but it was time for the *veda parayanam* [Vedic chanting in Ramana ashram] to begin.

Bhagavan, reaching for his stick, remarked before leaving:
There is a destiny guiding the course of events. One need not fret about anything, imagining oneself to be personally responsible for it.

Now the Master is in the body no more, but Swami Rajeshwarananda and myself (Gajapathi) wish to make the contents of these notebooks available to a wider audience. Swami Rajeshwarananda has discussed the idea with myself and he agreed to make a combined synopsis out of the notebooks, so that the Master's teachings shining in them may be published as a convenient teaching reference.

Sri Gajapathi's Notes

Reference Books and Translation

Much of the content presented here, showing Bhagavan reeling off verses from the Bible and other texts, is done so with the implicit assumption that the reader would naturally give himself to understand that Bhagavan was reading out from a book; certainly, Bhagavan did not burst out with these lines of prose or poetry from memory – at least, not in a majority of the cases.

I felt too lethargic to jot down every time Bhagavan asked the attendant to fetch this or that book from the bookcase in the Hall. When the attendant complied, Bhagavan then opened the book at the requisite page, without searching, and handed over the same to the interpreter with instructions to read out select portions to the Hall...and so forth.

Likewise, an interpreter – many times Mr TKS, occasionally

myself in those fortunate few months I dwelt continuously in Tiruvannamalai, or someone else – was used whenever the other person was to be spoken to in English (even if it was a long-standing devotee who lived within the ashram on a permanent basis, such as Chadwick or Cohen).

Bhagavan himself needed no interpreter. When Bhagavan himself speaks English the same is indicated in brackets here by me. There were times when, for a Caucasian language, no interpreter would be available. It was then that the Master would himself speak it, mellowly, placidly, and distinctly.

I have not pointed out separately conversations which were carried on through an interpreter in consideration of the length of this manuscript. Likewise, the names, cultural backgrounds, ethnicities, nationalities, and professed existing spiritual competencies of the various visitors who quizzed the Master have also been – largely – filtered out whilst preparing this manuscript. A lengthy manuscript may fizzle out the patience of a prospective publisher; also, I am aware that a book that appears tediously lengthy is – more often than not – ignored and bypassed at bookshops!

4th September 1936

Mrs Piggot Introduces Bhagavan and the Ashram

I had visited India on several occasions prior to this trip, but this was my maiden venture off the beaten track.

I was told of Sri Ramana Maharshi, and even from the little I heard, I knew I would travel anywhere and put up with any inconvenience in order to meet him and experience the sanctity of his presence. The friend who gave me the welcome news of the Maharshi's Existence offered to take me to him, and so we arrived at Tiruvannamalai late one afternoon.

Dakshinamurti [form of God Shiva] Shrine

On the way to the Maharshi's ashram, it is observed by me that our vehicle passes a simple stone shrine which stands dedicated to Shiva as Dakshinamurti, the most ancient of Yogis who teaches the Ineffable Absolute Truth through Silence of the Soul. He is a deity who perpetually faces south, and, consequent to the fact that south is the direction of death, he is also known as *Mrutyunjaya* [form of Shiva], the Conqueror of Death. Death, indubitably, is conquered by awakening to the ultimate truth of ourselves.

Just after passing the shrine of Dakshinamurti we reached our destination, announced by an archway bearing the words 'Sri Ramanasramam'. Having entered the grounds, we dismounted from our vehicle. The Maharshi's younger brother, Sri Nagasundaram, greeted us there. He was the ashram manager, known as the *sarvadhikari* or as Chinnaswami.

Meeting Bhagavan

He informed me that I could now have Bhagavan's *darshan* [the auspicious sight of a deity or saint]. I crossed a small courtyard and came to a long hall with all its doors and windows open. I went up a few steps and there, seated before me on a couch, was the sage of Arunachala. He is a slender, golden-skinned man in his late fifties. Except for a loincloth, he is completely nude.

In front of the couch sandalwood sticks were burning and a small brazier of hot coals, on which a special kind of incense was constantly being thrown. Although born a *Brahmin* [the highest caste in Hinduism], Bhagavan's features actually made him look like a docile country-side peasant. However, the awareness of the Absolute is marked out clearly on the face, making it profoundly serene and beautiful.

The splendour of Realisation is clearly evident from one look at his face. I now see that the psychological labels which the modern mind tended to affix to spiritual experience turn out to be irrelevant and unworthy when one is confronted with true achievement. I was so engrossed in my contemplation of Bhagavan that at first I did not hear when one of the attendants told me that I should take my place among the women, who sat on the Master's left. The men, who were more numerous, sat facing him down the length of the Hall.

The Hall in which the attendees found themselves was simply decorated and furnished. A frieze of blue flowers ran along the walls. A clock hung on the wall facing the devotees. Below it, on a shelf, there were a few tin containers. Presently, I saw Bhagavan take some nuts out of one of the containers for the squirrel that had run to him along the back of the couch.

Yet the banal setting could not detract from the grandeur of the Sage. He was exceptional first of all in just being himself. In every action he made, whether he was correcting a manuscript or reading a letter, there was a complete naturalness and absence of pose. This is very rarely seen, for few are those who, being rooted in their true identity, have no need to seek a flattering image of themselves or confirmation of what they are from the impression they make on others.

Lunch

At eleven o'clock Bhagavan and the devotees rose and left the Hall, for it was time for the main meal of the day. The meal was served in the communal dining hall where rows of freshly washed banana leaves had been laid out on the spotlessly clean stone floor. Bhagavan took his place among the devotees. The *Brahmins* sat on one side of him and the non-*Brahmins* on the other, thus respecting religious customs. Bhagavan, though, did not wear the *Brahmin's* sacred thread, and I remembered that on arriving in Tiruvannamalai he had thrown away the thread worn by the hereditary *Brahmin* race that indicated superiority over every other race.

I was served rice, vegetables, pepper water and milk curds. Bhagavan ate very frugally. He asked me courteously whether the food was not too pungent for me. These words of solicitude were the first words he spoke to me.

Hall Meeting

In the Hall I then joined the devotees who had come to spend the afternoon with Bhagavan. I did not see some of those who had been present in the morning, but several newcomers were there. I was surprised to hear that devotees might come into the Hall as early as four o'clock in the morning, though seven o'clock was the time most morning visitors gathered. Many spent only a few hours with him, but he was accessible to visitors all day long. As in the morning, the mood was rather informal. To those pupils aspiring to attain the highest grade of knowledge, Bhagavan apparently did not give any discourses. He replied to questions when they were put to him, usually very concisely, as if to let the one word or the few words he said make their way directly into the understanding of the questioner.

On the other hand, when a young man struggled to grasp what the Absolute Self was, Bhagavan, with great patience, guided him through his reasoning until at least he got some glimmering of what Bhagavan meant. Of course, the answer to the nature of the impersonal mind is only to be found on the intuitive level, but the breakthrough of intuition can be hampered by faulty reasoning. Apart from these exceptions to silence, there were long quiet moments when Bhagavan said and did nothing, but which were more effective in conveying transcendent Truth than any lecture or sermon would have been.

Coffee and the Evening Meeting

The afternoon ended with a twenty-minute break for the purpose of taking coffee, and presently Bhagavan got up and went for his evening walk. This was the signal for a general exodus, and we all trooped outside.

Bhagavan and the devotees gathered in the Hall again at five o'clock for the evening session. I found that the atmosphere now was quite different; much more solemn and charged with more energy than earlier on in the day. First there was the recitation of the *Vedas* [oldest Hindu scriptures] by a group of young *Brahmin* boys and their teacher. As the powerful Sanskrit syllables vibrated in the Hall, Bhagavan's appearance underwent a remarkable change. His expression became austere, his gaze turned inwards. His face appeared translucent as if lit by inner illumination, whilst the constant slight trembling of his body, which I had noticed earlier, had now completely stopped.

Yet even in this state it was evident that he was not oblivious of his surroundings, and that he had an awareness of both the inner and outer reality. After the *Vedas,* the devotees sang together a hymn to Arunachala. Then they sat in deep silence, capturing the force emanating from the Master, a force so strong as to be almost tangible. Bhagavan's ashram is a place where exclusively those people who have dedicated their entire lives to the spiritual quest may take up permanent residence.

Often there are no orders or binding rules, and anyone can come and go as he pleases. I discover to my pleasant surprise that most of the people living in the ashram speak English and are eager to greet me in a warm and friendly manner. On the day of my arrival, more than a dozen people tried to strike up a conversation with me. In their accented English, they wanted well-meaningly to know how I had heard of the Master and what brought me here.

A Dialogue with the Master

It was now several hours past the time night had fallen upon the little town. The occupants of the Hall spoke in low tones to one another, and a child was chattering to his mother; but soon these sounds ceased and there was quiet. I sat cross-legged on the floor with the others, though a chair had been thoughtfully provided for me.

I asked the Maharshi in a respectful hushed tone: "Thoughts cease suddenly, then 'I-I' rises up as suddenly and continues. It is only in the feeling and not in the intellect. Can it be right?" He was gracious enough to respond to me, saying that it was certainly right. Thereafter I tried gazing into his eyes. I repeatedly tried to capture his gaze. For a while nothing happened. I tried to concentrate my mind on the beingness of the formless Self.

Suddenly I became conscious that Bhagavan's eyes were fixed on me. They seemed, literally, like burning coals of fire piercing through one. They glittered in the dim light of the charcoal brazier burning by the side of the Sofa. Never before had I experienced anything so devastating – in fact, it was almost frightening. What I went through in that terrible half-hour, in a way of self-condemnation and scorn for the pettiness of my own life, would be difficult to describe.

Not that he criticised, even in silence – of that he was incapable – but in the light of perfection all imperfections are revealed. To place on record how little responsible he was for my feelings, I must mention here that he told me later on that doubting, self-distrust, and self-depreciation are some of the greatest hindrances to the Realisation of the Reality.

This is a record of the further conversations I had with him on the day after my first arrival at the ashram:

Q: Is a Realised Master necessary for Realisation?
B: Realisation is the result of Guru's Grace more than teachings, lectures, meditation, et cetera. They are only secondary aids, whereas the former is the primary and the essential cause.

Then Bhagavan ordered a certain treatise to be read out in the Hall, in which it was stated that as in all physical and intellectual training a teacher or instructor is sought, so in matters spiritual the same principle holds good.

The Master added that it was hard for a man to arrive at the goal without the aid of a Realised Master.

Q: Yet I have heard it said that you had no Guru *(teacher).*

A rustle of shocked horror ran through the Hall because I had inadvertently addressed him in the second person instead of referring to him as 'Bhagavan'. Yet the Maharshi was not in the least disturbed or offended. On the contrary, he looked at me with a twinkle in his eye. Then he threw back his head and gave a joyous, wholehearted laugh. It endeared him to me as nothing else could. A saint who can turn the laugh against himself is a saint indeed. Ultimately he did give a response to my impertinent remark:

B: Yes, but in the majority of cases, Guru is certainly necessary.

Q: How shall I find the Guru?

B: Intense meditation will impel you into the field of his presence automatically.

The Ashram

On the third day of my visit, one of the devotees offered to show me around the ashram, a cluster of small, whitewashed buildings and huts, all spotlessly clean, and joined together in some cases by a covered passageway. The ashram was picturesquely situated at the base of the famous holy mountain of Arunachala. It was on this mountain side that Bhagavan took up his abode more than thirty years ago, and ever since then it has been his home.

He must be aged about fifty years, but looks older, owing no doubt to the privations and austerities practised in early life. It was dark when I returned for the evening meditation, and most of the people not living permanently in the ashram had left. The Hall was compellingly still. The eyes of the holy one blazed no more. They were serene and introverted. All my troubles seemed smoothed out and difficulties melted away. Nothing that we of the world called important mattered. Time was forgotten. Life in its many aspects was now one.

(This text or extracts can be found in several publications – Ed)

Essential Teachings

Summa Iru [Be Still]

Aham Sphurana Extracts

A Typical Western Visitor

20th July 1936

Summma Iru [Be Still]

Q: How do I attain a Self-realised state for myself?
B: *Summa Iru* [be still]. That is the practice.

Q: Am I to be idle all the time? Is engaging in gainful or productive employment a crime?
B: The import of *Summa Iru* is, 'Keep your mind idle or asleep in the Beingness of the Self.' As for the body, it has its own *prarabdha* [destiny that effects our life now] to attend to. You have no right of say over the body. You cannot decide whether the body should work or remain idle. What is bound to happen will happen.

If the body is destined to remain without working, work cannot be obtained even if you hunt for it. If the body is destined to work you cannot alter such destiny, for the body will be forced to engage in it.

So leave it to the Higher Power. You cannot avoid or acquire work for the body as you choose. God has not permitted that freedom. Only one freedom is permitted to man – and that is the freedom to perish in his own Immortal Self. This is also the only free will.

Q: Can meditation or vichara *[Self-enquiry] be carried on in the midst of worldly activity?*
B: The feeling 'I am working' is the hindrance. Enquire, Who works? Remember to ask yourself, Who am I? every time such false notions of doership trouble you. Then no work can bind you; it will all go on automatically. Make no effort either to work or to renounce work. Your effort is the bondage. Simply perpetually remain as you ARE, mind merged in its source so as to be indistinguishable from the Beingness of the Self, and do not bother about the question of whether the body ought to work or to idle away. If you remain non-attached – neither attached nor detached, for both are voluntary actions – the body's *prarabdha* will effortlessly carry it through

whatever activities are meant for it in this life. You remain surrendered to the Self – everything else disappears. No more questions, doubts, or misgivings arise. This is the way for unshakeable *shanti* [peace].

(For the whole text – A Complete Layman p. 99 – Ed)

Aham Sphurana

Essential Extracts from the Manuscript

Q: So, is this state of consciousness steadily remaining merely as Itself, undisturbed by thought, called the Sahajastithi *[the natural state]?*
B: No. It is called *Aham Sphurana*.

Q: Then what is the Sahajastithi*?*
B: No description is possible. The reflected being – consciousness which is localised in a physical body – is destroyed; after this is destroyed, that alone remains which has always been. It is the Absolute Reality. It transcends dualities such as being and non-being, knowledge and ignorance, light and darkness, et cetera. It is THAT – WHICH – IS, that is all that can be said of it. That is what YAHWEH stands for in the Bible. Although there he seems to be a personal God, guiding the destiny of the children of Israel, the Talmudic Prophets of Old knew the transcendental aspect, as did the Christ. God told Moses, "I appeared to Abraham, to Isaac, and to Jacob as God Almighty, but by My name, Yahweh, I was not known to them." On the other hand, the term Yahweh occurs many times in Genesis. Is there a contradiction? No. Prophets before the time of Moses had known the personal God Yahweh, but Moses was the first to whom the transcendental, formless aspect was revealed.

The earlier prophets knew the name but not its significance. They loved God and cherished his name but did not understand the meaning or import of the name.

The name means 'I am that I am'. God revealed the meaning of the name to Moses, whereas the earlier prophets had only been given the name. The name means that one who is simply subjectively aware, without knowing any object, is absorbed or transformed into God. This is not an intellectual conviction or mental assertion. It is the blossoming of the heart-lotus [*hridayapundarikam*] of love from within.

Q: Bhagavan mentioned something known as the 'Aham Sphurana' *yesterday. Having reached this* Aham Sphurana, *how does one proceed from there to Self-realisation of the final* Sahajastithi*?*

B: Having reached *Aham Sphurana*, no further effort is possible. For one who has reached the *Sphurana* [pulsation], this question is impossible – as is any other question. No doubts arise because the doubter has long ago given himself up to the infinite Beingness that shines in his own Heart as the light of the true 'I'. One who has reached *Sphurana* and remains perpetually merged in it instead of being unsettled would never think, 'I have reached the *Aham Sphurana*. Now I wonder when Realisation of the Absolute Self is going to dawn on me.' Nor would he think any other thought.

The thinker gone, who is left to manufacture thoughts? The one who steadfastly remains in the *Sphurana* state does not crave Realisation – nor anything else – for he no more has any needs. Since a fall from it is always theoretically possible, the *Sphurana* is still classified as *sadhana* [spiritual practice] – however, it is the loftiest stage of *sadhana* for it is sustained without the least trace of effort or *sankalpa* [will] to remain in it.

Continuous *Sphurana* is possible only after the ego-sense has been finally given up. Before it manifests continuously it is possible for the *sadhaka* [spiritual seeker] to experience flashes of it. Instead of permitting these flashes to distract him, and instead of making deliberate effort to perpetuate it or voluntarily bring

it about again, he should calmly enquire, 'Who has experienced this?' until the *Sphurana* becomes continuous. Once the *Sphurana* becomes the permanent state, it is also, in due course, extinguished, like the combustion of a block of camphor is complete when neither camphor nor flame is seen anymore, and only Reality remains – that is the *Sahajastithi* [natural state] of the *jnanasiddha* [the one who has accomplished true knowledge] about which you are asking.

Q: What are the physical symptoms of the Sphurana*? Does it involve loss of functioning of the sensory organs? Does it cause loss of body consciousness?*
B: There may or may not be an involuntary spate of isolated breath retention; there would also be a throbbing or pulsating sensation – but why are you asking this question? Dive within and SEE for yourself. The important thing is that in the state of *Sphurana* there is no such thing as 'making a decision'. Everything is decided by the Higher Power...and your mind, having lost the ability to measure variety or make value judgements, stands reduced to mere consciousness of being. Sensory organs function normally, and the alienation of body consciousness is yet to be complete, but the events of the outer world are merely witnessed detachedly without any aversion or fascination, as one watching a cinema picture without the slightest interest. Actions are not pre-meditated but spontaneous.

The body becomes a tool in the hands of the Almighty, ecstasy floods the soul, and blinded by the spell of divine intoxication, one weeps and laughs, sings and shouts, without apparent purpose. These are only visible, external symptoms of the Deep pulling within, and may not manifest in all. I was like that in Madurai, shedding tears of longing at the Meenakshi Temple, without having the slightest clue why. Even the thought, 'Why are we crying?' did not occur. Not all may obtain the experience of weeping for God, not knowing whether they are weeping in the anguish of yearning or in the ecstasy of fulfilment, and not caring. The important thing is whether inwardly the *dehatmabuddhi* [the intellect that causes one to identify the Self with the body] or *kartritvabuddhi* [I-am-

the-doer-idea] has been broken or not. If the 'I am the body-mind complex' idea is completely abandoned, not a trace of *sankalpa* or volition remains. Bhagavan did not decide, 'Let us go to Arunachala.' Rather, (Gajapathi watched the figure on the Sofa gently touch his right shoulder with one delicate finger) **– come here – that is all.**

• —— •

Q: And how to recognise the Aham Sphurana *when it 'flashes forth'?*
B: There is no possibility of mistaking it when the experience actually occurs. Whatever description is given is not only useless but also counter-productive, because if a description of the experience of *Aham Sphurana* is given, the mind twists and contorts the present banal experience of outward-protruding, satiation-craving mental impulses into one that seems to perfectly match with the description given: because it wants to avoid getting destroyed. So, even if you have heard a description of the experience of the *Aham Sphurana* being furnished in this Hall, please make no effort to recollect it.

When the *Aham Sphurana* actually flashes forth, you will know it alright. Recognition of the *Aham Sphurana* is not based on intellectual corroboration – it is a direct experience of the Self, inferior only to the *Sahajastithi* of the *jnani.*

• —— •

Q: In Sat Darshana Bhashya *and* Talks with Maharshi (1932)*, it is said as follows:-*

> Realisation of *jnana* is always a *vritti.* There is a distinction between *jnana* [mental modifications, knowledge] or Realisation and *swaroopa* [essence] the real. *Swaroopa* is *jnana* itself, it is consciousness. *Swaroopa* is *sat chit,* which is infinite. It is always there self-attained. When you realise it, the Realisation is called truly *jnana.* It is only with reference to your Existence that you talk of Realisation or *jnana.* Therefore, when we talk of

> *jnana*, we always mean *vritti jnana* and not the *swaroopa jnana* [knowledge of the essence]; for *swaroopa* itself is *jnana* consciousness always.

I find this passage completely baffling. Would Bhagavan please explain it to me?
B: When the mind ceases to take any interest in the objective world and remains effortlessly abiding in its native, primeval state of pure beingness, it is *vrittijnanam* [turning the mind inwards]. One may be said to have reached the state of *vrittijnanam* only if and when his mind remains so not as the result of any motive or objective but because of the fact that now it does not know anything else. The mind, which was earlier consciousness concealed by a labyrinthine network of *vrittis* [mental habits], is now reduced into simple consciousness of being to which effort or objective is altogether alien. Then there is no question of straining oneself to remain still.

Stillness is now the natural state. This is *manonivritti* [freedom of mind structures] or *vrittijnanam*. In this state there is nothing available to deflect one's attention away from subjective awareness. The mind remains transfixed at the point of its origin. The light of 'I'-'I' can be clearly felt to be shining. The experience of the scintillation 'I'-'I' is called *Aham Sphurana*. Since this state is not brought about by means of expenditure of any mental effort, but rather on account of subsidence of mind, some books say that it is a transcendental state.

Q: Is that the state of the jnani?
B: No. When even the rarefied mind is destroyed in the Beyond, it is the *Sahajastithi* of the *jnani*. But you need not worry about all this. It is unnecessary. It is enough to lose the ego. Thereafter everything is automatic.

B: This phenomenon is called *Aham Sphurana* or 'I'-scintillation. It indicates that a state of incomplete or partial absorption in the Heart was prevailing at the time when such scintillation took place.

Complete absorption is the desirable state.

Q: How can I bring about such complete absorption?
B: Your efforts can extend only as far as the *Sphurana* [pulsation]. Abide continuously and incessantly in the *Sphurana*; leave the rest to God or Self.

Q: Often, even whilst the Sphurana *is going on, thoughts appear and distract me. What should I do at such moments?*
B: Gently extricate yourself from the thought; that is all. The mental faculty is not destroyed whilst the state of *Sphurana* is in operation; it is in a state of suppression; whenever it reasserts itself, look closely at the thought that caused such re-emergence and it will vanish. Steady, continuous practice is required until you have naturally become established in the *Sphurana* – that is, until you reach a state wherein no effort on your part is necessary any longer to keep up the *Sphurana*.

Plunge the mind in the *Sphurana* again and again and again and keep it submerged there until you find that the *Sphurana* is going on naturally and without any effort on your part. If there is a desire or resolve within the mind – 'I am carrying on with the *Sphurana* because doing so will earn me Liberation' – Liberation will never dawn. The *Sphurana* should not be the result of any mental process; it should be natural, motiveless, spontaneous and uncaused by anything. Only then will Liberation dawn. Those who expect or anticipate or want Liberation never find it. Abandon yourself to the *Sphurana* unconditionally and it will Liberate you.

Q: What is the difference between the state of Nirvikalpa Samadhi *[mind dissolved only Consciousness remains] and that of* Aham Sphurana *[a glimpse of Self-realisation] – if any? Which is the superior state amongst these two, and which is the supreme state?*
B: Both are equally worthy. In *Nirvikalpa Samadhi*, body-consciousness might be absent. *Nirvikalpa* + body-consciousness = *Aham*

***Sphurana*. However, *Aham Sphurana* is conducive for destruction of *vasanas*, whereas the same is not possible when the mind is temporarily sucked into the Heart, shutting out body-consciousness and precluding the possibility of sensory perception for the duration of the experience (of *Samadhi*).**

• —— •

Q: Yogis are said to divest themselves of body-consciousness and remain in its absence for decades together.

B: Yogis try to eliminate body-consciousness by practising *Kevala Kumbhaka* [breath retention] for abnormally large spans of time – but the trouble with adopting such an approach is that the volition or intent to remain bereft of body-consciousness remains still to be tackled. For this reason, it is better to not try to forcibly eradicate body-consciousness, which, after all, is only a harmless *upadhi* [limitation] once you have given up the notorious, delusory habit of false identification (of the Self with the not Self).

All possibility of volition and effort must be destroyed before *jnana* can dawn. As per the body's *prarabdha*, let the *upadhi* of body-consciousness drop off automatically. We need not bother about it, regarding it as any hindrance to be resolved or tackled. You need not try to destroy the body or somehow reduce it into nothingness. Simply cease to identify or associate with it in any manner; that will do. Trying to get rid of the body implies paying further attention to the body. Instead, channel attention away from the body and into the Self; that is the thing to be done. As for the supreme spiritual state, which you asked about, it is the *Sahajastithi* of the *jnani*. It cannot be attained by *sadhana*. No effort can reach it. Surrender yourself to it unconditionally and you will be absorbed into it. *Vichara* [Self-enquiry] is only to prepare the mind for unconditional surrender. If you can surrender absolutely, where is the need for *vichara* and where is the possibility – who would then be left to investigate?

• —— •

Q: Is the Self located on the right-hand side of the chest?

B: Only up until it is necessary for you to admit that you have a body. Do you?

Q: Yes. How can I deny it? Does not Bhagavan see this body talking to him?
B: The body does not say 'I am you.' You say that you are it. When you have weaned yourself away from this erroneous attitude that you are somehow linked with the body, then you will know where the Self is. The Self is not anywhere; it IS.

Q: What about Sri Bhagavan's idea that the hridayagranthi *[the knot of the heart] is represented by a physical spot in the body – if the Self is inherent only, doesn't this idea become invalid?*
B: Discover the non-dual Self and we can worry about its relation to the body later if need be: then, not now. It is true that there is an opening on the right-hand side of the chest, fashioned like a tiny hole. This contraption remains always closed, but it is opened by *vichara* – the consequence is that *Aham Sphurana* shines forth. However, all this is only from a relative point of view. In actual fact, the *jnani* who abides in the state of *ajata Advaita* [the Absolute] is quite irrevocably lost to 'physical reality'. These explanations are not for him; they are formulated only to satisfy the curiosity of ordinary citizens – their truth is only as true as the truth of your own bodily Existence, and no farther.

Q: Will vivisection of the body by a skilled anatomist reveal the presence of this organ?
B: No. It is on the subtle plane.

Q: Well, using a microscope then?
B: I meant to say that in my experience it is purely a locus for accumulation of mental energy. It might not have any physical coefficient. However, a physical sensation of pulsation or throbbing might be felt at the region. The fact is, such matters are not at all important. The thing to do, or rather un-do, is to Realise the Self. Whatever you experience is beside the point. Who is the experiencer?

That is the critical question.

Q: Is the Japanese concept of Satori the same as the Hindu concept of Moksha *[liberation]?*
B: No. Satori is *Spandabhraja Samadhi* [absorption in bliss] or *Aham Sphurana* ['I'-pulsation].

Q: What is this 'I'-'I'? Is it the same as jnana*?*
B: No. 'I'-'I' is the stage before the *Sahajastithi* of the *jnani*. It is known as *Aham Sphurana*. When the *Sphurana* becomes continuous, unstoppable, and spontaneous – that is, when it has solidified itself, so to speak, into a permanent phenomenon – it leads to the *Sahajastithi* [the state of the *jnani*]. In vedantic parlance *Aham Sphurana* is known as *vrittijnanam*. It may otherwise be known as cosmic consciousness. It is called 'cosmic' because the mind in that state is in a generic form. That is, it is not held captive by the *ahamvritti* ['I'-thought] for the duration of the experience. If the destruction of *poorvasamskaras* [latent predispositions] is incomplete, afterwards the *ahamvritti* reasserts itself and the flow of thoughts resumes itself as usual. The *Sphurana*, when held on to continuously, weakens the *ahamvritti* which alone is the cause of the *hridayagranthi* [knot between the sentient and the insentient – that is, the ego] and bestows *mukti* [freedom from embodiment and future births].

Q: How to hold on to the Sphurana *continuously?*
B: The effort or will or volition to do it is itself an obstacle to the shining of the *Sphurana*. If you remain as you ARE, the *Sphurana* shines forth of its own accord.

Q: Has Bhagavan said that the experience of the Sphurana *is accompanied by a prickly sensation on the right-hand side of the chest?*
B: Leave alone the physical sensation; it might be brought about

by the *Sphurana*, but it is profitless to think that merely having experienced the sensation means that you have accomplished something. The important thing is to always remain in the state of effortless-and-volitionless thoughtlessness. The subtle 'I', which witnesses the fact of the mind remaining in this state, must also vanish. Only then is Realisation made possible.

Q: Sometimes you talk about something called Aham Sphurana. *Is this the same as cosmic consciousness?*

B: Yes. It is called so because when in that state the subtle mind feels the Heart as a pulsating vibration; the accompanying physical sensation on the right-hand side of the chest may also manifest. But this sensation, on the whole, is not worthy of any deep consideration; it only serves as an indication that the mind, through long practice, has become largely subtle and serene. It is a symptom of progress but should not itself be mistaken to be the goal. The important thing is for the mind to always remain in its native state of effortless-and-volitionless absence of thought.

Q: When I investigate Who am I? I feel an intense, throbbing sensation in the heart-centre, which Sri Bhagavan talks about, on the right-hand side of the chest. It is like a sensation that a person would have who is overwhelmed with emotion; it brings tears to my eyes. Every time I investigate Who am I? I am drawn to this centre. Is it enough to hold on to this sensation? I ask this question because I have heard that it is Bhagavan's opinion that although concentration on this heart-centre is a beneficial spiritual exercise, it is not the same as vichara*; and I do not want to get side-tracked into doing anything that is not explicitly* vichara. *I am particularly anxious to get emancipated in this birth.*

B: Instead of trying to hold on to such sensation, remain unreactive. Why invent a spurious 'I' and then ask him to decide whether he wants to hold on to the sensation or not? If you try to hold on to such sensation, it will vanish. Do not try to 'do' anything with the

***Sphurana*. If you try to 'do' anything with it or catch hold of it, it will vanish and you will be left wondering where you went wrong and why the sensation has vanished. The *Sphurana* must be continuous. It will remain that way only if you leave it alone – that is, remain as you naturally ARE. Perfect absence of effort is what is needed to sustain the *Sphurana* continuously.**

Why? Because effort implies the existence of the ego making it, and if the ego resumes its activities the *Sphurana* will have to subside. Make every effort to remain totally without any effort. Who is that one who wants to hold on to the *Sphurana*? He is the mischievous imp known as the ego. So, do not permit the ego to disturb the *Sphurana*; let it go on indefinitely by means of exclusively remaining solely as It (the *Sphurana*) perpetually. This *Sphurana* is a partial experience of the Self. It is an indication of the coming Glory. But if it is to elevate into the Self it must be left undisturbed; it must be permitted to go on indefinitely. For that, the ego must be kept in check – by means of *vichara*. So, whenever you find the *Sphurana* subsiding, ask yourself Who am I? It will come aright in the end.

4th September 1936

A Typical Western Visitor's In-Depth Dialogue

Time and again I have observed that the Maharshi emphasises that Realisation was more the result of Guru's Grace rather than anything else. I had been in despair of ever again getting the Maharshi alone. It is hard to unburden the soul before a crowd.

One morning I resolutely made my way into the Hall a few hours earlier than usual and found him there unattended, emanating his usual wonderful stillness and ineffable peace. I asked quietly if I might talk with him. He nodded, smiling, and sent for someone to translate. On the arrival of a devotee, I put my first question.

Q: What are the obstacles which hinder Realisation of the Self?
B: They are habits of mind [*vasanas*].

Q: How to overcome these mental habits?
B: By Realising the Self.

Q: That is a vicious circle.
B: It is the mind which brings about such difficulties, creating obstacles and then suffering from the perplexity of apparent paradoxes. Find out who makes the enquiries and the Self will be found.

Q: What are the aids for Realisation?
B: Introversion of mind is the one and only aid.

Q: How can I achieve the same?
B: By preventing the mind from straying out after thoughts, desires and imagined objects of sensory perception.

Q: If the world is a dream, am I making efforts to Realise the Self within a dream?
B: Yes.

Q: But there will always be other dreams! Do we have to make efforts to Realise within each and every dream?
B: If effort is going on to Realise the Self within this dream, it means that the same effort is going on within all other dreams also.

Q: Discussions, lectures and meditations: are they not useful for attaining Realisation?
B: All these are only secondary aids, whereas the essential aid is

Guru's Grace.

Q: How long will it take for one to get Realisation?
B: Why do you desire to know?

Q: To give me hope.
B: Such a desire is also an obstacle. The Self is ever there, there is nothing without it. Be the Self and the desires and doubts will disappear. The Self is the witness in sleep, dream and waking states of Existence. These states belong to the ego. The Self transcends the ego. Ego or no ego, the Self remains always. It is ever as It is. Did you not exist in sleep? Did you know then that you were asleep? Was there awareness of the world in sleep? In sleep you remained without a body and without a world. Why do you now hanker after these? In *jagrat* [watchfulness] you also remain aloof from body and world. It is only in *jagrat* that you describe the experience of sleep as being unawareness; therefore, the consciousness when asleep is the same as that when awake.

If you know what this waking consciousness is, you will know the consciousness that witnesses all the three states; such absolute consciousness is found by means of seeking the source of pure consciousness.

Q: In attempting to trace back pure consciousness to its source, I am overwhelmed by sleep and soon fall into slumber.
B: No harm!

Q: I still maintain that to me sleep is nothing but a mere blank.
B: For whom is the blank? Find out. You cannot deny your Existence at any time. The Self is ever there and continues in all states.

Q: Should I remain as if in sleep and be watchful at the same time?
B: Yes. Alert watchfulness is the true waking state. Therefore, the state of *jagratsushupti* [waking deep sleep] will not be one of sleep, but sleepless sleep. If you go the way of your thoughts, you will be

carried away by them and you will find yourself in an endless maze.

Q: So, then, I must go back, tracing the source of thoughts.
B: Quite so; in that way the thoughts will disappear and the Self alone will remain.

Q: Does the practice Who am I? lead to any spot inside the body?
B: There is no inside or outside for the Self. These concepts are merely mental projections of the ego. The Self is pure and absolute. However, till Realisation is gained, it may be said that consciousness has a locus in the body, which is located on the right-hand side of the chest.

Q: Is not intellect a help for Realisation?
B: Yes, up to a certain stage. Even so, realise that the Self transcends the intellect; the latter must itself vanish in order that the Self might be Realised.

Q: Does my Realisation help others?
B: Yes, certainly. It is the best help possible. However, the actual truth is that there are no others to be helped, for an emancipated soul sees only the Self in everything, just like a goldsmith estimating the gold in various jewels sees gold and nothing but gold. When you identify yourself with the body, forms and shapes are to be found. But when you transcend your body the others in the world disappear along with your body-consciousness.

Q: Is it so with plants, trees, et cetera?
B: Do they exist at all apart from the Self? Find out. You think that you see them. The thought is projected out from the mind. Find out from where the mind rises. Thoughts will cease to rise and the Self alone will remain.

Q: I understand theoretically. But thoughts refuse to subside.
B: Thought is nothing but mental excitement. Mind is only a bubble

floating on the Self. Break the bubble and you are the ocean.

Q: Is it the mind that creates the world we see?
B: Yes. It is like a cinema show. There is the light on the screen and the shadows flitting across impress the audience as the enactment of some screenplay. If in the same screenplay an audience also is shown, what is the position? The seer and the seen will then only be the screen. Apply this analogy to yourself. You are the screen, the Self has created the ego, and the ego has its additions of thoughts which are displayed as the world, the trees, plants, et cetera about which you are asking.

The truth is that all these are nothing but the Self. If you see the Self, the same will be found to be all, everywhere and always. Nothing but the Self exists.

Q: Yes, but I still understand only theoretically. Yet the answers are simple, beautiful and convincing.
B: Even the thought, 'I do not Realise' is a hindrance. The Self alone IS and HE alone could ever BE.

Q: What are vasanas*?*
B: Habits of thought, accumulated tendencies of mind, and intellectual predispositions.

Q: How does one get rid of these hindrances?
B: Seek the Self through meditation in this manner: trace every thought back to its point of origin, which is only the mind. Never allow thought to run on. If you do so, it will be unending. Take it back to its starting place – the mind's essence of pure consciousness – again and again, and thought and thinker will both die of inaction eventually.

The mind only exists by reason of thought. Stop thought and there is no mind. As each doubt or depressing thought arises, ask yourself, 'Who is it that doubts? What is it that is depressed?' Go back constantly to the question, 'Who or what is this thing called

'I'? Where is the source of the mind?' Tear everything out and go on discarding until there is nothing but the Source of all left. And then live always in That and only in It.

There is no past or future, save in the mind. Only present exists. Yes, even the present is mere imagination. It IS. That is all. Ehyeh Asher Ehyeh (Hebrew: I am that I am).

Q: *How can I help another with his or her problems and troubles?*
B: What is this talk of another? There is only the One. Try and realise there is no 'I' no 'he' no 'you', only the One Self which is all. If you believe in the problem of another, you are believing in something outside the Self. You will help him better by realising the oneness of everything than by any outward activity. The ego masks the Reality.

All mental activities during the states of *jagrat* and *swapna* [dream] are the handiwork of the ego only. The emotions and intellect are merely mind-manufactured fictions. In deep sleep the body is lost, but yet the Self is there. It is the distracting, active mind that veils the real Self.

Q: What meditation will help me?
B: No meditation on any kind of object is helpful. You must learn to realise the subject and object as one. In meditating on an object, whether concrete or abstract, you are destroying the sense of oneness and creating duality.

Meditate on what you are in Reality. Try to realise that the body is not you, the emotions are not you, and the intellect is not you. When all these stand discarded you will find That.

Q: What is 'That'?
B: You will discover it yourself. It is not for me to say what any individual experience ought to be. 'That' will reveal itself to the mature aspirant automatically. When It does reveal itself, hold on to It without ceasing.

Q: I still maintain that in trying to still the mind, I am likely to fall asleep.

B: It does not matter. Put yourself into the condition that is in deep sleep, but with awareness. Then watch yourself to ensure that no thought arises to disturb your peace. Be asleep consciously, instead of unconsciously. There will be then only one consciousness.

From that time onwards, I started a routine that was to be the same for many weeks. The rickety cart would turn up at six in the morning. It took me up to the ashram and came back again at seven-thirty in the evening for the return journey.

Up at the ashram I was given a small hut, seven feet by seven, for my use during the day. In it was a wooden plank, a chair and a table on which were a basin, towel and soap. Not luxurious, but the thought and care with which it had been provided touched me more than I can say.

There were two chief meals at the ashram, one at eleven-thirty in the morning and the other around eight in the evening. I ate with the others at the morning one. The food was more or less the same at both – rice, with an assortment of vegetables and milk curd. Everybody sat on the floor in front of an individual strip of banana leaf.

The question of food, especially the strict vegetarian meals that were served in the ashram and the diet prescribed conducive for the spiritual seeker by Bhagavan himself, was something a Caucasian would necessarily question. So I sought decisive clarification from the Master on this practice.

Q: What diet is prescribed for a spiritual seeker?
B: *Sattvic* [clear, light] food in limited quantities.

Q: What is sattvic *food?*
B: Wheat, rice, vegetables, fruits, nuts, et cetera.

Q: Some Brahmins *take fish in Northern India. May it be done?*
No answer was made by Bhagavan.

Q: We Caucasians (western people) are accustomed to a particular diet;

change of diet affects health and weakens the mind. Is it not necessary to keep up physical health?

B: Quite necessary. The weaker the body the stronger the mind grows.

Q: In the absence of our usual diet our health suffers, and the mind loses strength.

B: What do you mean by strength of mind?

Q: The power to eliminate worldly attachment.

B: The quality of food influences the mind. The mind feeds on the food consumed.

Q: Really! How can the Caucasian adjust himself to sattvic *food only?*

B: (Asking another Caucasian who was seated in the vicinity) You have been taking our food. Do you feel uncomfortable on that account?

The gentleman responded by saying that he was comfortable with the food served in the ashram, owing to the fact that he was accustomed to it.

Q: What about those not so accustomed?

B: Habit is only adjustment to the environment. It is the mind that matters. The fact is that the mind has been trained to think of certain foods as being tasty and good.

The food material is to be had both in vegetarian and non-vegetarian diet equally well. But the mind desires flesh-food as it is accustomed to the same and considers it tasty.

Q: Are there restrictions for the emancipated soul in a similar manner?

B: No. He is steady and not influenced by the food he takes.

Q: Is not killing life to prepare meat-foods unethical?

B: For the *mumukshu* [seeker of liberation], yes. *Ahimsa* [non-violence] stands foremost in the code of discipline for yogis.

Q: But even plants have life.
B: So too the slabs you sit on!

Q: May we gradually get ourselves accustomed to vegetarian food?
B: Yes. That is the way. Food affects the mind. Certain kinds make it more *sattvic*. For the practice of any kind of yoga, vegetarianism is absolutely necessary.

Q: Why do you take milk, but not eggs?
B: The domesticated cows yield more milk than necessary for their calves, and they find it a pleasure to be relieved of the milk.

Q: But likewise the hen cannot contain her eggs!
B: But there are potential lives in them.

Q: Could one experience spiritual illumination whilst normally eating flesh foods?
B: Provided you slowly wean yourself away from them and gradually accustom the body to purer types of food. But in any case, once you have attained Illumination, it will make little difference what you eat. It is the early stages that are important. On a great fire it is immaterial what fuel is heaped.

Meditate on the Self, and on that alone. There is no other goal.

The Maharshi's philosophy and teaching is the purest form of *Advaita* [non-duality], known as *ajata Advaita* [the Absolute is *aja*, the unborn eternal non-duality].

As the days passed, I saw more and more clearly that this was no theoretical philosophy. He himself lived it continuously and joyously. He was one of the few I have met who were not only perpetually happy but also completely untroubled by the world.

(This dialogue has appeared in a Ramana Ashram publication – Ed.)

The Dialogues
in the
Diary Date Order – Summer 1936

6th July 1936

Who am I? Explained to Major Chadwick

Q: Who is a jnani*? What does he do? What does he see that others do not?*
B: One who does not know anything is called a *jnani*. He does not do anything and he does not see anything.

Q: What is the secret of Self-realisation?
B: Self-surrender.

Q: Is it not jnanavichara*?*
B: The variation is in phraseology only.

Q: Does jnanavichara *require a Guru?*
B: Yes.

Q: Guru's assistance is said to be a an essential condition for achieving Realisation. Is it so in all the margas *[paths]?*
B: Yes.

Q: Is free will only a myth?
B: Yes.

Q: What does Bhagavan think about abolition of the caste system and

removal of caste differences? Are not all of God's children created equally? Is not all creation equal before the eye of God?
B: His eye sees no creation.

Q: If Advaita *is the only truth, then why did Madvacharya talk about* Dvaita *[dual]?*
B: It may be better to ask him.

Q: But he is dead!
B: So am I.

Q: What is the significance of going around the Arunachala Hill?
B: The noose of Grace tightens and tightens and tightens around the neck of the Ego until it suffocates and eventually snaps.

Q: Will it alone do in the absence of any other sadhana, *to reach Bhagavan's High State?*
B: Yes.

Q: How many times should I go around the Hill to reach Final Liberation?
B: Until you are no longer able to stop (going around).

Q: The Aghori Swamis *of Benares, I hear, are cannibalistic. Is it not disgusting and abhorrent? Are there not plenty of other, good things to eat? Why eat human flesh and ordure?*
B: The purpose is to root out the idea, 'I am this body made of flesh and blood.' One who is content with his apparent bodily Existence never Realises the Self.

Q: Would Bhagavan have me turn into a cannibal, then?
B: You practise your method and let others practise theirs. The world would be a very sorry place indeed if only what you thought was right was allowed to be done. Each one wants to impose his ideas of moral rightness on the world. Die and let die – that should be the attitude!

A Tamil *pandit* [learned man] asked*: Your Self-realisation experience in a few words?*
B: I came. I saw. I was conquered.

Q: The summit of all knowledge?
B: Absence of all (objective) knowledge.

Q: The king of all virtues?
B: Compassion.

Q: The summit of all compassion?
B: (does not say anything)

Q: Is it Silence?
B: Yes.

Q: The indestructible wealth?
B: Poverty.

Q: The permanent happiness?
B: (The true import of) I!

Q: The eternal misery?
B: Want.

Q: The truly inseparable couple?
B: *Meipporulum prakrirtiyum* [Absolute truth and primordial nature]

Q: The eternally mutually antagonistic couple?
B: *Atrium urakkamum* [knowledge and sleep]

Q: The eternal secret?
B: Arunachala!

Q: That which eternally remains incapable of being spoken?

B: *Sadhvasthu* [true substratum].

Q: The sweetest ragam *[song]?*
B: *Thannunarvu* [Self-consciousness].

Q: The loftiest Siddhi *[magical power]?*
B: Self-abidance.

Q: The true nature of God?
B: Love.

The poet Muruganar was sitting in the Hall. At the end of the dialogue, his eyes were seen to be moist with feeling.

Q: I am a simple layman who is in search of realism. Swami, I ask you, having a longing, will you please teach me a simple and quick path to attain Mukti *[salvation]?*
B: *Irukkai* is the source from which emanates the thinking. Merge with that source.

Q: But what does it mean?
B: It means to remain permanently submerged in the Shining of the Heart (that is to say, the Beingness of the Self). The *irukkai* is the source from which emanates the thinking or accepting phase of the mind; it is of the nature of formless consciousness or of consciousness uncontaminated by thought. If we merge into the source from which emanates the thinking and manage to keep ourselves there once and for all, our troubles would be over.

Q: Is the Self or Heart pure Subjective Consciousness itself, or is pure Subjective Consciousness one of its attributes?
B: Neither statement is correct. Pure Subjective Consciousness is beyond the realm of thought, and the Self or Heart is beyond even pure Subjective Consciousness; pure Subjective Consciousness

proceeds from it, as does a ray of light from the sun.

Q: How then shall I reach the Self?
B: By going on investigating this thing that appears calling itself 'I'.

Q: Many seem to try. Not many seem to obtain a successful result.
B: It has to be done intensely and without stopping or pause. If a stray splinter of wood has pierced the gums, does the tongue keep quiet until it has been extracted?

Q: So, I should go on making effort until Realisation dawns?
B: Yes. Ceaseless practice of *vichara* is necessary until one obtains without the least effort that natural and primal state of mind that is wholly free from thought and intention.

Q: But Bhagavan seems to have said yesterday that we are already that, here and now, and that all we have to do to obtain Realisation is to give up the thought that we are not Realised. He also seems to have given the parable of the ten ignorant men crossing a river who lamented the loss of the drowned man, when in fact none of them had drowned, and that of the lady searching for the missing necklace, which had never left her neck, to illustrate his point.

Today Bhagavan is saying something that contradicts his previous statement. I am very confused between these contrasting positions. Please help me by throwing some light on the matter.
B: Constant, intense effort is absolutely necessary right up until the moment of Realisation. Those in the parables are in agony until the right knowledge dawns on them.

Your present state is one of constant changing of mind. When mind becomes steady in introversion owing to long practice, it is no longer willing to jump out at objects, whether sensory or of intellectual manufacture.

It is then that the dormant power asserts itself. 'The Absolute is already Realised' is a safeguard against the wrong idea that there is something new to be gained – that is all. The one that pulls back

cloud does not create sky. But if the sky has to be seen, the clouds have to be rolled away.

Chadwick was reading aloud to the Hall an English summary he had prepared from Bhagavan's essay *Who am I?*

> Since attainment of *Samadhi* is our goal, in order so as to unambiguously reach, the remembrance Who am I? should be held on to all the time; the means to so hold on is, when other (distracting) thoughts arise, one is not to pursue them, but ought to inquire as to whom they have arisen. No matter how many thoughts arise, with conscientiousness, each of them, even as they arise, if confronted with the question, to whom has this thought arisen, will lead to the answer, to me.
>
> If one enquires Who am I?, the mind goes back to its source and the thought also subsides. As one continuously practises on the above lines, the power of the mind to stay in its source is intensified. When, in this manner, the mind stays submerged in the Shining of the Heart, the thought that serves as the foundation for or underlying substance of all thought, the 'I'-thought, is discovered to be false (or incapable of Existence and thus non-existent or mythical), and THAT which always is alone shines forth.
>
> So long as (the discerning eye that is) the mind beholds impressions of objects, up until that time the before mentioned practice of Self-enquiry is necessary to be employed. As many thoughts there do that arise in (or gush forth with rapidity from) the mind, all, each and every one of them, without even a single one being spared, as and when they arise, then and there, at their very source, through the dint of Self-enquiry, should be comprehensively annihilated.

> If one were to permanently inhere in the Awareness of one's immediate sense of True Self, the sensation of 'I'-'I', that alone would do. (so as to have reached the state of freedom from the illusionary appearance of being ensnared in the cycle of birth and death and of separateness, described as True Immortality, which is simply abidance as pure and undifferentiated consciousness of Being, or Being One with the One Reality).

The above content is not reproduced from memory; I copied it out from Chadwick on a scrap of paper, and am now rewriting it in this notebook.

Bhagavan asked him: Have you prepared this synopsis so that you can memorise it and repeat it to yourself often?

Chadwick responded in the affirmative.
B: There is no harm in it if you felt the necessity, but actual practice alone will lead the way to Illumination.

C: Practice means encountering every thought with the counter-thought, 'To whom has this thought arisen?' Am I correct?
B: Asking Who am I? should return the mind to its primordial nature of Naked Beingness. That is its purpose and goal.

C: Beingness or subjective awareness uncontaminated by thought is also a component of mind. It remains after asking Who am I? Thus, when Bhagavan propounds that asking the question leads to destruction of mind, I am puzzled by the statement.
B: Beingness is not a component of the mind; it is its substratum. When that uncontaminated awareness remains so permanently, having once-and-for-all lost all volition to spill itself over into the realm of thought, it is also destroyed, but you have no role in that final destruction, nor do you have any power to bring it about. It is left entirely to the Beyond.

C: After that final destruction, what is left?
B: The Beyond. It is known as *Parabrahman* [Supreme Truth]. It cannot be described. The mind cannot imagine it. Yet it is your true Self.

C: So, our final aim is only this 'Parabrahman'*. Attaining it is called Self-realisation. Am I correct?*
B: There is no attaining it. If the reflected consciousness is cleared away, only the original consciousness remains. Destruction of the reflecting phenomenon, namely the delusive ego-mind, is the goal, or rather reveals the Goal. That is Self-realisation.

C.: Once attained, can Self-realisation be lost?
B: The phraseology used should be clear. Even a glimpse of *Brahman* by the mind in the realm of subjective awareness, can be called Self-realisation. Does it lead to freedom from rebirth or embodiment? No. A man cannot become a high officer merely by visiting one, making note of his educational qualifications, and mimicking his costume. The exceedingly rare state of *sahajajnanastithi* [establishing or dwelling in *Brahman*] is available only to one who has no *vrittis* [structures of the mind] left in the mind. Desires, attachments, opinions, preferences, traits of personality, et cetera, et cetera, are all examples of *vrittis*.

They cause pure Subjective Consciousness to spill over into the deceptive realm of thought, and trap one in the vicious cycle of births and deaths – that is, of embodiment. In those whose bondage is strong, *vrittis* are found to have impregnated themselves so strongly and deeply that they manifest as *vishayavasanas* [desires after sense objects]. *Vishayavasanas* are difficult to eradicate because they carry a pretentious, duplicitous sense of legitimacy about them. For instance, if a man is starving, try to go and tell him, 'It is all in the imagination,' you will likely be placing yourself at the receiving end of a few well-aimed blows...

C: (laughs) But then surely the basic requirements of bodily sustenance – food, water, clothes, a modest roof over one's head – surely these can be

considered reasonable?
B: Do not think that they are your requirements. They are the body's.

C: I am not the body, yet it is my duty to take reasonable care of the body. Am I correct? Not all have the Herculean spiritual strength to throw themselves into an abandoned underground cellar filled with centipedes and rats and focus on the Self only!
B: There is no need to fall into any cellar. If the 'body-am-I' idea is given up, and one surrenders oneself unconditionally to the mercy of the Higher Power, then responsibility for the body's maintenance is automatically thrown on the Higher Power and He carries on from there. You should not think, 'I have the duty of taking care of the body.' You have entrusted yourself to him; leave everything including the body to him. He manages everything supremely well. His ways are mysterious but in the end the job is done.

C: I have heard Bhagavan saying that the total destruction of all vasanas *is possible only in the final* Sahajastithi *[natural state]. I have also heard him say that without such destruction being effected the said state cannot be gained. It sounds paradoxical.*
B: It is paradoxical on the spurious, apparently-real level of the ego only; the ego is a self-contained illusion; when it goes away you find that it never existed.

C: I do not understand.
B: If Zeno's paradox of the race course were to be true, we should find it impossible to move from one place to another. Yet so far as the paradox is concerned, it appears sincerely true when studied or considered in isolated intellectual light. Is our day-to-day life experience compatible with the inference that is to be drawn from the paradox? Do we not find motion possible? Likewise, when pondered over using the intellect the question of Self-realisation is an annoying paradox; if the intellect is bypassed or transcended only the realm of Being remains. Therein no questions arise and only Silence reigns.

C: Vasanas *are a decisive obstacle to Self-realisation; yet repeated and continuous practice of* vichara *roots out the* vasanas *and Liberation is ultimately gained; so far it is clear.*

Can Bhagavan please tell me how the vasanas *arose out of what was originally pure Subjective Consciousness?*

B: The idea that *vasanas* are at present irrevocably tied together with consciousness, and that removing them through *sadhana* involves splitting these two ordinarily intertwined components of mind, is an incorrect understanding. *Vasanas* are seed-like impressions that direct consciousness along the narrow, finite channel known as the intellect.

***Vasanas* are tiny, insentient, imaginary layers that appear to have gathered atop the Self and prevent it from shining. They are neither real nor natural. Only Being is Real. You may dive into or submerge yourself in the Shining of the Heart and forget about destroying the *vasanas*.**

Abiding in that state in which mind has permanently been rendered one and identical with the Beingness of the Self, one need not worry about the fact that the mind is yet to die a conclusive death – let *granthinasam* [destruction of the knot] happen when it is destined to happen. You remain attending to ensuring absence of promiscuity of thought, and that is enough. When thoughts about *vasanas* perturb you, see whose *vasanas* they are.

C: The Self is the Almighty; such tiny vasanas *are able to obscure it!*

B: The obscuration is self-notional only. There is no ignorance in fact. Yet whilst *vasanas* remain, the final state will never be gained.

The Master read out from *Kaivalya Navaneetham* [Advaita classic in Tamil]:

> **• This foul thing called *vasana*, the never-ending temptation to indulge in enjoyment of sensual and sensuous worldly objects, is the bright indicator of the Existence of the Ignorance, which is the root-cause of the so-called cycles**

of sorrowful births and deaths, *samsara* [cycle of birth and death caused by *karma*]; whereas, the bright indicator of TRUE KNOWLEDGE is desireless.

• Ignorance means identifying one's Self with non-Self. By this means, the ego is caused to be developed; so also, the doer and the enjoyer, the *jiva* [the individual self]. Thus, the only obstacle that blocks Realisation of the true Self is this foul thing called *vasana*, which blocks It like dark clouds in a rainy season block the brightest Sun.

• The ego or *ahamvritti* [pure 'I am'-feeling] produces the enjoyment-thought patterns called *sankalpas* [will]. *Sankalpas*, when they are fully fattened, themselves become the bundles of desire stored in the form of *vasanas*, the evil store-houses of desire, in the memory location of the *jiva*. When relevant or appropriate place and time come, these fetid *vasanas*, one by one, tempt the *jiva* to jump into the noxious ocean of never-ending, ever-painful actions and reactions and make him reap the results thereof, the sorrows and perturbations, the births and deaths, of *samsara*.

• *Vasana prakshyo moekshaha* – the complete eradication or destruction of *vasana* or the memory-pattern of desires is called Emancipation.

• Due to the gigantic size and immense resistance of the heap of *vasanas* accumulated in the memory of the *jiva*, the negative potency of

mental impressions accumulated over countless hundreds of thousands of past incarnations, forcibly pull the aspirant outwardly towards the enjoyments of sensuous and sensual objects. So, it becomes natural to the mind to run outwardly, to fall into the deep ditch of sensuous and sensual enjoyments.

• With the mighty power of *vivegam* [prudence] and *vairagya* [detachment], the extroverted mind is stopped, introverted, subjugated and made to stay relentlessly, persistently, ever on the Self, the Witness. This is true *sadhana*.

Chadwick seemed overjoyed with the detailed explanation furnished by the Master. He bowed his imposing frame low before the Master, thanked the interpreter, and left the Hall.

• —— •

A visitor scrupulously juxtapositioning himself close to the Sofa and, perched there, speaking in a small, subdued tone.

Q: Why is everyone calling you Maharshi and Bhagavan, and giving you special treatment? Have you grown a horn like a rhinoceros on your head?
B: (bursting out laughing) I am as clueless as you are!

Q: Can I also become a Maharshi?
B: Yes, surely!

• —— •

Q: I have heard Bhagavan saying that vairagya *is necessary for the* sadhsishya *[true disciple]. What is* vairagya *[detachment]? Is it the attitude of non-attachment or dispassion towards worldly cares?*
B: What is merely an attitude of mind cannot be true *vairagya*. What is true *vairagya*? It is mental derailment.

Q: What?! Should we all become mad persons to attain Self-realisation?
B: Mental derailment is the total loss of belief in the objective reality of the world.

Q: One who is incapable, even at the intellectual level, of understanding or appreciating the Impersonal Absolute or Brahman, *but steadfastly worships and loves a personal God, will he be able to Realise the Self?*
B: God will appear to Him in the form of a *Satguru* [true Guru] and lead him to the Truth.

Q: How shall I obtain peace of mind?
B: The term 'peace of mind' is an illusion. It is the mind that obstructs your natural state of peace. While there is yet a mind, real peace is not to be had.

Q: In that case, how to get rid of the mind?
B: Only by tracing thought to its source and discovering that there is no mind to be got rid of.

Q: Is Self-realisation for all or only for those whose prarabdha karma *will allow it?*
B: Realisation is with the mind. *Karma* is for the body only.

Q: What is the cause of my birth? Is it karma*? How does one get rid of* karma*?*
B: What is birth?

Q: When the body comes into Existence, I call it birth.
B: Nothing comes into Existence or goes out of Existence. Existence was never created; it can never be destroyed. That which people commonly refer to as 'birth' is not the commencement of Existence but the assumption of limitations. On the other hand, 'death' is not dissolution or destruction of the body but Revelation of the Real Self.

Q: How to transcend the limitations?
B: See to whom they have arisen.

Q: Again, I feel like asking – Why was I born? I want to know the actual reason.
B: Who was born? If you were really born, should the question not arise in deep slumber also? Why does it not arise then?

Q: The mind is inactive in deep slumber.
B: Exactly! Thus, we discover that birth and death are in the mind only: they are only mental conceptions.

Q: Trailanga Swami of Benares was three times the size of the average man's girth; yet I have heard that he had the ability to fly up high in the air. Also, his age at the time of death was estimated to be 450 years. How are these supernatural phenomena to be explained?
B: Supernatural phenomena have been termed so because they can never be explained to the satisfaction of the intellect.

Q: Will Bhagavan not impress us by displaying any fantastic siddhis *which defy the known laws of physics?*
B: Loss of the personal 'I' is the supreme *siddhi*.

Q: Is hathayoga *[system of physical yoga techniques] of any benefit to the aspirant?*
B: In the early stages of *sadhana*, it might be. It is not indispensable.

Q: What is Sri Bhagavan's opinion on the theory of reincarnation? Is there rebirth?
B: Are you born now?

Q: Yes, I am aware of my Existence in this body.
B: Does the awareness of the body remain in deep slumber?

Q: The mind was inactive in sleep; so it could not be aware of the body – but the next morning again there is the same body. Is it all mere illusion?

B: Yes.

Q: If everything is an illusion, then how did the illusion arise? How did I get trapped in it?
B: Ask yourself to whom the illusion arose and you will discover there never was any illusion.

Q: So, it is 'illusory illusion'?
B: Exactly.

Q: But why did the Self fall from his natural state and become the ego?
B: The Self remains always in His natural state. It is you who are running away from Him!

Q: Who am I, apart from Him?
B: That is it – find out!

Q: If I surrender my apparent individuality to the Self, will Self-realisation be the consequence?
B: Unconditional surrender is the Goal itself.

As Bhagavan finished speaking a piece of railway track was heard noisely banging against stone. It was lunch time at the Sage's hermitage. **'Oh! Already!'** exclaimed the Maharshi sweetly. Then he rose and left the Hall.

In the evening, an old man wearing traditional caste marks came and stood near Bhagavan and addressed him:

Q: I have read the Advaita *philosophy, but it has no appeal to me. I am not interested in taking up Bhagavan's* atmavichara *[Self-enquiry] method. All I want is to see* Rama *[The Lord]. I want to be with* Rama *all the time. Even thinking of* Rama *fills me with Bliss. I want to go to* Rama. *Will Bhagavan tell me the route to him or not? I care nothing for the Impersonal* Brahman. *All I want is* Rama. *Where is* Rama? *Please tell me, Bhagavan.*

I want to go to Rama. *Will Bhagavan please show me the way to* Rama? Rama! Rama! Rama! *Where is* Rama*?* (Every time the visitor said '*Rama*' his face lit up in ecstasy. He seemed to be moved to tears at the mere thought of *Rama*.)

B: (cryptically but emphatically) Soon *Rama* will recall you to His Kingdom.

This terse assurance seemed to satisfy the old man. He prostrated and left.

• —— •

Q: I meditate continuously on the pranava *[cosmic sound] or* omkara [OM] *sound. Is it sufficient for Self-realisation or is* vichara *also needed?*

B: Makes no response.

Q: (after some time, as if struck by Realisation) Yes, now I understand.

• —— •

Q: If I uninterruptedly stay in Bhagavan's physical presence or proximity for twelve continuous years, commencing with today, will I be able to Realise the Self automatically? It is said that satsangam *[association with spiritual teacher] is necessary and sufficient to Realise.*

B: No such guarantee can be given.

Q: Many Gurus claim that their mere physical presence enlightens their pupils.

B: Then why come here and waste your time, instead of going to those Gurus?

Q: I want to know what Bhagavan thinks about it – if Bhagavan thinks their claims are genuine or otherwise.

B: Bhagavan does not think about it.

Q: How to tell if a Guru is genuine or not?

B: Makes no response.

11th July 1936

Samuel Cohen Asking Questions

Bhagavan's *prarabdha* [destiny], however, it seemed, was that his throat should have no rest that day. A man, whom I noticed almost every day at the Hall, perhaps an American, wearing North Indian clothes and a ridiculous cap, seated at the rear of the Hall, presently rose and came forward to an empty place on the floor, and started asking his questions one after the other.

Q: Some succeed in Realising the Real; others fail, though effort might be the same in both cases. Can we say prarabdha *is the reason and dismiss the matter at that?*
B: The more one turns inward, the more he succeeds in transcending the three-fold *karma*, because only his body is bound by it, and he identifies himself less and less with the body as his Self-absorption in Being-Consciousness becomes more and more continuous and intense. Finally any sort of bodily or other identification becomes impossible, and he quietly reposes in the Shining of the Heart always, whether his body is idle or active.

Q: But what is the answer to my question?
B: No, *prarabdha* cannot be said to be the reason.

Q: Then what is the reason?
B: When a man is told he is neither the body nor the mind, he is initially puzzled, because all along his life his experience of self has been confined to these two only. When he hears the words of the *Jnanaguru* [true Guru] for the first time, he learns to his shock that these two are suddenly to be regarded as unreal, insignificant and immaterial, and Consciousness of Being alone is to be treated as Real and material.

To one whose understanding of the world is sustained by conceptual knowledge and whose life is ruled by subject–object

relationships, this can be too much of a shock to bear. He either laughs off the *ajata Advaita* [the Absolute is *aja*, the unborn eternal; non-duality] doctrine as sheer nonsense developed by mischievous minds that have nothing better to do or takes it seriously and is shocked by the implications – everything he has ever known and cherished in his life is now suddenly revealed to be meaningless, replaceable, shortlived, and fickle, and so unreal and unworthy of consideration.

Whereas what he had never before paid attention to is revealed as the only permanent, abiding Reality. To one who has up until that point in time been regarding himself as a subject, finite across time and space, occupying an objective world, this revelation comes as a great emotional and mental upheaval, because he is attached to the things of the world.

One whose past *sadhanas* have weakened all attachment takes naturally to the idea that the world is a dream – either way it is not going to matter to him because he is not interested in it. The idea that the world does not exist as a collection of independent objects, but rather depends upon perception for its apparent Existence, shocks some people.

The evidence of the five sensory organs is merely random 'information'. It does not denote that any such object is actually 'out there'; there is no 'out there'. The inlet of consciousness is only one; therefore, all perceived depends upon the perceiver only; this consciousness, turned outside, is the world and its perceiver; turned inside it finds that it is the Self. *Jagratprama* is the *prama* [knowledge of the world] of *jagratpramata* [the knower of the world]. Apart from the perceiver there is no such thing as the perceived. The *pramata* [the subjective knower] believes he knows so many things about the world; he is merely accessing the contents of his own mind.

All thoughts and perceptions are intra-mental modifications. The light of the Self falls on the *ahamvritti* [pure 'I am'-feeling, 'I'-thought] and its children and a *jiva* [individual soul] is born. (In this context, Sri Bhagavan refers to the other *vrittis* originating from the *ahamvritti* as the children of the *ahamvritti*.) **It is for the aspirant to destroy all the other *vrittis*. The Self takes care of the nude *ahamvritti* – that is, destroys it. Then it will remain without reflection.**

Q: This is pure Egoism – To be is to be.
B: The Egoist says the mind is real, that everything, including the world and thoughts, that proceed from it is a phantom or shadow. He does not question the reality of the mind itself.

I am asking you to go even further. I say that the mind itself is a shadow or phantom proceeding from the Self. You will discover this as a matter of direct experience – if only you will probe into the source of the mind. You ask why some do not Realise. You wonder whether *prarabdha* [destiny that effects our life now] might be the reason. No. *Prarabdha* has no power to pull back into the world a *jiva* that is adamantly determined to disappear in its source forever. Then what is the reason, you ask.

This is the reason – clinging fast to objective knowledge. There are learned *pandits* [learned men] who have written rich commentaries – volume after volume – upon various *advaitic* texts which directly propound the *ajata Advaita* doctrine – *Ashtavakra Gita, Ribhu Gita, Panchadasi, Kaivalya Navaneetham, Ozhivil Odukkam*, et cetera…Go to their houses when a much-loved, much-feted child has died, and ask how they feel. You may be met with a hostile stare. If you sit down then and there and explain all this, you may count yourself lucky if permitted to leave with your life.

Where does the problem lie? All the learning has been in vain, because it has stopped at the level of the intellect. It is unable to crush the ego, because there was no practice. The only effort made was to read more books, go on writing commentaries, and go on receiving distinctions for being 'an expert in the field of *Advaita*', thus making the ego grow bigger and bigger. Never was effort made to still the ceaseless waves of thought. Even some effort in that direction might have brought a reciprocal flow of Grace from the Self. But no.

Read, write, receive shawls at book-launch festivals, imagine

oneself to be acting in a highly intelligent manner in saying the words, 'No, no, it is all God's work. I am an instrument in his hands, that is all.' Receive applause, and inflate the ego further and further. The Sun and the Earth may one day decide to interchange their positions out of boredom, but such people, who are infatuated with the poisonous wine of love for book-learning, cannot obtain True Knowledge.

Objective knowledge and book-learning are the most deadly enemies on the path to Self-realisation, because they are expertly disguised as sweet friends, and the disguise runs deep indeed.

Q: If I Realise, one reflection is destroyed. What about the others living in the world? When will everyone wake up?

B: You first do it and see and then raise the question afterwards if need be. After waking up from a dream, do you ponder, 'Oh! I dreamt of so many people drowning, I wonder if anyone has rescued them or whether they perished?'

Q: So I alone am ignorant – rather, I alone am! But then I should feel hopelessly lonely.

B: Being alone means remaining without thinking thoughts, and that includes remaining without the thought, 'I am alone' or 'I am lonely'.

Q: When told I am the Self why do I not rest content in that knowledge? Why do I continue to stray into the realm of thought?

B: There is a dishonest sense of legitimacy attached to the *ahamvritti*. This is the cause of your trouble; it must go before good results can follow. This may be termed the 'Weltanschauung' (world view) of the ego. It is to the *ahamvritti* what the brain is to the heart. Without the heart, there would be no supply of oxygen to the brain and the body's survival would not be possible; without the operation of that portion of the brain which regulates involuntary muscular activity, the heart would not find contraction and expansion possible because the neuro-electrical impulses that propel its function would not be available, likewise rendering the

body's continued survival impossible.

Killing the one, kills the other. Killing either of them, kills the body beyond the point of resuscitation. Likewise here. Killing the 'Weltanschauung' kills the *ahamvritti*, and vice versa. Killing either of them destroys the ego once and for all. The *bhakta* [a devotee of God] who surrenders, completely destroys thereby any importance 'I' has for itself – thus he uproots the 'Weltanschauung'. The *jnanasadhaka* [a true spiritual seeker] keeps on trying to find 'I' – thus he uproots the *ahamvritti.* Note that this explanation is for analytical purposes only. To explain to you the two parallel approaches I have created this intellectual division.

Actually world view and *ahamvritti* are simply two different shades or aspects of the ego, just like how a chameleon changes colour depending upon the colour of the immediate environment, but is in fact the same chameleon. The *ahamvritti* is the thought 'I'; the 'Weltanschauung' is the intellectual framework which legitimises the apparent, illusory, individual existence of this thought 'I' by making it associate itself with equally fictitious objects or surroundings. This is because the thought 'I' cannot remain in the absence of such association.

Thus killing the 'I' causes intellection or association to end automatically, and putting an end to the habit of intellection or association kills the 'I' automatically. 'I' and its objectifying or associative tendency amount therefore to one and the same thing, but its destruction may be carried out either way, depending upon the individual's psychological temperament. If you are unsure (laughing) mount a two-pronged attack! When Alexander the Great invaded India, King Purushottama, emperor of the Punjab, who is said to have been Alexander's most formidable enemy, was defeated by him in this manner when all other tactics failed. There is no escape from between the twin jaws of a crocodile.

Whenever the ego seems too noisy and difficult, and refuses to surrender itself, tackle it with *vichara*; whenever you feel you are too mentally beleaguered and weakened to take up *vichara*, surrender! A battle of annihilation on one side, and a battle of

attrition on the other – that ought to win the war! But remember – all this, whilst your body is engaged in its worldly activities! Never use *ajata Advaita* as an excuse to deliberately avoid your duties, telling yourself, 'Everything is an illusion; why should I make any effort if everything is a dream?'

Q: Yes, that is what I was about to ask! Sri Bhagavan has read my mind with uncannily acute accuracy!
B: Giving up worldly duties will lead to more complications than you might be able to presently imagine. You will be jumping from the frying pan, straight into the fire!

Q: Is it possible to keep the mind on the Self, and yet attend to one's work as usual?
B: Why not?

Q: For a spiritual Hercules like Sri Bhagavan it is doubtless child's play. What about me?
B: Yes, what about you?

Q: How can one remaining without thinking, which is what is meant by fixation of attention on the Self, carry on worldly duties? As an example of the point I am trying to make, suppose during the course of my vocation I have often to perform arithmetic operations involving sets of large numbers – this would involve accessing and using logarithmic tables; so, what do I do? Does it not become necessary to employ the mind – at least part of it? Can one use logarithmic tables without the mind?
B: The problem is that you are so used to bodily-identification that you think you are the doer of the actions your body performs. It is the Higher Power who does everything. You just appropriate credit or merit for yourself. A little practice will make you see the truth. Do you have the habit of riding bicycles?

Q: (surprised) Certainly – why, does using a bicycle somehow strengthen the ego?!

B: (laughing genially) No, no! Listen! Do you sometimes sing as you ride?

Q: (astonished at the Maharshi's clairvoyance) Why, yes! How does Bhagavan know all this?!

B: I heard it from somebody. Now, the point is – has it been your experience or not that on familiar terrain, sometimes you are so absorbed in the delightful song that is being sung by you, that you find that you have reached your intended destination, although the route was a complicated one, although there were buffalos and bullock carts that needed to be dodged along the way, and although the weather was far from perfect when you were travelling?

Q: (nearly laughing in stupefied wonder) Yes! Good heavens, yes! But what has it got to do with...?

B: Yet if anyone asks you to travel without paying attention to what you are doing, you would doubtless consider him mad?

Q: Meaning no disrespect – certainly yes.

B: Thus you see my point. We set too much store by our intellect. We think we make choices. We think we are in control. We think we do everything the body does. We think we make the body move, speak and behave the way it does. It is a cleverly constructed sham! Everything happens of its own accord, including bodily movements. So there is no such thing as 'acting on a decision'. Free-will is an illusion. The world of events and the world of thought both lie in the mind, but are not connected and are not mutually interdependent.

You say that you make a decision, and then act upon it. Consider what actually happens. The action is decided by *prarabdha*. Whichever way you decide, the outcome of the decision will ultimately be only the destined action, and nothing else! Thus the decision does not count at all. So, no action is ever the outcome of man's decision. We delude ourselves into thinking so. Since knowledge of the future is excluded from man,

he cannot possibly know whether actions follow thoughts or whether thoughts simply fall in line before forthcoming actions, like iron filings before a bar magnet, so creating an illusory cause–consequence relationship between thoughts and actions, whereas, in fact, it might be a consequence–cause relationship...

'Man can do what he wants, but he cannot will what he wills,' Schopenhauer has said; the same truth of what I am saying may be put this way also. In either case the inference drawn is that free will could not possibly exist. Once you cease to believe in free-will, the grip of the ego loosens automatically.

Q: (doubtfully) It was alright in case of riding a bicycle, physical coordination was enough. But extending it to all cases of activity (shakes his head thoughtfully).

B: I repeat – practice will reveal the truth of what I am saying. Practise remaining as pure Subjective Consciousness of Being and see whether actions go on by themselves or not.

Q: What if the actions are not according to my liking?

B: You aspire for Self-realisation. Yet you want to live life on your own terms! No other aspiration can meaningfully co-exist with the aspiration for Self-realisation. In due course, even the aspiration for Self-realisation becomes an obstacle to blossoming into Self-realisation – for whatever shall we do with the aspirant? Thus, as *sadhana* gains in momentum, even the aspiration for Self-realisation must be given up. Once you are in the hands of the Higher Power, your own will or opinion is not permitted to stand in the way. You become clay in his hands. Every last notion is demolished, every learned thing unlearned, all objective knowledge undone, despoiled, and destroyed, to reveal the pure substratum shining underneath as 'I'-'I'.

Concerning the question of physical renunciation, life in the world is to be kept up as before – if it be the will of the Higher Power. If you remain in the world, you do so on his terms; if you renounce, again it is only on his terms. He decides whether you stay

in the home or forest or both. To you it is altogether immaterial where the body is or what it is doing. So far as you are concerned, you gave up everything you had, or believed yourself to have, the day you renounced your ego to the Self, and that includes the body.

Your renunciation is complete then and there. The confusing collection of name and form that is called 'world' is revealed to be none other than sweet, lovely Self, once the ego perishes in the light of true Self-knowledge. This is *jnana* [spiritual knowledge].

13th July 1936

Samadhi from Major Chadwick's Notebook

A Moslem gentleman asked –

Q: Bhagavan used two different terms yesterday – Self-realisation and Sahajastithi *[natural state]. Is there a difference? Is the former a translated version of the latter?*

B: Once the mind apprehends *Brahman* in the realm of Subjective Experience, it is no longer interested in the quirks of the world. It stays aloof from sensory experiences, thinking of them neither as a burden nor as a pleasure. The *sadhaka* who has understood the impermanent, illusory, and transitory nature of manifestation, after a prolonged period of *vichara abhyasa* [Self-enquiry practice], perceives the world only as a dream, and sees objects of the world as merely mental projections (whereas the *jnani* would see the Self only).

Such a one may be called Self-realised. However, his mind is not destroyed and *vasanas* remaining in seed-form cause inevitable

rebirth. He cannot be said to possess the Transcendental Awareness that the *jnani* is always in. When, by the compassionate Grace of God or Guru the remaining *vasanas* which pose an impediment are also destroyed, the mind is pulled into the Heart. There it perishes like a salt doll thrown into the ocean. This is the final *Sahajastithi* [natural state] of the *jnani*, and this alone confers freedom from future births.

Q: Yesterday Bhagavan clarified about the three kinds of Samadhi. *I have been thinking about it. I want to ask – is it necessary to go through the trance-like* nirvikalpa *before moving on to the* Sahaja*?*
Bhagavan called Chadwick to his side and said something to him. Chadwick exited the Hall and presently returned with a notebook,

Chadwick reads out as follows notes he had made from an early conversation with Bhagavan:

> I asked my Master if He would mind giving me a detailed explanation concerning the term *Samadhi*, and its various kinds. The Lord Ramana graciously assented and sweetly spoke the following words:-
> **The meaning of the word *Samadhi* is generally given as Union with Reality, but it is not so. *Samadhi* means the State of non-differentiation from Reality or THAT – WHICH – IS. The following are its kinds:**
>
> **1. *Savikalpa Samadhi* [thoughts still exist but they do not affect] – mind is forced by effort of will to hold on to pure BEING – without such deliberate attentiveness or volition, the mind starts straying into world of sense-objects or realm of thoughts again – *vrittis* or concepts remain in latent-form or seed-form – if concentration is sufficiently advanced one**

progresses from here to *Aham Sphurana.* This is generally not characterised by loss of body-consciousness – 'I'-'I' pulsation is distinctly felt – bliss experienced – continuous inherence in *Aham Sphurana* leads to *Sahaja* [spontaneous enlightenment] *Samadhi* thus bypassing requirement for *Kevala Nirvikalpa Samadhi.*

2. *Kevala Nirvikalpa Samadhi* – mind temporarily merged in *Parabrahman* – like bucket dropped into a well, but rope attached using which to haul it up again – rope represents *vasanas* or *vrittis* or *samskaras* [mental imprints] – concepts or *vrittis* are merely in suspension; they merely temporarily disappear only to reappear after the trance comes to an end – nor was possibility of 'I'-'I' pulsation or any other sensation to be known during the duration of the trance – for that duration of time there is no one whom it can occur to – when the word 'time' is used, it refers to the experience (not actual experience, for that is only Being, but apparent impression formed by an extroverted mind) of the onlooker, of time passing.

People immersed in *Kevala Samadhi* are not conscious of passage of time because for that duration, as marked only by the observer, he is dead as an individual and alive only as Reality – no mind during *kevala* trance – thus, not possible to cognise anything known as 'time' – complete absence of body-consciousness – even involuntary bodily functions cease – body becomes cadaver – no way to tell apart from actual cadaver – occupant body may be abandoned for good due to the intensity of

the bliss experienced – if so, taking up of new body, gross/subtle, inevitable, because *vrittis* remain in seed-form. The difference between *yoganidra* [yogic sleep] and *Kevala Samadhi* – *yoganidra* brought about based on Patanjali's teachings or *rajayoga* [royal path] method misapplied – deadliest of all stumbles on spiritual path – must be very careful to avoid – simply a long spell of sleep-like condition.

Story of man doing what he thought was *tapas* [austerities], on banks of river Ganges – asks disciple to fetch water from river to drink and goes into trance – wakes up 1000 years later – no river to be found – landscape has changed completely and finds his body immersed in a swamp – first thought that occurs to him after waking from trance – I want water to drink – therefore 1000 years totally wasted.

Yogi thinks experience of pleasure or bliss by him means Salvation – nothing could be more absurd – many doing *vichara* think they have found Reality and fall into this trap – very difficult to leave – more addictive than cocaine, morphine, etc. – how to find out if one is confronted with this danger – just after a heavy meal where favourite dishes have been served, one is relaxing – there is a pleasant lull in the mind – no thoughts – just pleasure which stands on the threshold of drowsiness – this is precisely similar to condition of *yoganidra*, only intensity of the pleasure is heightened manifold – mind not thinking, not sleeping, not dreaming, not cut-off to sensory-perceptions totally, but yet NOT Self-aware – just a blank mind.

Many poor souls when asked to remain

without thinking go to this state because this is the only thought-free state they know. They think this is the goal of Self-enquiry – think this is liberation – but this is a dead end – worst thing that could happen to a *sadhaka* – once mind gets used to this sort of poisonous pleasure, would find coming out less and less desirable and therefore progressively less and less possible – no rescue possible after the initial stage – *tamasic* [darkness] nature grows on increasing – Eternal Damnation.

To avoid, mind must focus not on pleasure, or happiness, or joy but on ensuring absence of distractions to BE-ing – after certain critical limit of *tamas* [dark, inertia] reached and exceeded, *rajas* [passion] and sattva [clear, light] reduced to negligible quantities – thus taking on body to alter the balance between the *gunas* [attributes] so that Realisation can be reached by making *sattva* only predominant *guna*, no longer possible because not adequate *sattva* and *rajas* left to work with to form body gross or subtle – no help possible.

***Tamas* grows and grows – body becomes a vegetable and then rots away – mind's *tamas* is on the decline – unless *Ishwara* [the supreme Being] himself takes pity and adds *rajas* to favourably balance the mix, thus putting the poor soul in some primitive body, so that he can go on from there, increasing sattva, no deliverance possible – great danger in *rajayoga* [royal path] and *kundalini* [divine energy] yoga method.**

That is why Bhagavan does not encourage – danger exists even for *vichara*

practitioners who want pleasure or bliss more than freedom from bondage – whilst living on the Hill Bhagavan encountered one such yogi Adhityanath – body falling into pieces on account of neglect – everyone thought he was in *Samadhi*, revered him.

Bhagavan could see the truth – he had lost himself in a yogic trance [*yoganiththirai*] – Bhagavan tried to help him once – man angrily pushed Bhagavan away, had become addicted to the pleasure, would never give it up – Bhagavan left him to his fate and came away because nothing could be done.

That is why it is important that AWARENESS OF BEING be sustained throughout the *sadhana* – the moment Self-awareness started to fluctuate or lull tried to take control, one had to stubbornly pull mind back into realm of Being – pleasure or bliss not the goal – only one true goal – destroy possibility of manifestation – consciousness free from *upadhis* has got to be sustained throughout *sadhana* for it to succeed – birth man's greatest disease – common man thinks birth = commencement-of-Existence – nothing could be further from the truth – birth = assumption-of-limitations – this had to be understood at intellectual level before any meaningful *sadhana* could begin.

3. *Sahaja Nirvikalpa Samadhi* [the mind is dead, resolved into the Self] – no description in words could do justice. No concepts, no sensations, no experience, no bliss, no cosmos, no person, no God, no nothing. HE IS THAT in which manifestation and its absence are

contained and that by virtue of which presence or absence of manifestation is able to be perceived – experience of the Self by the mind is blissful – Self itself neither bliss nor agony – it is as it is – words *trupthi* [satiatedness] or *shanti* more meaningfully describe Self than *ananda* [bliss], though descriptions cannot afford a glimpse into that state – state known as *Sahajastiti*, not newly created – even now it is there and you are THAT.

But mind veils it – search for mind – mind never existed, but it is to be practically discovered not to exist so as for Realisation to occur – discoverer himself does not remain to say I have made discovery – only Self remains – end of all effort – ONLY means of freedom from rebirth lies in this state.

<u>Additional Notes: *Kevala Samadhi* state,</u> though not as bad as *nidra* [sleep] state, not in fact desirable – does not happen to all aspirants – it is a waste of time that could otherwise be used to destroy *vasanas* that prevent one from reaching the final goal – goal not to attain Self – what nonsense, who can attain Self – besides the Self what could exist – are there two Selves – goal to destroy illusory not-Self so that Self alone remains.

***Kevala Samadhi* generally achieved by faithful followers of Patanjali or *ashtanga* [the eight limbs of yoga] yoga school – again some danger – aspirant would think final goal has been reached once mind has known *Brahman* once – sheer absurdity – temptation to go into *Kevala Samadhi* instead of rooting out *vasanas* intensely because of the terrific bliss felt – thus**

final goal delayed – right Master has to arrive to convince him this is not final state – problem is, would call himself a *brahmajnani* [person with knowledge of the Self], think himself to be a knower of *Brahman*, allow his ego to decline, would not listen to right advice – insensitive behaviour may come on – thus this state best avoided – family-members may be alarmed, may cremate body, no telling when body-consciousness might return – *vicharamarga* [path of Self-enquiry] by-passes this stage.

***Aham Sphurana* already described serves as substitute – *Kevala Samadhi* in fact a by-lane, not to be aspired for – those who want Bliss of *Brahman* without losing personality or individuality, *Kevala Samadhi* last threshold for them – *jnanamarga* does not embrace desire for bliss – *vicharamarga* aspirant must not aspire at all – remaining naturally without desire is the hallmark of ideal *jnanamarga* aspirant – even desire for Enlightenment is a serious hindrance – just like you forego other desires, forego desire for trance or bliss or Enlightenment also, by asking, to whom same has occurred.**

REMAIN AS YOU ARE – free from thoughts, ideas, desires and all other sorts of *vrittis* – remaining in natural state alone true freedom, because this state cannot complain about embodiment or bondage – why *sahaja Samadhi* [the natural state of being] explained only as negation – it is that which is beyond the ultimate – here no one besides the Self exists to experience the bliss of the Self, and the Self is not capable of experiencing anything, not even Itself – no question of perceiving anything –

nothing apart from Him for Him to percieve – that is why called *Advaita* and not *ekatva* [unity] – no question of *jivatman* ever reaching *Parabrahman* – if He be pleased with aspirant's sincerity, He himself reaches out and destroys him – this action naturally happens – no faculty of volition present in *Parabrahman* to decide, let us give this *jivatman* liberation or destroy him.

If *jivatman* approaches close enough, automatically sucked in and annihilated – but for this *jivatman* has to approach very very close – Master gives example of asteroids passing close to the sun in orbit – the energy with (or velocity at or whatever it is) which the body is going around the sun and its distance from the sun would usually suffice to ensure that it was not pulled in by the massive gravity of the sun; progressive reduction in either of these two factors would make it more and more likely that the body might crash into the sun – likewise, according to Bhagavan 'I'-thought and its objectifying tendency were two factors that prevented ego from merging into Self – crush one of them totally, and that was enough – Guru's Grace like friction-action of debris that gradually reduces the speed of the body and gradually alters the course of its orbit so that it will eventually surely gravitate toward Sun – devotional path snapped ego's brain, the objectifying tendency – investigation path snapped ego's heart.

The 'I'-thought – these two are aspects of same ego – killing one would kill the other and kill the ego – some aspirants ask I am ready

for liberation why am I yet to be liberated – it shows they are not ready at all – the truly ready aspirant has no *sankalpa* [will] or volition left to make any such communication, for the extent of his Self-surrender is total – what is surrender – to surrender is to cease to have any cares, leaving it to the Lord to do as he likes with you.

The truly surrendered one asks nothing because he feels no need, no desire – he does not even want non-Existence of misery, much less aspire for release from *samsara* – *jnani* is always in *Samadhi* whether body moves about or is stationary or is dead – *jnani* cannot see his body – there is only one thing that He can do and know and that is to BE the Self – people say so-and-so is a *jnani* – from the *jnani's* own point of view this has no meaning – nothing in him to manufacture the assertion I am a *jnani* – there is simply no one there localised in terms of that body – the wise *sadhaka* does not decide to quit the household – nor does he decide to move into the jungle – he silently surrenders his faculty of volition to the Higher Power and is meekly led by it wherever it takes him, jungle or household, heaven or hell – since he has already freed himself from the body-am-I idea, he would not think, 'I am being taken somewhere.'

Unselfish Love for God is called *bhakti* – unselfish love is not for the sake of acquisition of material possessions, nor for attainment of heavenly realms, nor for attainment of Salvation, nor for breaking free from the wheel of births-and-deaths, nor for fulfilment of altruistic or philanthropic motives concerning upliftment of Humanity – unselfish love is not

even accompanied by the hope or expectation of being loved in return; it has nothing to ask – unselfish love simply knows to love, that is all – the earnest *bhakta* is not affected by the presence or absence of all or any of the worlds – his own apparent Existence is an inexplicable embarrassment for him, for to him everything is the Lord's.

His will becomes entirely non-existent, the Lord's will taking its place – that is the love Job in the Bible had for God, that the *gopis* [*female devotees*] had for *Krishna* [supreme God, eighth avatar of *Vishnu*], that Karna had for Duryodhana, love that knows to love only – if you are able to cultivate this kind of mad, all-consuming Love for God, the resultant intoxication will ensure that worries about employment, means-of-livelihood, et cetera, are kept well away from your mind – the truly surrendered one has no hopes or expectations as to what he wants the future to be; whatever happens, he accepts the same as the will of his Lord; indeed, he sees only the Lord Himself in all the objects and events that he experiences in the *jagrat* and *swapna* states – you can never make him experience pain, because the moment his body feels distress, he tells himself, 'It pleases the Lord to cause one of his possessions to undergo such-and-such sensations; who are we to question His will and why would we need to bother ourselves with the propriety of His decisions? It is for us to meekly submit to Him, and, keeping quiet, leave the rest to Him; that is all.

Cultivate this attitude and then no worry can touch you – you were not born by reason

> **of your own volition; remain unconcerned, indifferent and disentangled also from everything that follows birth; this is the true renunciation – remaining as One with the Heart is neither a goal to be reached nor can it meaningfully be the object of any ambition or aspiration; it is the natural state of one and all; to remain as this pure undifferentiated Being, in which the faculty of otherness-causing differentiation is dead, and in which there are no concepts, is no accomplishment: it is THAT with which you are identical; it is you; YOU ARE THAT – what is liberation – complete bondage to God is known as liberation.**

Major Chadwick from England is a long-standing senior devotee of the Maharshi. He arrived a year before me (Gajapathi Aiyyer) and was fortunate enough to stay at the Ashram right till the Master's death. What you see above are the original notes made by Major Chadwick directly from the Sage's words. On this occasion, the gentleman was requested by Bhagavan only to read those portions of his notes that dealt with the topic of *Samadhi*.

Accordingly, he did so, reading out quickly sentences from the notes you find enclosed above. Since he spoke quickly, I had difficulty following him. Since I wanted the information, I later approached the gentleman and explained that I had failed to properly follow what he had read in the Hall, and that if I might read his notes I would be glad to do so. He accordingly consented and handed over to me a sheaf of papers, and I quickly copied out the notes contained in them.

I was so enchanted by Bhagavan's words that I copied all of the notes the Major had made as contained in the said sheets, and not merely the portions pertaining to *Samadhi*. I have faithfully reproduced those very notes here, though they certainly extend beyond the scope of the conversations that took place at the Hall on this date, since I am confident the gentle reader will welcome any opportunity not to miss the Master's words.

Whilst compiling this manuscript I wondered if I might convert these short hints into sentences; then I decided against it because I myself was not present when these statements were made by the Sage, and therefore, in the interest of preservation of authenticity, it struck me that it might be a better idea to leave them in their original, precise, concise form. I do not think any of the Master's devotees would encounter any difficulty in ingesting, digesting, and assimilating these quick, penetrating bites of wisdom.

15th July 1936

The World is Only in the Mind

Samuel Cohen has returned!

Q: I have heard Bhagavan saying 'Knowledge of the world is exclusively knowledge of the knower of the world.' What does it mean?

B: That the world is only in the mind – that the appearance of any world, or the phenomenon of manifestation, is not possible in isolation from your mind.

Q: Are there as many minds in the world as there are people? Are all these minds emanating from the Self at the same time?

B: There are not multiple minds. Only your mind emerges from the Self, styles itself 'I', makes the assumption that the objects it perceives through the senses are apart from it and have an objective Existence independent of its perception of them, generates desires towards those objects, feels frustrated when those desires are prevented from being fulfilled, asks questions about the meaning

and purpose of life, and finally raises as respects itself the doubt Who am I?, as a result of which it subsides quietly back into the Self.

The entirety of this cycle is happening only from the point of view of the mind. The Self is not aware of any change. Since all perception (sensory or intellectual) is perception only of what does not exist, and since the idea of 'other minds' is only an inference that forms the subject-matter of a mental perception, there are no other minds. Yours is the only mind that appears to be, and if you go on closely and intensely investigating it for a prolonged and intermittent period of time, that will also vanish, leaving behind only the substratum that always was.

Q: How can that be? Just as I have a mind, so too must the others in this Hall – except Bhagavan, of course, who has successfully eradicated it.
B: The scene appearing in front of your eyes is a fabrication of your own mind only.

Q: Is there any proof for this?
B: The world and mind arise and set together as one. Consider the state of *sushupti* [deep sleep]. Did multiplicity exist for you then?

Q: The universe may exist in sleep but go unperceived.
B: The perceiver is the only creator and the one exclusive cause for manifestation – and in his absence there is nothing but Bliss.

Q: I understand this line of reasoning. But again I ask – how can it be proven?
B: The entity hankering after proof is the mind. Can mind discover proof of its own non-Existence? No. You can never find mind through mind. Surrender it and you will be absorbed into the Beyond. The entity competent to ascertain or pass judgement on the question of the mind's Existence – and therefore the question of the Existence of manifestation – cannot be the mind itself. Mind can know only mind, whereas in the state of no-mind there is a clear (unambiguous) absence of mind.

Q: Who recognises the absence of mind in the state of no-mind?
B: Since there is no mind to carry out any recognition or to be subject to it, the question of the recognition or non-recognition of the Existence or non-Existence of mind never arises in the state of no-mind. The suggestion of the fact that the mind is a perishable entity gives rise to a mental curiosity to discover the substratum that is left, if any and whatever it might be, after the mind has been destroyed. This curiosity, known as *atmajignasa* [to enquire about the Absolute Truth], causes the mind to become introverted and thus brings about Realisation.

Q: Do all jivas *have this curiosity?*
B: No.

Q: How to get it?
B: By the Grace of the Guru.

Q: And how is that obtained?
B: If you go on working with the light available you will meet your Guru, as he will himself be seeking you.

•——•

Q: I have some doubts about what I have read in the Bible, in particular concerning the actions and sayings of Jesus. May I clarify them with Sri Bhagavan, whom I consider to be a living embodiment of the Christ himself? Bhagavan indicated his assent with a patient nod of his head. *What does 'Ego eimi' (I am) mean, coming from the mouth of Jesus?*
B: Among all the names of God, the one that most efficaciously captures the essence of the only direct means to Realise Him is the name 'ehyeh asher ehyeh' (I am who I am), which is revealed to Moses from the burning bush. To those who know the significance of the name is revealed the means of Realisation, because they are one and the same:

> **Because he hath set his love upon me, therefore will I deliver him: I will set him on high, because he hath known my name.**

Jesus is reassuring his followers, and indeed anybody willing to listen, that Emancipation is obtained not by good works but by God's Grace alone, and that such Grace does not come swiftly but to those who have heard God's name and understood its significance. The significance is that complete introversion is the direction that the mind needs to be channelled or yoked into, so as to make Realisation possible. 'I-am that I-am' implies that the mind is not aware of anything other than itself – it is the state of *Samadhi*. 'I am this or that...' is *jagratswapna* [daydreaming], where the mind is occupied with name and form, memory and belief, otherness and separation. 'I-am' is the Noumenon that is the substratum from which the mind derives its Existence and into which it resolves. 'I-am' is a reference to a state in which there cannot be any externality. This is the state that prevails prior to and underneath the mind.

In solemnly declaring 'I-am', Jesus is not deliberately blaspheming the Jewish belief system corresponding to the period of Herod's Temple; he is indicating that his state transcends time and space:

Before Abraham was, I am.

The purpose, inasmuch as there can be any such thing attributed to the deeds of one whose mind is dead, of speaking those words is to proclaim that the state in which concepts of time and space have been given up is verily the one and only state that is worthy of being the object of our effort to cultivate. 'I-am' – here lending itself to the interpretation of being the state of mind that does not see or recognise anything external to itself – is the way, the truth, and the life.

Q: What did Jesus mean when he said,

> *Unto you it is given to know the mystery of the kingdom of God: but unto them that are without, all these things are done in parables: that seeing they may see, and not perceive; and hearing they may hear, and not understand; lest at any time they should be converted, and their sins should be forgiven them.*

Surely He did not mean that people should suffer for not being able to understand His words?
B: Many people arrive at Ramana Ashram, pick up the Pamphlet *Who am I?*, come here, prostrate before the Sofa, ask me for benediction and go away. Do all of them attain *jnana*?

Q: Meaning it is necessary to continuously remain in the physical presence of Sri Bhagavan for years at a time, to stand a genuine chance of Realising?
B: The mental presence is what counts.

Q: I do not understand.
B: Sri Ramakrishna has said – 'Complete sincerity is necessary to Realise God.' One man may keep on doing *tapas* [austerities] all the hours of day and night, but if he has not freed himself from the idea 'I am doing tapas', he is not going to reap any spiritual benefit. Another may remain in the thick of the world attending to various tasks that constitute the *prarabdha* of his body to attend to, without thinking that he is doing anything, having surrendered mind and body, heart and soul, to God.

To such a one Realisation comes effortlessly. What Jesus means is not that he is deliberately trying to keep anyone in the dark about his teachings, but that to those whose ego has not subsided, his teachings would be incomprehensible. It (the passage) means that one who still arrogantly thinks 'I', even after being told to surrender, deserves no mercy and that he will certainly find the path to Realisation closed to him.

Q: Bhagavan says in Verse 30 of the Ulladhu Narpadhu *poem that the quest for Reality begins in the mind. Yet, when people ask him for practical guidance on the quest, he speaks of the Heart. What is the explanation? Is the Heart the last stage of the practice or the Goal itself?*

B: The *sadhaka* begins the practice with the mind turned inward to oppose the attack of the dangerous, rushing thoughts which plague him day and night and leave him without peace. By virtue of the practice, he eventually comes to locate the sensation of 'I' through feeling-recollection. When the mind eventually sinks into the Heart, undisturbed bliss is overwhelmingly felt. There is then the feeling of 'I', having nothing to do with the intellect, which is not divorced from pure Subjective Consciousness. So, mind must get subsumed into the Heart. The Heart cannot be felt as the object of your practice. Its Realisation dawns only when the mind has become finally lost of all distracting and wierd tendencies.

Q: In Verse 266 of Vivekachudamani, *Sri Adi Shankaracharya (8*[th] *century - famous* Advaita Vedanta *teacher) says that* Brahman *can be Realised by* buddhi, *the subtle intellect, which means that the intellect must be of immense help in Realisation. While it seems to be Shankara's opinion that the purified* buddhi *is indispensable to Realisation, Bhagavan is of the opinion that it must be destroyed before Realisation dawns. Is that not so?*

B: The word '*buddhi*' is rightly translated by you as 'the subtle intellect'; that is the usual meaning; but in this verse it could also specifically mean 'the cave of the Heart'.

Bhagavan then asked somebody in the Hall to read out aloud Verse 266:

> In the cave of the *buddhi* there is the *Brahman*, distinct from gross and subtle, the Existence Absolute, Supreme, the One without a second. For one who lives in this cave as *Brahman*, O Beloved, there is no more entrance into a woman's womb.

B: *Buddhi*, in the sense of referring to the faculty of discrimination between right and wrong, good and bad, must certainly vanish

prior to the dawn of Realisation. *Buddhi* in the sense of referring to the subtle intellect helps the mind to incessantly hunt for its own source, and therefore leads the *sadhaka* to Realisation. The purified *chittam* [mind] or mind cleansed of *vrittis* automatically leads to Realisation of the Self.

Q: If I lose the ability to distinguish between right and wrong, good and bad, would it not be dangerous for me? I may harm others, not knowing that I am doing so and that it is bad. I may be unable to prevent others harming me, not knowing that I am being harmed and that it is good to protect myself against harm.

B: As you advance deeper in your practice, you will, of your own accord, make the discovery that such things as good, bad, right, wrong, evil, morality, et cetera, do not exist. That is what I meant. In the world, the usual worldly standards of behaviour are to be maintained.

Q: But doesn't that amount to a double standard, implying hypocrisy?

B: No. Once a certain stage of mental introversion has been attained, you will come to discover that your spontaneous behaviour in dealing with others is based not on your mind but theirs.

Q: Just some time back Sri Bhagavan told me that mine was the only mind that existed.

B: The apparent appearances are to be met with apparent responses on the same plane of imagination.

Q: I don't understand.

B: *Advaita* is meant for internal, mental application. It is like the story of King Janaka who was questioned why the elephant was taken to the building allocated for stationing elephants, the cow to the cow-shed, and the dog to its kennel. If you try to apply *Advaita* in the world, you will get into serious trouble.

16th July 1936

Vichara, Self-Enquiry

Major Chadwick Shares his Doubts

Q: What are the indicators based on which I shall be enabled to find out for myself whether I am doing vichara *[Self-enquiry] correctly or not?*
B: If *vichara* has resulted in a state of mind wherein it abides as identical with pure Subjective Consciousness, then you have done it correctly.

However, it is not easy for the novice to tell whether his mind is presently abiding as identical with pure Subjective Consciousness, because the dull mental state of *manolaya* [loss of awareness] is often mistakenly regarded as being the tabula rasa (clean slate) mental state of pure Subjective Consciousness.

When mind abides as identical with pure Subjective Consciousness, it unmistakeably scintillates 'I'-'I'. So, the definitive answer to your question is that *vichara* has been done correctly when doing it has resulted in the *Aham Sphurana* flashing forward.

Q: And how to recognise the Aham Sphurana *when it 'flashes forward'?*
B: There is no possibility of mistaking it when the experience actually occurs. Whatever description is given is not only useless but also counter-productive, because if a description of the experience of *Aham Sphurana* is given, the mind twists and contorts the present banal experience of outward-protruding, situation-craving mental impulses into one that seems to perfectly match with the description given: because it wants to avoid getting destroyed.

So, even if you have heard a description of the experience of the *Aham Sphurana* being furnished in this Hall, please make no effort to recollect it. When the *Aham Sphurana* actually flashes forth, you will know it alright. Cognition of the *Aham Sphurana* is not based on intellectual agreement. It is a direct experience of the Self, inferior only to the *Sahajastithi* [natural state] of the *jnani*.

Q: Is the Aham Sphurana *something that is felt only by ripe souls?*
B: Yes.

Q: What are the others to do then?
B: (smiling) Ripen themselves!

Q: How?
B: *Vichara abhyasa* [Self-enquiry practice] is the way.

Q: I would now like to ask a slightly different, but related, question. Please tell me how I can find out how much progress I am making with respect to the vichara abhyasa.
B: The length of time for which you are able to keep the mind in a state wherein it abides as identical with pure Subjective Consciousness is the yardstick by which you can find out how efficaciously you are practising *vichara*.

However, more pragmatically, the degree of the absence of both thought (imagining this and that) and mental dullness is the means to measure progress. However, the desire to progress is an obstacle – get rid of it. Ask yourself who it is that wants to measure progress.

Chadwick: (unhappily) I have been staying here for months. I see no improvement in me. If anything, my condition seems to be taking a turn for the worse. The viscosity of my thoughts is on the decline. I am consistently using Bhagavan's vichara *method.*

Yet there is no diminution in the strength of the army of thought that I am attacked by day after day. I am desperate to Realise in this lifetime. Or, if I am born again, Bhagavan must also agree to be born again to help me Realise in the next life. Without Bhagavan what can I do?

Someone from the back of the Hall called out: *'He is a* jivan-mukta *[liberated being]. Where is the possibility of further birth for him? Is not the suggestion absurd?'* Chadwick merely ignored him.
B: Give up the idea that you are striving for Realisation.

C: (appalled) What?! Bhagavan would have me abandon the quest? Has he decided I am unworthy to Realise?
B: Did you pay attention to what was said to you? You were not asked to abandon the quest. You were asked to abandon the spurious idea that there is a 'you' which is trying to merge with a 'super-you'.

C: (dejectedly) I understand nothing.
B: Throw away the belief in the Existence of the personal self. It is only on that erroneous basis that you are now asking questions.

C: But I must remain to perform sadhana*!*
B: What is the objective of *sadhana*?

C: Destruction of the ego.
B: No, transcendence of the idea of its Existence.

C: So, if I just free myself from the idea that I exist as an individual person, the Who am I? method is not needed?
B: First discard that erroneous idea. Having discarded that idea, do not bring in any other idea in its place, such as *Aham Brahmasmi* [I am Brahman], and so forth. Remain free from all ideas, that is, from all mental identification. Let the mind remain in the state of pure Subjective Consciousness free from all objectification or identification.

Then, as and when thoughts arise, tackle them with the counter thought, 'To whom has this thought arisen?' This arrests the further development of the thought. Then return the mind to its native state of pure Subjective Consciousness. This is the way.

C: Bhagavan has been quoted as saying that certain qualifications are necessary for those intending to successfully pursue vichara*. Will Bhagavan please explain those qualifications?*
B: It is enough to intuitively recognise that the three states are passing phenomena not having any reality. But again, consequent to steadfast and intermittent practise of *vichara*, such intuition dawns

unasked. So, there is really no need, prior to commencing practice, to sit down and endlessly reflect whether you are competent enough to pursue the practice so as to result in the outcome of success. If you find that it attracts you, you can certainly go on to practising *vichara.*

Q: Before taking up vichara, *is it necessary to first qualify myself or prepare myself using preliminary practices such as breathing techniques, visualisations of pleasant mental imagery, and so forth? Or can I plunge into* vichara *straightaway?*

B: The best preparation for *vichara* is *vichara.* The other practices are for those to whom *vichara* – for some reason – does not appeal favourably.

Q: I am a man who is utterly new to spiritual practice. Should I begin with vichara*? Or should I begin with an easier method, such as watching the breath, for instance, and move on to* vichara *once my mind has acquired sufficient maturity?*

B: No method is per se easy or difficult. Depending upon one's temperament, what one finds easy the next man finds difficult. The thing to do is to stick to what fascinates you. Never mind which method is best. Which method appeals to you?

Q: I like to meditate, however Bhagavan has opined that vichara *is the only means to pierce the veil of ignorance. So, I tend to castigate myself that I am following a method, which, according to Bhagavan, does not lead me to Realisation.*

B: Who said that I disapprove of other methods? You may go on following your present method until you yourself feel, intuitively rather than intellectually, that the time has come for you to give up the *sadhana* [practice]. At that point in time the mind will automatically begin to gravitate towards incessantly reflecting upon 'I'.

Fascination with 'I' leads to spontaneous *vichara. Vichara,* if not done for its own sake, does not bring forth a successful result. If

a splinter of wood is stuck in your gum, your tongue will of its own accord go on trying to uproot it, without the need for any conscious effort on your part.

***Vichara* will succeed only when there is that degree of spontaneity. The tongue knows that the splinter is a foreign body and must go. It will go on fighting until the alien appendage comes loose. Likewise, the mind must be able naturally to discern the ego, to which it owes its apparent Existence, as being an unnatural and alien entity.**

This preciseness will come only after prolonged practice. That *abhyasa* may take up any form which appeals to you. Whatever road you are pursuing now will of its own accord lead you to *vichara* when the moment is ripe, provided you are sincere and unrelenting in your effort.

Q: When thoughts occur, I should revert my attention back to pure Subjective Consciousness. That is the point of vichara. *Is that right?*
B: What you mention is without doubt *vichara*. But there is more to it.

Q: Please explain.
B: Once the practice of *vichara* has brought about a sufficient degree of ripeness (maturity or steadiness in introversion), the mind is loathing to think thoughts and is now content to remain merged in the Beingness of the Self.

Even then, however, there is the subtle 'I' who spectates the fact of the mind remaining so merged. Catch hold of him and continuously watch him – and when he vanishes, *jnana* alone remains.

Q: I have been investigating Who am I? for several years. I see no result. What is the reason? Where am I going wrong? What am I doing wrong? Please help me.
B: What is meant by *vichara*? Is it to intellectually analyse oneself along the lines of the question, Who am I?

Q: Isn't that it?

B: No. *Vichara* means effort to trace thought back to its source, culmination of which effort is discovery of such source as being the Shining of the Self-resplendent Heart that is, the Beingness of the Self. The penultimate triumph in *vichara* has come about when effort is needed in order to leave the Shining of the Heart rather than in order to plunge and merge into It.

If you continuously hold on to the source of thought, there will come a time when emergence from such source becomes altogether impossible; the embodiment of this state is what *vichara sadhana* seeks to achieve. *Vichara* means hunting for the source of thought so that we might abide exclusively and permanently there as and therein. To practise *vichara* is simply this: seek from where within yourself it is that thought arises; having found such source, stay there once and for all.

Q: Some practise vichara *for a short while and succeed in Realising. Others try for decades; their efforts are rewarded only with failure. What is the explanation?*

B: What matters is extent of intensity of introversion of mind. There must be desperation to Realise the Self. The thirst to discover Reality, the yearning, the longing must burn brightly in the mind, burn with enough force to reduce the mind into ashes. Half-baked and half-hearted efforts are not going to get you anywhere.

Once you know that all this is fiction, can you remain content until and unless Reality is gained? The more actually unacceptable the mundane Existence is, as opposed to the mere intellectual understanding or conceptual notion that Existence in the form of the body is undesirable to you, the greater your chances are of Realising the Absolute Existence. Perfection in *vairagyam* [renunciation], automatically brings about *jnana* in its wake.

16th July 1936

Time and Science

The Moslem gentleman again.

Q: I want to effect Self-realisation as quickly as possible so that I can escape from the sorrow of samsara. *Will the Who am I? method suffice by itself?*

B: Yes.

Q: I wonder how much time it is going to take for me to Realise?

B: What is time?

Q: One measures it by looking at the clock and the calendar.

B: But what is it?

Q: I leave it to the all-knowing Bhagavan to enlighten me.

B: Time is only a mental idea. Consider the following story from *The Mahabarata*:-

> **Revati was the only daughter of King Kakudmi, a powerful monarch who ruled Kusasthali, a prosperous and advanced kingdom under the bed of the ocean floor. Thinking that no one could prove to be good enough to marry his beautiful daughter in the earthly realm, Kakudmi took Revati with him to *Brahmaloka* [the abode of god *Brahma* and his consort *Saraswati*] to ask *Brahma's* [the creator] advice about finding a suitable husband for her. *Brahma* was listening to a musical performance when they arrived, and so they waited patiently until the performance was finished.**
>
> **King Kakudmi bowed and made his request: "O *Brahma*! To whom shall I betroth this daughter? I have come to you to ask on this**

> point. I have searched for many princes and seen also a good many of them and none of them is to my liking and so my mind is not at rest." *Brahma* laughed at the foolishness of the King. "O King! The princes that you thought would become the bridegroom of your daughter have all died; their sons and grandsons and their friends even have all passed away." Time, *Brahma* goes on to explain, runs differently on different planes of Existence. During the time they had waited in *Brahmaloka* to see him, twenty-seven *chaturyugas* [a full time cycle of Hindu cosmology] had passed on Earth.
>
> Everything that Kakudmi had and owned, his friends and family, his sons and wife, his armies and treasures, had vanished with the time that had passed. The King and his daughter were overcome with astonishment and grief for everything they had lost, but *Brahma* comforted them, and recommended a worthy husband currently on Earth: Balarama, the twin brother of *Krishna*.

Today, we so often think of time to be an arrow moving in one direction, with a beginning, middle, and end. However, ancient Hindu philosophy was familiar with the concept that time is relative and many passages in the *Vedic* scriptures repeatedly point out that the cosmic time of the gods is different than the time on Earth.

What Kakudmi and Revathy thought were just minutes in front of *Brahma*, were in fact millennia in terms of our time. Thus, aeons had passed away at home. When they came back, they did so to a vastly different place, which they could not recognise at all.

Q: What is the moral of the story?

B: Time and space are purely irrational mental conceptualisations. They are totally unreal. Einstein's Relativity has already done away

the ideas of absolute time and absolute space. Only the speed of light in vacuum is said to be a constant. Likewise, in his 1930 publication, *The Physical Principles of the Quantum Theory*, Heisenberg writes:-

> **In classical physical theories it has always been assumed either that (the interaction between observer and object) is negligibly small, or else that its effect can be eliminated from the result by calculations based on 'control' experiments.**
>
> **This assumption is not permissible in atomic physics; the interaction between observer and object causes uncontrollable and large changes in the system being observed, because of the discontinuous changes characteristic of atomic processes. The immediate consequence of this circumstance is that in general every experiment performed to determine some numerical quantity renders the knowledge of others illusory, since the uncontrollable disorder of the observed system alters the values of previously determined quantities.**

His theory postulates that the more precisely the position of some particle is determined, the less precisely its momentum can be known, and vice versa. What does it all mean? Till now, the physicist thought, 'I want to know more about it. So, let me go close to it and measure it, that I may study it.' However, when he tries to adopt the same approach at the sub-atomic level, nature is not so agreeable. The very act of measurement seems to influence – if not bring into Existence – the data that is measured! Any pursuit of information concerning the position of the particle prior to the time of measurement is mere mental hypothesis.

The only way to determine or ascertain information about the particle is to carry out a measurement; measurement contributes to generation of the same information the extraction of which had

been the objective of the act of measurement, in which case we are not measuring but creating. Measurement (or observation) and creation have thus become inextricably interlinked.

Aeons ago our Sages had discovered this and given it the name *drishti-srishti-vada* [creation through perception]. The physicist Bohr seems to feel that an experimental observation instantaneously collapses the inherently uncertain state of the particle in such a manner as to make its future evolution consistent with what we observe experimentally.

For instance, take a particle that is observed or detected or measured at a certain specific location. Thus, the probability of its being detected in any other place suddenly becomes zero. Up until that point, the particle's position is inherently uncertain and unpredictable, an uncertainty which only disappears when it is observed and measured. This immediate transition from a multi-faceted potentiality to a single actuality, according to Bohr, need not necessarily warrant an inevitable inference that there ought to be only one precise point at which such a collapse occurred. Thus, Bohr argues, it is necessary to discard the laws governing individual events in favour of a direct statement of the laws governing aggregations and probabilities. According to Bohr's model, there is no deep quantum reality and no actual world of particles – but only a description of the world in these terms.

Thus, science is reduced to merely affording us a formalism that we can use to predict events and the properties of matter. The laws developed by Bohr and Heisenberg seem to suggest that particles exist in a combination-of-all-possible-states-at-once, lacking even basic properties such as a definite location, and instead existing everywhere and nowhere at once. Only when a particle is measured does it suddenly materialise, seeming to decide on its position as if by a roll of the dice. Thus, their interpretation is essentially a pragmatic view, effectively saying that it really does not matter exactly what science means; the important thing being that it 'works', in the sense that it correlates with reality in all possible experimental situations.

Einstein, on the other hand, keeps arguing that the physical world must have real properties, whether or not one measures them; he seems to particularly dislike Bohr's claim that a complete understanding of reality lies forever beyond the capabilities of rational thought, insisting that the idea that a particle's position before observation is inherently unknowable is nonsense and makes a mockery of the whole of physics. The good gentleman is apparently still convinced in his brilliant mind that the positions and states of particles must already have been established before observation...

Q: From all this I gather that Bhagavan himself sees the world as some sort of dream?

B: There is really no world for Bhagavan to see. He abides as the Self and sees only the Self.

I couldn't follow the lines about Einstein's Relativity and Heisenberg's Quantum Mechanics. I have reproduced them here to the best of my ability. It is for the Reader to make sense of them, if he so happens to possess knowledge concerning the field. I wonder who gave Bhagavan Einstein's and Bohr's and Heisenberg's scientific papers to read! He is unlikely to have himself taken the trouble to procure them, for He was really not interested in any reading.

Whenever He read anything, it was only to explain to a devotee some teaching or point of His. The fact that He was in a position to understand the modern complex physics of this era (1930s) does not surprise me, notwithstanding the fact that I am aware He is an exponent of the *ajata Advaita* [the Absolute is *aja*, the unborn eternal non-duality] philosophy. He is Bhagavan the Omniscient.

(In the 1930s particle physics was a popular topic that Bhagavan could have read about in his newspaper. He was rumoured to have scientists visit him – Ed)

17th July 1936

Surrender

Q: Is surrender a means to overcome and vanquish the *vasanas* [tendencies of the mind], thus resulting in Realisation?
B: Yes: provided it is unconditional, surrender is a foolproof way to Realise the Self.

Q: What is the guarantee that I shall Realise the Self if I surrender?
B: You are missing the point of surrender.

Q: How so?
B: To surrender is to let go of everything without anticipating or expecting anything in return. Letting go of everything also encompasses abandoning the aspiration to Realise the Self. Suppose you are holding a red-hot iron ball. Your hand is quivering in unbearable pain. Somebody suggests to you that you let go.

If your response is, 'What benefit will I obtain if I let go?' will not the other person wonder, 'Poor fellow! The pain of holding that dreadful thing in his hand – has it addled his brains?'

That is how it is to me having now listened to your question. *Samsara* is intolerably painful. Why look for reasons to let go of it? If *samsara* still appears as being acceptable to one – no matter however remotely or infinitesimally so – can he Realise the Self? One who does not see *samsara* as actually being the horribly excruciating misery that it indeed really is – will he Realise the Self?

Q: Suppose I surrender yet fail to Realise the Self – what then?
B: Yes, that possibility is always there from the ego's point of view.

Q: But just now you said that surrender is a fool proof way to Realise the Self.
B: What did the preceding words say? Surrender works only if it is unconditional. That means your mind must be genuinely reconciled to the possibility that anything can happen or not happen, including

one's failure to Realise the Self.

Q: So, success in Realising the Self is made possible only if I wholeheartedly accept the possibility that I may fail to Realise the Self?
B: Such acceptance must be natural or genuine. For instance, it must not be self-imposed so that the condition for Realisation to be made possible, the mind ought to stand reconciled to the possibility that anything can happen or not happen, including one's failure to Realise the Self may be attempted to be rendered satisfied.

Q: The path of surrender seems less careful compared to Who am I? Have I made a correct observation?
B: You say you find surrender suitable for your temperament. Adopt it.

Q: In the Who am I? path, if a thought occurs, one asks 'To whom has this thought occurred?' Likewise, in the surrender method?
B: In the initial stages you may counter worldly thoughts with the counter-thought, 'This is God's business, since I have surrendered all to Him. What reason have I to involve myself in it?' As one's mind ripens, however, the need to achieve control over thoughts by using other thoughts gradually tapers off.

As soon as a thought arises, it is directly reined in. Be it surrender or Self-enquiry, in either case the purpose of the practice is only to arrest further development of the thought, and the mind should be returned to its native state of pure Subjective Consciousness, sustained effortlessly and without will, as soon as the disciple observes that the mind has begun to depart from that state.

Q: The idea sounds complicated.
B: On the other hand, it is so utterly simple that trying to communicate it semantically leads us into a hopeless quagmire of complicated-sounding ideas. TOTALLY LET GO and the Self stands Realised: that is all there is to Realisation.

20th July 1936

Day by Day with a Jnani

The Caucasian gentleman returned early in the morning to quiz Bhagavan.

Q: Does the jnani *have no sensory perceptions? For instance, if Bhagavan inadvertently stubs his toe against a brick, is there no sensation?*
B: The sensation is there, but not the idea, 'I am feeling this sensation.' The *jnani's* state can be correctly comprehended only by the *jnani*; others merely wonder about it with complicated-sounding words without actually Knowing. The *jnani* or *jivanmuktha* is said to be like a person fast asleep inside a house whose doors and windows are wide open.

Q: I fail to comprehend the example.
B: His senses are fully awake and alert, yet fully inactive.

Q: It seems paradoxical.
B: His sensory organs perceive, yet there is nothing for them to perceive because mind is dead. A new-born infant sees and hears quite well, but it never really understands anything. It knows only joy, although people may even treat it cruelly. Likewise with the *jnani*. He does not know anything apart from *Parabrahman* [the supreme Self].

Q: Bhagavan explains to us the details of various philosophical texts in expert fashion. How is it possible without the intellect? If mind is no more, how can the intellect, which is a component of the mind, survive in isolation from it?
B: It is like shadow puppetry. Someone else is moving the strings. There is no such thing called 'I' that has any role to play anywhere with reference to the *jnani's* actions.

Q: Who is this mysterious 'someone else'?
B: Some call him God, some call him Randomness, some call him Fate, and some call him Causality. One who sees events, actions,

and circumstances inquires the reason for that. The seer does not see himself – thus his own apparent separate Existence is an inexplicable mystery. Yet, ignoring this primary question of what his Self is, he goes around questioning everything else.

So, in order to satisfy his curiosity all sorts of ridiculous theories are spun by philosophers and *Vedantic pandits* [learned men]. The Truth is that there is no-thing to see, because there is no-one to see anything. The explanation of God, Providence, et cetera being in control of the world's events is kindergarten-level spiritual advice. The *jnani* who does not see anything has no questions; he knows the Truth – that nothing was ever created.

Q: But I see a solid world around me! What does Bhagavan mean in saying that it is not there? For instance, Bhagavan is sitting on the Sofa. Is the Sofa invisible to his eyes? What is he sitting upon then?! Is he floating in the air?!
B: Is there any seeing to be done in sleep?

Q: First let us finish discussing the jagrat *[waking] state.*
B: This body is sitting upon the Sofa, you say. But the Sofa, this body, this Hall, the Hill yonder, and everything else is inferred Existence. Thus it is not Existence at all, but fiction, like asking the question, 'Santa Claus (the mythicised caricature of St. Nicholas popular in the collective imagination of the Western public) wears a golden pince-nez (old fashioned glasses). I wonder if I may know what the strength of the corrective lenses amounts to?'

Can there be an answer to the question? At best, you can say, 'Since there is really no Santa Claus at all, the question never arises.' Actual Existence is not to be seen. It is Being, which you always are. Do not think about it, but BE it: this is the way for attainment of Realisation.

Q: How to be the Self? That is the question. The Self seems to be like the carrot dangled in front of the foolish mule – very close yet altogether unattainable.
B: You (as the personal self) are sitting on top of the (Real) Self. Get up and clear off. That will do.

Q: How is that to be done?
B: Permanently cease to believe in the Existence of the personal self. Then the magic will unwind of its own accord.

Q: Am I to understand that my personal self is unreal and non-existent? This is the self I have always known. Now I am being told it is non-existent. I have never known or even seen the Impersonal Absolute, the Brahman. *Yet I am expected to believe that I am it and that it alone exists in Truth.*
B: You are not asked to believe in anything. When asked to abandon all belief, you ask which belief you should take up instead. I said, 'Cease to believe in the Existence of the personal self.' You have interpreted it incorrectly to mean, 'Believe in the non-Existence of the personal self.'

Q: The linguistic difference is merely owing to variations in sentence – construction and grammatical formation.
B: No. Abandon ALL belief. Only the Self remains. Relinquishment of belief cannot be brought about by another belief to the effect that such relinquishment must take place; it can only be brought about by letting go of everything you think you know and everything you hold dear.

Q: J. Krishnamurti has said: "Total negation is the essence of the positive."
B: Exactly.

Q: Is J. Krishnamurti the incarnation of Lord Maitreya, as the Theosophists would have us believe?
B: If your belief be so, so he is.

C: Leadbeater's judgement has been proven correct; he IS the World Teacher. THAT is why he dissolved the order. People criticize him in their unwisdom. I was reading one of his poems the other day.

Reads out from a slender magazine or newsletter:-

I have no name;
I am as the fresh breeze of the mountains.
I have no shelter;
I am as the wandering waters.
I have no sanctuary, like the dark gods;
Nor am I in the shadow of deep temples.

I have no sacred books;
Nor am I well-seasoned in tradition.
I am not in the incense burning upon the high altars;
Nor in the pomp of ceremonies.
I am neither in the graven image;
Nor in the rich chant of a melodious voice.

I am not bound by theories;
Nor corrupted by beliefs.
I am not held in the bondage of religions;
Nor in the pious agony of their priests.
I am not entrapped by philosophies;
Nor held in the power of their sects.

I am neither low nor high;
I am the worshipper and the worshipped.
I am free.

My song is the song of the river calling for the open seas;
Wandering, wandering;

I am Life.

Sri Bhagavan commended the verses as to their lofty spiritual quality.

20th July 1936

A Complete Layman

Q: Yes, it is clear now. But I am not finished with my questions. I, a complete layman, want to become a jnani *like Bhagavan or Swami Vivekananda. What should I do?*

B: If you want to shine like the sun, first burn like it! Practice more practice, further practice, and still yet more practice alone will reveal the Truth.

Q: What should I practise doing?

B: All that is necessary for obtaining *jnana* is to intermittently abide as one and identical with the Beingness of the Self.

Q: Does the jnani *do anything to ensure that more people in the world blossom into* jnana*? Does he have an agenda that, within his lifetime, he should awaken at least one person besides himself into Realisation of the Real?*

B: (roaring with laughter) What does it matter to the *jnani* how many people succeed in Realising their true nature or fail to do so? And why should he do anything to spread any teaching? Why should he feel the need to do anything at all? 'Doing' is not the characteristic of the *jnani*.

The man of the world is judged by the deeds he has done. The *jnani* does not do anything – he cannot do anything. Thus, it is impossible to judge him. That is why the Christ said, 'My Kingdom is not of this world.' You will be more successful in measuring the sky than in understanding a *jnani*. Also, for the *jnani*, there is no 'besides himself'. All is He.

Q: How do I attain this state for myself?

B: *Summa Iru* [be still]. That is the practice.

Q: Am I to be idle all the time? Is engaging in gainful or productive employment a crime?

B: The import of *Summa Iru* is, 'Keep your mind idle or asleep in the Beingness of the Self.' As for the body, it has its own *prarabdha* [destiny] to attend to. You have no right of say over the body. You cannot decide whether the body should work or remain idle. What is bound to happen will happen. If the body is destined to remain without working, work cannot be had even if you hunt for it. If the body is destined to work you cannot alter such destiny, for the body will be forced to engage in it.

So, leave it to the Higher Power. You cannot avoid or acquire work for the body as you choose. God has not permitted that freedom. Only one freedom is permitted to man – and that is the freedom to perish in his own Immortal Self. This is also the only free will.

Q: Can meditation or vichara *be carried on in the midst of worldly activity?*
B: The feeling 'I am working' is the hindrance. Enquire, 'Who works?' Remember to ask yourself Who am I? every time such false notions of doer ship trouble you. Then no work can bind you; it will all go on automatically. Make no effort either to work or to renounce work. Your effort is the bondage. Simply perpetually remain as you ARE, mind merged in its source so as to be indistinguishable from the Beingness of the Self, and do not bother about the question of whether the body ought to work or to idle away.

If you remain non-attached (neither attached nor detached, for both are volitionary), the body's *prarabdha* will effortlessly carry it through whatever activities are meant for it in this life. You remain surrendered to the Self – everything else disappears. No more questions, doubts, or misgivings arise. This is the way for unshakeable *shanti* [peace].

Q: Back at home, they have introduced the following new prayer in my local church after the Vesper service – 'My Lord, give me the courage to change what requires to be altered, the serenity to accept what cannot be helped, and the insight to be able to tell the one from the other.' Is this not what Bhagavan calls surrender of the responsibility for one's life to God?
B: What you describe is a small step towards unconditional surrender,

which is quite unequivocally absolute and does not ask this or that. Letting go of everything is called surrender. The one whose mind has totally surrendered would have nothing to ask. He may simply think 'I let go' once, and thereafter abides as the eternally silent one whose ego remains perpetually merged in its source. The prayer you describe is a partial surrender. If the strength of the *sadhaka's vairagya* [renunciation] be maintained, throughout all hours of waking and dream, at an all-consuming level of intensity, then partial surrender leads to absolute surrender. Absolute surrender is the goal of all spiritual practice.

Q: For one who has completely surrendered, is vichara *unnecessary?*
B: Having surrendered without the slightest reserve, who should be left to make the *vichara*?

Q: Is it true that by coming around this Hill repeatedly, Realisation can be gained in a relatively short span of time?
B: Provided you unconditionally surrender yourself to the Hill.

Q: Does Bhagavan have any parting instruction for me?
B: Only the usual.

Q: Which is?
B: To perpetually abide in the state of *Summa Iru* [be still] that is, the state in which the ego is merged in its source.

1st August 1936

A Dog and a Monkey

The man seemed to want to argue further, but before he could say anything more, a compelling diversion arrived: a pair of unrestrained animals rushed into the Hall making, one might think, enough noise to make the roof quaver. A dog was furiously chasing a monkey. The monkey, sensing Bhagavan was the only safety for it, shot straight up to his Sofa, leaped on to the Master's lap, and from there clambered onto his shoulders. The attendant rushed forwards with a stick kept in the Hall for the purpose of threatening monkeys. Bhagavan would not allow any to be actually beaten.

Bhagavan stopped the attendant with a firm gesture of the hand, and there sat the monkey on the Master, merrily grimacing and leering and rumbling to its heart's content at the dog barking away to glory below. The Master kept compassionately stroking the creature's tail. With a sad droop of its tail, the dog finally went away after exhausting its energy on countless pointless barks. The monkey gave a triumphant look around the Hall and majestically made its exit through the window.

B: These simple creatures are indeed more blessed than man, whose head is filled with worries such as, 'What is the origin of my race? Which other breed surviving today is its best representative?' Their concerns are happily rudimentary, restricted only to the basic requirements of bodily sustenance.

They do not accumulate wealth and then worry, 'What will happen to all this after me? Will someone cart it all away one day?' They are content if something is found to eat and water to drink. They live as God has intended them to live: without accumulation, be it of memories or of worldly possessions.

Q: But man alone is endowed with the ability to attain brahmajnana *[knowledge of Brahman].*

B: That is your opinion.

Q: Can then an animal Realise the Self?
B: It is not unheard of.

Bhagavan now looked at Chadwick, who was present in the Hall, squarely in the eye, and said: **When you came here first, you asked how the Guru's help is useful in bringing about Realisation. You were told that it makes the poisonous fangs of *samsara* ineffective. Now do you see?**

Chadwick merely looked uncomprehendingly vacant.

B: Whilst the monkey was seated on this (pointing to his body), it was quite beyond the reach of the dog. Howl as it might, the dog could not sink its teeth into the monkey's flesh. It had to go away disappointed.

Likewise, one who has firmly caught hold of the Guru's glance of compassionate Grace has placed himself quite irrevocably beyond the reach of *samsara. Samsara* can then only severely bark at him; it is powerless to bite. For this, unconditional surrender is necessary.

C: How can I tell whether my surrender is perfect or not?
B: Questions or doubts, such as these included, arise no more. There are no more wants or cares.

9th August 1936

I Have a Body

Q: So, it is the thought 'I have a body' that is responsible for creating the false impression that I have a body, whereas in truth I have none. Am I correct?
B: Yes.

Q: In that case, if I think 'I have no body', the body should disappear, but it does not disappear. Why is this so?
B: Intensely thinking about the disappearance of the body does make it disappear; but acquisition of such worthless *siddhis* [psychic powers] is not our objective. You were asked to remove the idea 'I have a body' and keep quiet. Instead, you remove that idea and in its place introduce the idea 'I have no body'. *Jnana* is the disappearance of all ideas. 'All ideas must disappear' is also an idea. Abandon that idea also and keep quiet.

Q: How will day-to-day life go on in the absence of thoughts?
B: Many times better than it is going on now.

Q: Can we move or speak without thinking?
B: Once the ego is burnt away in the fire of *jnana*, all actions become automatic.

Q: This is the jnani's *point of view. Can it apply to an* ajnani *[non-Realised]?*
B: Never mind *jnanis* and *ajnanis*. Keep quiet and see whether your body's actions are not spontaneously guided by a deep Higher Power.

Q: Can the Higher Power be trusted to always act in accordance with my interest?
B: He always does the right thing. What he does may or may not coincide with your world view and your understanding of or preference for how things ought to go or events ought to unfold.

His actions may even seem unwise in your eye. What you should do is to close the eye of perception or judgement once and for all and open the eye of wisdom once and for all. Let the Master take care of the body and the circumstances, favourable or unfavourable, that it is destined to face.

You remain permanently submerged in the Heart and lose yourself there. Then it will not matter whether the body is drenched in rain or roasted in the sun or buried in the bowels of the earth; you remain unaffected, irrevocably and irretrievably lost in supreme *shanti* [peace] and not knowing anything apart from that.

Q: Only a jnani *could be so indifferent to the body.*
B: Be a *jnani*, then.

Q: But it is said to be the hardest of all attainments.
B: On the other hand, it is always your natural state.

Q: If so why am I unaware of the same?
B: Because you think you are unaware.

Q: How to remedy the affliction?
B: Stop thinking.

Q: How is that done?
B: Every time a thought arises, ask yourself, 'To whom has this thought arisen?' and then take the mind back to its origin, which is the primordial state of subjective awareness sustained effortlessly and volitionlessly.

Q: The thought 'To whom has this thought arisen?' is also a thought.
B: The stick which is used to stir a burning pyre (cremation fire) – what is its ultimate fate?

Q: Generally, it is thrown into the pyre itself to burn.
B: Exactly.

10th August 1936

What is the Purpose of Life?

Q: What is the purpose of life?
B: It is to discover the correct answer to this question.

Q: What is the correct answer?
B: Life.

Q: I do not understand?
B: Life does not question its own purpose. It has no questions to ask. It has no complaint to raise. It has no grudge to bear. Therefore, it is in perpetual peace. You, on the other hand, seem to lack peace; that is why you are raising these questions, evidently. So, if you make yourself indistinguishable and inseparable from Life, no more questions about Life or anything else will arise so as to throw you into the uneasy marsh of inner tumult and worry. Thus, you will remain in Peace. So, the purpose of life is to subsume your life into Life so that torments such as this question cease to distress you. Then you will abide as Life or Peace itself. Thus, the purpose of life is Life.

Q: I find Bhagvan's words cryptic.
B: Go around the Hill this evening. You will find the peace you are looking for.

Q: I shall do as advised. Is this Hill God?
B: Yes.

Q: Is not everything God?
B: All parts of your body, evenly, are made up substantially only of the elements oxygen, carbon, hydrogen and nitrogen. Can you use the anus for eating and the mouth for excreting?

Q: (laughs impertinently) So far, I have not tried the novel proposition. So,

this mountain has a special function to play in the spiritual destiny of the world or mankind?
B: Undoubtedly.

Q: Does this mountain bestow jnana *upon those who think of him but once?*
B: At least eventually.

Q: What is the agreement to be followed in order to win jnana–siddhi *[accomplishment of knowledge] from this mountain?*
B: *Poorna sharanagathi* [complete surrender].

Q: It means?
B: Totally cease to care about anything. Let what may, happen. What comes, let it come. What goes let it go. See what remains.

Q: You are – in effect – asking me to throw away my life, Sir.
B: Yes. 'He that findeth his life shall lose it: and he that loses his life for my sake shall find it.'

Q: (again the same insolent laugh) May I know why I am being expected to want to lose my life for your sake? I assure Bhagavan that my mental faculties are quite sound, despite coming here.
B: One who wants Immortality must perish therein.

Q: Then what is the point of Immortality?
B: Immortality is already immortal. Your mortality is the obstacle to Realisation of the same. Kill that mortality and Immortality shines forth.

Q: How to do this?
B: By following the investigation Who am I? Its import is not verbally or mentally articulating the question, but is only this: You say 'I am'. Find out who 'is'. Find the source of thought. Stay there once and for all.

11th August 1936

Jaws of the Tiger

Q: Has anyone succeeded in winning the admiration of Maharshi himself?
B: Oh! Yes.

Q: Who?
B: You.

Q: (face proudly lights up with pompous joy, but manages to modestly utter) How can that be? I am a spectacularly worthless creature. Even after years of repeatedly visiting the sacred soil of Tiruvannamalai, I remain an unenlightened person.
B: That is it.

Q: I do not understand. I am good for nothing. What is there for the great Maharshi to admire in me?
B: The tenacity and perseverance of your ego. This weak creature came here, and he was conquered and vanquished in a moment. You have managed to hold out for so long against the infinitely mighty power of Arunachala. Still, you continue to fight. You seem tireless. How strong you are, especially compared to this coward who gave up without a fight as soon as he merely heard the name of this mountain! Entirely admirable. What immense strength and endurance characterise your person! Even the gods envy you for it (laughs).

Q: (despondent) Oh! I see; Maharshi is making fun of me.
B: (laughing) Oh! no. It is no easy feat to persist in this *arul poerattum* [struggle for grace]. To untiringly wage war against Lord Arunachala himself is no joke. He is intent upon devouring your soul, but you have managed to hold out for so long against him and still vigorously continue to resist him.

I surrendered or fell conquered the moment I heard the name. My weakness is proverbial. But see your strength! From the heavens

the *devas* [divine beings] are watching you wonder-struck for it, thinking, 'Why, here is a man who seems a challenge to the might of the Lord himself!'

Q: Ultimately, I shall lose of course?
B: Yes, it is a mere question of time in your case. Once the jaws of the tiger have clamped down upon the goat's head, there is no return to life for the goat. Some goats wisely see the futility of fighting such an incalculably massively powerful enemy and quickly stop struggling after one or two vain escapes to break free; then the tiger at once twists his jaws so that the other animal's neck snaps and his agony meets an expedited end.

Other goats go on struggling until the point in time arrives where loss of blood finally results in unconsciousness. In these latter cases also, it is within the tiger's power to bring the goat's suffering to a prompt end, but since the goat wants to play for some time he also does not mind the good fun. After all, the goat does not seem to mind his own pain, and is perhaps enjoying it; why then should he, the tiger mind? Maybe it is the goat's cherished last wish to play-act at escaping; why deny it to the poor doomed creature?

Whichever kind of goat he might happen to be, once his head has entered the tiger's mouth his fate is sealed. Some take longer to die than others; it is (obviously) immaterial since the end is the same for all trapped goats: total destruction. It must be admitted that this tiger is very choosy in selecting his prey; but once he has selected, that is the certain beginning of the inevitable end.

Q: I find the parable fascinating. Dying in the jaws of the tiger means Realisation! Am I correct?!
B: Yes.

Q: The goat is the ego. Am I correct?
B: Yes

Q: The tiger is the Guru's glance of Grace, as mentioned in Bhagavan's

Nan Yar [Who am I?]? *Am I correct?*
B: What was now elucidated was the specific compensating power of Arunachala.

Q: I want to be marked out as prey.
B: Come around this Hill as often as you possibly can. That is enough.

11th August 1936

Non-Doing

Q: If I stay at the root of the mind or abide as pure consciousness, will I Realise the Self?
B: The question shows that the irrational mental conceptualisation, 'Realising the Self', is still present in the mind. Staying in the root of the mind should be a matter of course; it must be the natural state. On the other hand, you are trying to deliberately do it so that you can thereby gain the reward you call 'Self-realisation'. Can it work? No.

Stillness cannot be reached with the mind. Water cannot be made dry water. Subside as the mind and Stillness alone is left over. People want to know how this may be done. It cannot be done because doing is the antithesis of it. Do not do anything with the mind. That is Realisation.

Doing cannot bring about non-doing; absence of doing is known as non-doing. Non-doing is not an exotic variety of doing; it is simply not doing. Abstinence from or relinquishment of thought is not a positive act. It should therefore not require to be attended to with effort or volition. If there is any effort or volition involved, you are still stuck in the realm of doing. The transition from the realm of doing to that of non-doing should be a natural collapse. It is pointless if forced.

12th August 1936

Guru's Grace

Q: The terms Aham-Sphurana *['I'-Pulsation] and* Sahaja-asamprajnatha-Samadhi *[oneness with God] are synonymous. Am I correct?*
B: No.

Q: Why not?
B: Sometime after a fire is lit underneath a pot containing water, only an empty pot will be left. Yet, the space inside the pot is always vulnerable to being filled up again. If the pot is smashed into pieces, it is quite ruined and there can be no scope any more for depositing anything into it.

***Sphurana* indicates that the exhaustive emptying of the contents of the pot is nearing completion. *Sphurana* involves not merely a clarity in the state of subjective-awareness-sustained-effortlessly-and-volitionlessly; it also evokes a response from the Deep; therefore, we may say that it encompasses a transcendental aspect; even so, it is still a state of subtle duality.**

Duality ceases only after the mind has been irredeemably destroyed. Continuous and unbroken abiding in the *Sphurana* is possible only after the ego has finally surrendered. One who is in such a state of agelessness alone is eligible to awaken into *jnana*; such an egoless one cannot want *jnana* and neither can he want anything else; this is why it is said that those who want *jnana* do not get it. So, when *jnana* finally dawns it makes no difference to the *sadhaka* [practitioner]**. *Jnana* shines forth only well after the ego has been finally given up.**

Q: The fire underneath the pot is the Guru's Grace. Am I correct?
B: Yes.

Q: The pot is the mind. Is that not so?
B: Yes.

Q: The contents of the pot are vrittis *[structures] of the mind. Have I not made a correct observation?*
B: Yes.

Q: Can the pot be smashed whilst its contents are yet to be boiled away?
B: It's usually impossible. It is not safe for destruction to be suddenly forced upon the mind. The mind must wane and wane and only after it has been reduced into an infinitesimally tiny speck that is incapable of offering any resistance is it finally destroyed by the Self. A motorcar is going at an enormously high speed. If it suddenly encounters a large and heavy obstacle round the bend of a corner, what will happen?

Q: The occupants of the motorcar will all be killed.
B: If the driver had applied brakes slowly and steadily over some distance prior and reduced the speed before the obstacle had to be encountered?

Q: Nothing will happen to them.
B: Likewise with the mind. For countless births your mental habits have been cherished by you. They will not go down without a fight. The fight does involve pain. Pain is inevitable. Also, these habits will not disappear overnight; do not expect them to vanish all of a sudden.

You will need the patience of the bird that recklessly laid its eggs in mid-flight whilst gliding over the ocean, and then, being unable to dive into the water as far down as the ocean bed, kept furiously flapping its wings over the surface of the waves, in the hope that one day the effort might make the ocean dry up and reveal her young ones.

Q: It is absurd. How can the bird's effort succeed?
B: Saying, 'I shall reach the Self with the mind' is just as ridiculous.

Q: But how then shall I attain jnana*? Seeing Bhagavan's noble and saintly countenance, I am also inspired to become a* jnani *like him. Is the ambition immoral?*

B: If you will have Realisation you must be prepared to irrevocably relinquish everything you think you have including yourself first and foremost. Every last thing precious in your sight shall have to be given up. What is being spoken of here does not amount to advice to physically remove yourself from your incumbent surroundings. What actually matters is that the mind must be insulated and isolated from its familiar worlds of sense perceptions and intellect fabricated labyrinths, and whisked away into the Heart.

Q: How then shall I cultivate detachment towards the world?
B: It is non-attachment that is needed, not detachment, which is merely attachment to the perceived virtue of non-attachment or aversion to the perceived vice of attachment. To be non-attached implies to be non-detached also. Absence of modification of mind is the one and only genuine non-attachment.

Q: If I give up my fondness for the things of the world, if I mentally give up everything I think I own or cherish, will jnana *be bestowed upon me in return?*
B: In return, you may or may not obtain *jnana*. The matter rests at the discretion of the mercy of the Higher Power. In giving up everything, you must give up also your ambition for *jnana*. Then this question also cannot arise.

Q: These are harsh terms.
B: Yes. But did anybody hold a dagger to your throat and force you to Realise? The honest fact is, those who go crazy with the pain of *samsara* [cycle of birth and death caused by karma] invariably and inevitably Realise. When the mundane Existence has become altogether intolerable and even inconceivable, then Realisation is not far away.

If *samsara* is still acceptable or reckonable to you, will it be possible for you to Realise? One who does not recognise the blatantly self-evident truth that *samsara* is a curse, not a blessing: can he Realise? There are those who clearly see the patently poisonous

nature of *samsara*; Realisation comes to them in a trice.
Others go on discussing, 'I wonder what *sadhana* I shall perform to Realise the Self? Shall I practise Sri Ramana Bhagavan's technique to Realise or Sri Aurobindo's technique?' And so on.

If a piece of live coal falls into your hand, will your first instinct be to drop it, or to ponder, 'Now, I wonder if this is charcoal, peat or coke...'? Yet men manage to hold on tenaciously to *samsara* – how? Because the glove of *avidya maya* [illusion caused by ignorance] shields the man from the whole of the impact of the pain.

If he felt the pain at its unmitigated, full impact, he would drop the pain-causing affliction at once, and Reality would be deprived of its fictitious complimentary counterpart, *maya* [illusion].

Since the pain seems, at first sight, manageable, and to alternate with so-called pleasures – which, unbeknown to him, are also of the nature of doing and therefore only pain in disguise – man deceives himself into believing that by holding on to the glowing piece of coal with which he has been forcibly thrust he is fulfilling a heroic, enjoyable challenge called life, as a reward for which he is going to avail for himself the wages he calls pleasure.

Thus, the man in ordinary society, although he may imagine himself to be comfortably off, lives in pain all the time, ignoring his true nature of Absolute Bliss. Man is led to the belief that *samsara* is somehow 'manageable'; for this reason he never really makes any effort to break out of it.

When the Guru's Grace commences to plunge into operation, the glove of ignorance begins to rupture. Then that fortunate one who is earmarked for total destruction in his current lifetime begins to suffer like never before. His old stance concerning *samsara* tries to convince him that these bad circumstances are only passing clouds of bad weather, and that soon matters would improve; but no signs of improvement arrive.

Meanwhile, the rupture in the glove has become larger; his hand is squirming with the unbearably scorching blaze of what he had once fondly regarded as a 'challenge'. Finally, just as the glove is sundered, he sees the pointlessness of offering any more resistance

and disgustedly throws away the glowing ember known as *samsara*. This is the secret of how Guru's Grace brings about Realisation: he does not bring about Realisation from anywhere, he merely removes the obstacles to it by speeding up the devotee's absolute surrender. Even prior to the latter's present birth the benign and compassionate *Satguru* carries out an artful selection from the devotee's *karma* to bring about in that very lifetime the Liberation of the innocent, child-like devotee who has placed the entirety of his trust in Him.

So as to make him surrender heart and soul, mind and body – by the dint of merciless and brutal bombardment of his life with misfortune and misfortune only – he brings him to his feet totally by implanting in him strong aversion to and disgust for *samsara*. The *Satguru* takes the liberty to adopt this radical approach only in the case of those devotees who have completely placed their lives in his care.

To others, he politely says, 'Please carry on with your *sadhana* [practice],' and then keeps quiet. Know that if the *Satguru* has decided to grant Liberation to a devotee, even *Brahma* is powerless to raise any objection. The one fail-proof way to obtain Liberation, therefore, is to win the grace of the *Satguru*.

Q: (shedding emotional tears) Yes, I am now prepared to renounce samsara *completely. Please do with me as you like. Please introduce misfortune in my life if necessary. I shall not resent it.*

I want to Realise somehow in this very lifetime. I am prepared to pay any price. Let everything I have ever considered my own be burnt and reduced into smoldering ashes. Let me die as a leper.

But oh! pray, let me have Realisation in this lifetime!

The man was given some water to drink by Bhagavan's attendant and soon he calmed down.
Bhagavan smiled but did not say anything.

14th August 1936

The Answer is to Enquire, Who am I?

A curious, altogether ridiculous personality has arrived at the ashram gaudily dressed in a three-piece suit, a beaver hat, and an ascot cravat. In this weather, his skin ought to catch fire; I wonder how it still seems to be intact. He carries an ebony walking stick mounted with a miniature bronze, roaring lion's head.

He is attracting curious glances everywhere. Apparently the *sarvadhikari* [ashram manager – Ramana's brother] had fallen down in a fit of fright upon first seeing the man and his walking stick. Thinking he must be polite to his hosts, he is taking off his hat whenever he meets anyone in the ashram, with the result that people here have come to the conclusion that some madman has been let loose upon them. Thinking they are going to be attacked, everyone runs away from him as soon as he is spotted.

His head is abnormally large and looks like a gigantic ostrich egg. The rest of his body is malnourished and thin. He sports a completely bald head and a pencil moustache. A comical goatee adds the finishing touches to the eccentricity of his appearance. Bizarrely, his protuberant eyes look hilariously tragic – they convey the impression of a man who is unable to take himself seriously, but has always longed to.

He entered the Hall and bowed low to Bhagavan, hat clasped in hand tucked against tummy, monocle dangling in the air and all. Bhagavan seemed to survey him with quiet interest. He introduced himself, with Chadwick acting as his interpreter. His name is Monsieur Pierre Géant, but he is known as 'L'affolé néant' (the maddened nothingness) by his friends. He comes all the way from the Republic of Greater Lebanon, formerly part of Turkey; a descendant since the conclusion of the Great War. He was always interested in Mysticism and the prospect of experiencing a personal union with God Almighty.

In 1896 he had arrived at a turning point in his life: he met Swami Vivekananda in England. Vivekananda had recommended the study of his Guru's life, as well as of *Vedanta*. Then the distraught one had engrossed himself in Sri Ramakrishna and *Vedanta* for years. Sri Ramakrishna's experiences thrilled him to the core and he wanted them replicated in his own case. Just when he was feeling hopelessly dejected and agitated that Ramakrishna was in the flesh no more, Paul Brunton's book was read out to him, quite casually, by an English-speaking friend, and the 'Maharishi' in it interested him profusely. So he had come straightaway in a steamer, the next available one. He had questions for Bhagavan.

Q: Is your teaching the same as Sri Ramakrishna's?
B: Absolutely.

Q: If I-am-God is the Truth, does it not amount to arrogance?
B: It does not mean you, as you imagine yourself to be, are God. It means, God is the Real 'I'.

Q: There is a self which is coexistent with the personality and attaches itself to the body. This is known as the mind. Then there is the Parabrahman *[Supreme Being] mentioned in* Vedanta. *This is known as the Impersonal Essence of man. Which is my true self? Can I have more than one self?*
B: The mind is a phantom. In the Impersonal Essence the mind is nowhere to be found.

Q: How to reach it?
B: There is nobody there to reach it. Thus, there is no reaching it. Subside and let the Light shine forth. Subside as the mind and shine as the Self.

Q: Practically, what is the method for it?
B: The investigation, Who am I?

Q: But this investigation also is made with mind only.
B: It commences, no doubt, in the mind. It ends in no-mind.

Bhagavan asked Chadwick to read out *Who am I?* to him in French.

This was done and he listened carefully, cocking his huge head against a meagre shoulder, so that his left ear should be better exposed to the sounds emanating from Chadwick's lips. Presently he extracted a small ear-trumpet from the folds of his laborious clothes and held the ear-piece to his left ear.

The bell of the gadget was positioned to face Chadwick's direction. Bhagavan looked at the surprised faces in the Hall and laughed.

Q: What is the authority for saying that the world is a dream? Where is the proof, I mean?
B: Did you exist in sleep?

Q: Yes.
B: Do you exist now?

Q: Yes.
B: Then what is the difference (in the two states)?

Q: I am not aware of my body and world in sleep.
B: Being aware of the body and world is called dreaming. Remain unaware of them now also. That truly is *jnana* or Reality. This alone is the state of true wakefulness.

Q: But how can we call this world a dream?
B: Why not?

Q: There are so many people on the Earth. If it is a dream, whose dream might it be?
B: Yours.

Q: But why pick me out specifically? For instance, it may even be the dream of the amiable Monsieur Chadwick here.
B: Only you are there.

Q: What about you, then, Sir?
B: No, I am not here or there. I AM. There is no here or there or anywhere. I AM THAT I AM.

Q: I comprehend not.
B: Evidence produced by the sensory organs is merely mental in nature. All knowledge of diversity is fictitious mental information. Your Being is Real. There is nothing else.

Q: I want proof.
B: If proof is given to you, how will you be able to believe it?

Q: I comprehend not.
B: The proof given to you, if any, is also going to be mere mental information only.

Q: What can be believed, then, as true?
B: Whatever is believed is false only. Truth is in Being only.

Q: How to attain this Being?
B: By giving up the idea that there could be anything to be attained and all other ideas.

Q: Practically, how can I go about it?
B: Investigate Who am I?

Q: Will repetition of sacred syllables not be helpful? Do not the sacred incantations of your religion hold some sort of latent spiritual power? By unlocking this power or energy can we not reach the state of Enlightenment?
B: You have been appraised of the direct method.

Q: The others are by-lanes or diversions?
B: Yes.

Q: Should food restrictions be followed by a seeker after Enlightenment?

Can I eat pork?
B: Try to thrive on grain and fruit.

Q: Can the investigation of Who am I? be done in your presence only? If I do it elsewhere, would I able to succeed in Enlightening myself? Is your physical presence needed? In order so as to bring about a successful outcome to the practice, I mean?
B: It is the mind that matters. If the mind is kept steadily poised in introversion, such questions cannot even arise.

Q: Is worship of, or even belief in, a personal God permissible?
B: Yes.

Q: Does it not sabotage one's progress toward Enlightenment?
B: When you become ripe enough, you will no longer feel that it is you who are praying.

Q: Is philanthropy a distraction or ought one try to help the suffering world?
B: It varies according to the temperament of the individual's psyche.

Q: I see. What about my case?
B: When you see suffering, what thought first crosses your mind?

Q: I wish God had created a world in which there was no suffering.
B: Those destined to help think – foolishly – 'Let me see what I can do here.'

Q: Is there any need to officially renounce my affirmed affiliation into the La Rochelle Temple?
B: No.

Q: Occasionally I become frightened when my health takes a turn for the worse. How to remain free from such fears?
B: You already know that for this perishable body made of the elements, destruction is certain one day. Why stall over the inevitable?

Q: But how do I keep fear at bay?
B: By not identifying the Self with the body or mind.

Q: But how to get rid of such erroneous identification?
B: Only by relentless pursuit of the investigation, Who am I?

15th August 1936

We have no Right to Judge Anyone

Q: How did Bhagavan finally persuade that boy, Vishwanatha Aiyyer, to return home?

B: I did not. On that night when he was sleeping outside the ashram, I was sitting some distance away from the boy when I noticed that Shabarigirisan, the languor (monkey), was sitting blissfully alone on the roof of the ashram, staring at the full moon in great contentment. When I looked at him, he leaped down, pressed some ginger shoots into my hands and took them back.

Then he climbed back and was for some time ingesting them. Then he did something nobody will believe. He came near us, poised himself on the floor in the *bakasanam* [a type of yoga posture] and softly began whistling (or screeching), perfectly, the tune corresponding to *Endaro Mahanubhavulu* ["Lots of Great Souls"].

The boy sat bolt upright. When he saw what was happening, he burst into tears and caught hold of my feet. "Oh! *Rama*, you have saved me from the great sin of unfairly deserting my delicate mother. If I had done so hell would surely have been my miserable lot. But oh! compassionate *Rama*, by showing me this miracle through Lord *Hanuman* [monkey god], you have saved me from such a perverse fate! *Rama*!

"I will ever remain a bond-slave to your blessed feet! Please bless me! I shall never think of running away again! Oh! *Rama*, I surrender myself at your holy feet! Please bless me!" Shabarigirisan went away with a satisfied grimace.

The next morning the boy returned to town as soon as the sun peeped into the sky, without even waiting to take any food.

Gajapathy: How did Bhagavan get the monkey to sing?
B: I have got nothing to do with it. There is some Mysterious Power in this place which defies all possibility of understanding. Each one gets what he deserves here. The mature ones obtain Emancipation.

G: But then how did he suddenly render the tune? Did he possess any yogic siddhis*?*
B: He was really an extraordinary fellow in countless ways. Other monkeys would eat the lice on their bodies, but Shabarigirisan would gingerly pick them up and set them on a tree branch. He was certainly spiritually inclined; there cannot be any doubt about it.

G: When did Bhagavan see the singer-boy again?
B: Never. They say he has become a regular singer now. But yesterday – where is that *Amanda Vihaan* (weekly magazine published in Chennai)?

The Master rose from his perch and began to rummage at the contents of the bookcase. At length he said, **"Well, somebody seems to have taken it away,"** and returned to his couch.

G: Why, did it contain anything on Bhagavan? Shall I go to town and buy a copy for the ashram?
B: Oh! no. This was an old issue. I was casually skimming through it last night. In one article the humourist Kalki has made fun of a cinematographic picture released last year called *Bhakta Nandanar*.

G: Nandanar is the saint Tirunalaippovar, is that not so?
B: Yes. But this picture is not based on the traditional account in the *Periyapuranam* (Tamil epic poem). Evidently, they have alerted themselves to the likelihood of facing a social backlash if one belonging to the *panchamabandham* [lowest human caste] were to be depicted as entering a fire and emerging from it as a *Brahmin*.

So, they have ignored the account in the *Periyapuranam* and wisely opted to base the script on the *Nandanar Saritthiram*, a novel written by Gopalakrishna Bharathiyar, which presents an egalitarian version of the story. Otherwise, it would be classed as incendiary material and someone might try to stall the exhibition of the film, by means of approaching the judiciary or by 'direct confrontational' means (laughs).

G: He has found the time to perform for cinematographic pictures. Why not come to the ashram to pay Bhagavan a visit?
B: (sternly) Keep quiet. This is what I don't like. Do you know everything? Judge (by external appearances). This is how men lose their peace of mind.

G: Oh! Sorry, very sorry.
B: *Parava illai* (it doesn't matter). In future do not formulate judgements upon others. We have no right to judge anyone. There is a Supreme Judge for all. Leave the judging to him.

G: Yes...I comply, certainly. Are there any more interesting incidents concerning the monkey Shabarigirisan?
B: Oh! Yes, many. We could go on talking throughout the year.

G: Bhagavan has mentioned other monkeys like Nondi-Payyan that were petted by him whilst he was staying on the Hill ashram. Did Shabari condescend to mingle with them?
B: I told you, he was aloof. Other monkeys, whether common ones or languors, used to avoid him. They seemed to hold him in awe or reverence. Nayana used to say that in many places in the scriptures it

has been mentioned that an advanced *tapasvin* [one who performs Tapas] can be identified by the brilliant *tejas* [illumination] on his face. The Bible also mentions it:

> **...Moses wist not that the skin of his face shone while he talked with him.' '...behold, the skin of his face shone; and they were afraid to come nigh him.**

G: Yes, everyone sees it in Bhagavan.
B: (laughs) Is Bhagavan a *tapasvin*? For whose Deliverance shall Bhagavan do *tapas*, since he sees only the bliss of Liberation everywhere?

G: So, according to Bhagavan, there are no ajnanis *[ignorant persons] anywhere?*
B: The *jnani* sees no one as *ajnani*. All are only *jnanis* in his sight. Why? Because the Self is pure *jnana* and nothing else. The *jnani* cannot know anything apart from the Self.

G: But the languor has a black face. Can it shine?
B: (laughing) Charcoal is black. Does it not glow red when radiant? *Tejas* is not physical. It is the feeling of peace; it is freedom from thought waves that the ordinary man finds himself continually disturbed by.

G: It must be on account of Bhagavan's positive influence that the languor developed such an exalted spiritual status. Did Bhagavan, teach him atma-vidya*?*
B: He was no stranger to it himself. Once he came there I said, "If the discovery that there is no such thing as 'I' is to be made, the mind must be made nude. So, all *vrittis* [mind structures], including the belief you have mentioned, must be relinquished."
Apparently on hearing this, Shabarigirisan made his spine erect, closed his eyes and lapsed into *kevala kumbhaka* [breath retention]

for some time. Perumal remarked, "See, he has gone into *Samadhi!* This monkey is the Ramana Maharshi amongst monkeys!" and we all laughed. Those days we would have good fun every day. There was no ashram, sofa, and so on. Now all this property has come in and I am trapped! (laughs)

(There are many stories illustrating Bhagavan's close rapport with animals, an important teaching in light of man's ongoing extinction of nature and his dangerous notion that man is separate from nature – Ed)

18th August 1936

Unrealise the not-Self

Q: If the theological pronouncements of the Christians are to be believed, we are all born mired in sin. Is the doctrine of original sin correct?
B: What is born is born only in sin. The Unborn is sinless; therefore, He is never born. Birth into *samsara* is the announcer of agony. In fact, you are the one original Absolute. But apparently you have now assumed limitations and taken on the form of this perishable body. Your true Self knows neither beginning nor end. But now you seemingly were born and shall die. Why?

Q: I don't know.
B: Find out.

Q: If I surrender my life to the Almighty, can I remain carefree thereafter?
B: One who has surrendered would not raise this question or any other question. Surrender is not a means to an end. Something that

involves 'doing' cannot be surrender. Give up everything and stop caring for anything (on the mental plane) – that is surrender. Some, when asked to surrender, reply, 'Done, Swami. Now, when am I going to Realise the Self?' It is absurd. To surrender is to abandon even the fundamental or random-mental conceptualisation, the *aham vritti* ['I'-thought]. If you are yourself not there, who is going to raise doubts or questions? After true surrender, only Silence remains.

Q: What is the crux of Bhagavan's teachings?
B: You say 'I am'; find out who is. Find the source of thought; stay there once and for all.

Q: How do I know that this whole thing about Self-realisation isn't just one big scam?
B: That is just what it is.

Q: What?! Then why are you running this ashram and misguiding people?
B: I am not running any ashram. People come here and ask how the Self is to be Realised. They are told something and they go away contented for the time being. As far as I know, there cannot be anything to form the subject-matter of Realisation. The Self is always in Realisation. The Sun cannot know darkness.

There is nothing besides the Self to Realise the Self. There are not two Selves, so that they may Realise each other. So, who is to Realise what? If everything (including the renouncer foremost) is abandoned, the Self stands Revealed. But people will not understand this and want to 'Realise the Self'. What can I do? How to Realise that alone which is Real? Can you impart reality to Reality? Is it not ridiculous? All that is possible to do is to Unrealise the not-Self. Then the Self alone remains.

Q: According to Bhagavan the inevitability of predestination is unalterably undeniable. This pronouncement seems to be severely discouraging for sadhakas *[seekers of truth]. If only what is destined to happen is going to*

happen, what is the point in performing any sadhana*? It may be that I am simply destined not to Realise at all.*
B: Do you know what your destiny has in store for you? Are you capable of knowing it beforehand?

Q: No.
B: (smiling) Continue with your *sadhana*.

Q: What is the use in it, if I am destined to not Realise?
B: If it is going to turn out to be useless, let it. What does it matter? The effort is only made by the ego, which is from the beginning non-existent or fictitious. What is Real cannot make any effort. When you do at last Realise, even then all this effort (that you are talking about) can only ever be described as a waste, for you will then find that you have expended effort to discover the most self-obvious and self-evident natural state! Just how ridiculous the idea of *sadhana* is you will see only then.

Q: So, according to Bhagavan, ultimately the ego's mirage-like Existence is, on the whole, just a complete waste?
B: Yes. But do not take Bhagavan's word for it. All that is possible to do is to unrealise the not-Self. Ascertain the truth of the fact for yourself, exclusively by means of relying upon your own insight into the matter. Why should you depend upon the opinion of others? Opinions obtained from others will also go as they came.

Q: But I trust in Bhagavan's words.
B: Only one's own Experience can Reveal the Truth. The blossoming or revelation of the light of Truth from within can only be the result of one opening one's own eye of wisdom. Others can only show you the way. The horse can only be led to the pond.

Q: Faith in the Guru's words is enough to lead to Deliverance, say the books.
B: Yes, but you must act upon the words. Can the Guru's Grace act as a substitute for our own effort? Some reassure themselves with

the notion that their Guru takes care of them come what may. Then they remain easy going. The Guru is (himself) used as an excuse for not making any effort. Some believe that when the appropriate time arrives, the Guru will himself call them and hand over their Realisation to them on a platter. The Guru cannot spoon-feed you with Realisation. I have shown the way. It is up to you to do the rest.

Q: But I am a weak creature.
B: No. Weakness is only an idea or thought. Swami Vivekananda said:

> **Whatever you think, that you will be.**
> **If you think yourself weak, weak you will be;**
> **if you think yourself strong, strong you will be.**

So, if you think nothing, your ego will be reduced to nothing. People imagine themselves to be weak because it conveniently allows them to be easy going. This pretended weakness is used as an excuse for remaining idle. Idleness is the antithesis of stillness. Idleness is trance or dullness. Stillness is motionless alertness. Who said you are weak? The fact is, you never realise how strong you are until the option of being weak has been taken away from you already. When it is no longer open to you to imagine that you are weak, strong is the only way to BE. Struggle madly until you strike the Light within. Sri Ramakrishna said:

> **The citadel of the Kingdom of God must be**
> **seized by storm.**

21st August 1936
Sri Gajapathi Healed

It is well past midnight, but since I am feeling inexplicably feverish, I have not returned to my lodgings near the temple today. The Hall is dark and quiet; the only sound found to be embellishing the electrifying silence permeating this hallowed Temple of the Presence is the gentle breathing of the young men sleeping at the back of the Hall. The Master is as usual seated upright upon the Sofa, his eyes as unimpressionable and starry as ever. These lustrous eyes are brightly lit with a light that is not of this world. I am reminded of the words of the Christ: 'My kingdom is not of this world.' These wonderful eyes evidently belong to a human, but the Immortal-being which gazes through and out of them is clearly inhuman.

One look into those eyes is enough to convey the truth that this man is really not here at all, that he has been devoured without trace by the Beyond, that he is quiet, quite lost in that supreme Divinity, perpetually elusive to sensory perception, which man is wont to call God. In this duration of merely seven weeks or so, I reflect in joyously surprised contemplation, how much he has altered me for the better, hopelessly incorrigible idler that I was. Peering into those fathomlessly deep eyes, I remember with wry bemusement how petty my life's concerns had been before meeting him.

Precisely at that moment, unexpectedly, a deluge of loving gratitude for everything he is and everything he has done for me suddenly bursts through my mind, like raging water exploding out of a pulverised reservoir whose flood far beyond capacity has resulted in its utter collapse. I am racked and convulsed with silent, helpless sobs. Those great eyes slowly turn and look at me, as though just then registering my presence. A smile of enchanting sweetness gently comes to play on the Maharshi's lips.

G: 'You know I do not deserve your Grace, Master. Why then give it to me? Is that not wrong?' I ask him from within my mind.
The Master laughs like a child and says softly,

B: The saving power of Love alone makes one worthy of Grace. If you have a heart that knows to truly Love, be assured that you have the instrument in your hands with which to win over Emancipation. Love alone is the crowbar with which to prise open the terrifically strong knot of the Heart.

The words make the hairs all over my body stand on end; a thrill of sheer, ecstatic joy runs up my spine, and I shudder involuntarily. My body trembles and shivers with the strain of maintaining continual eye-contact; but I am unable to resist the temptation to go on looking, for here is an ocean of supreme, sovereign Serenity, and immersion in her blissful waters provides my abandoned, wearied soul with unrivaled refreshment and rejuvenation that is truly 'the peace of God, which passeth all understanding'. For the first time, I understand practically, as an insight, the meaning of the Master's oft-repeated maxim:-

> **You may imagine to yourself that you have parted from God, but know that He never parts from you.**

Then, without warning, a spasm of pain crossed my abdomen and moments later I lay flat on the floor, whimpering in alarm.
B: Do not be discomposed. That which has been aimed at the head: let it carry the turban away. You may collect some *Thiruneer* [sacred ash] from the Matrubuteshwara shrine. Dissolve a small quantity in water and drink it whenever you have this sort of trouble (affliction of the gastroenterological system). Also, you may resume chanting the *Hanuman Chalisa* [devotional hymn].

I did not ask how he knew; I am now convinced that the body on the couch before me is simply a mask or vehicle for God Himself to guide me, and he is Himself that God.

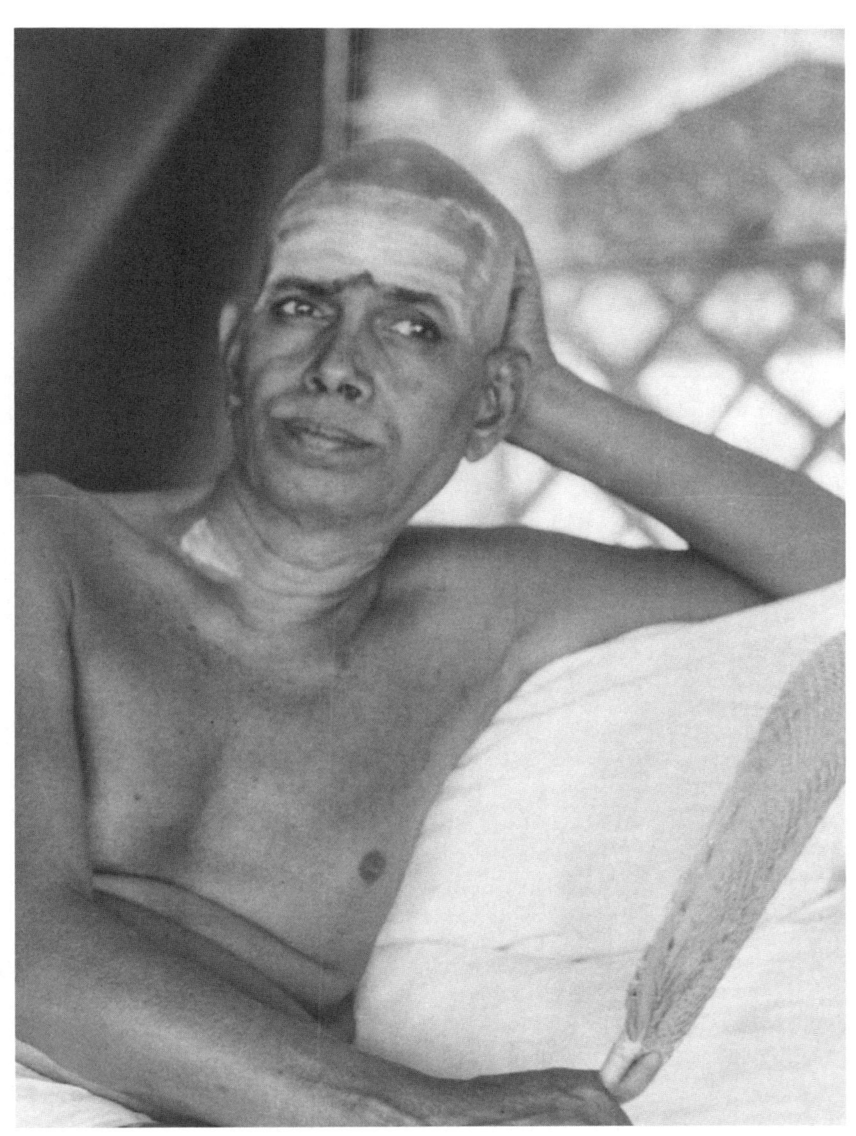

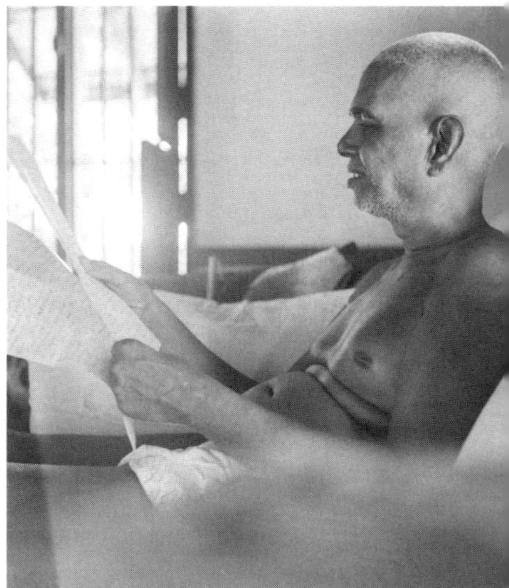

Bhagavan with Paul Brunton and Ella Maillart to the left

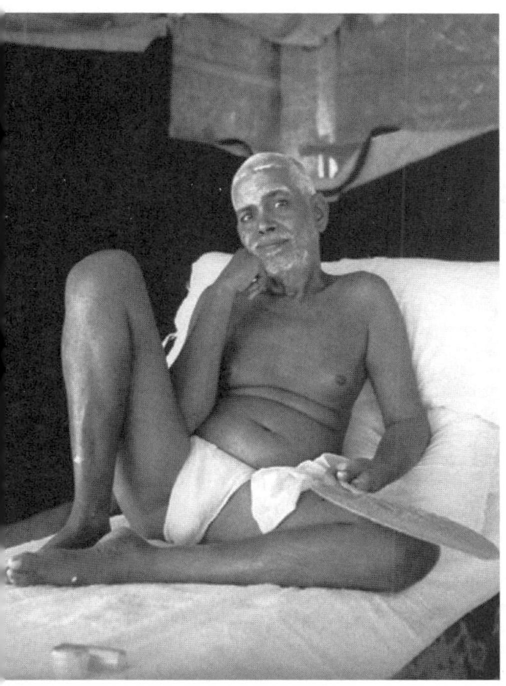

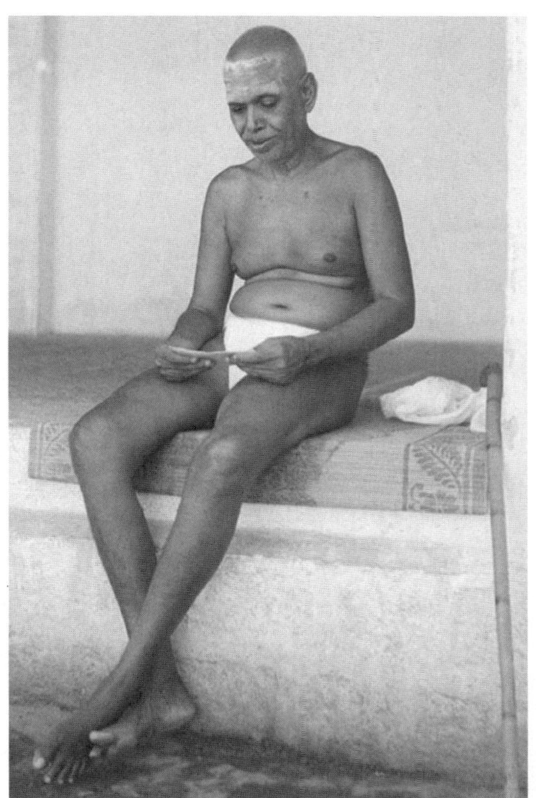

aul Brunton next to Bhagavan

Bhagavan sitting with Annamalai Swami (on the left)

Bhagavan with cow Lakshmi

23rd August 1936

Love Is

This morning when I entered the Hall, Sri Bhagavan smiled at me sweetly, like a child, and handed me a letter, saying, **'See, you will like this!'**

Piqued, I unfolded it and read it. It was from a Monsieur Alfred E Sorensen (Sunyata – Ed), and it ran so (reproduced from memory):

> *The moment your eyes fell on me, I became motionless like you and immersed me in my own intrinsic inner state of Absolute Being, which in truth is only You.*
>
> *I kiss the dust of your sacred feet every day, for by drowning me once and for all in the deep ocean of exaltation which is truly You, you have consumed my unfaithful mind forever. Now I live only as Love-of-You. I have happily lost myself in You, who are Love Itself. Never ever will the miseries of the world manage to hunt me out again, for I see only Lovely you in them.*
>
> *When your omniscient eyes bored into mine and said 'THERE IS NO ANYTHING,' my Heart tugged from within, and, knowing it was you who was calling, I meekly followed. There I was made nothing; now I am NOT. Now I roam around the universe like an unbridled wild animal, knowing not what I am doing nor why. Now all I know is you in which there is no me.*
>
> *My Master has been kind enough to send word through Mr Hurst (Paul Brunton – Ed) that he regards me as a* sahajajnani *[always the same], or natural mystic. Although now there is no question of anything remaining apart from my Master, my heart aches to set eyes upon his physical frame again. May Sri Bhagavan hastily fulfil my wish! Bhagavan's Love.*

(Sorensen/Sunyata was unlikely to use this form of 'I' – Ed)

Gajapthi: Who is this man?
B: He came here earlier this year, perhaps at Mr Brunton's invitation.

G: Bhagavan took one look at him, and he attained the Final State?!
B: (twinkling) Bhagavan does not cause anything to happen. Why, are you thinking along the lines of 'Oh! I am sitting in the Hall every day, hearing reports of people obtaining lofty, transformative, spiritual experiences from Bhagavan every day, and excitedly listening to Bhagavan's teachings every day – when is all this going to bear fruit, and when shall I become a *jnani*?' Is the attraction of *jnana* sorely tempting you?! (laughs)

G: Oh! No. The moment I came here and Bhagavan looked at me, I forgot all about myself. Now I think only of Bhagavan, who is already a jnani. *So, for whom am I to ask* jnana*?*
B: The secret of *jnana* is *bhakti*. Unselfish Love – motiveless, ceaseless, stubborn Love – is the key that unlocks the Gate of the Heart once and for all. Long and yearn for him fervently not so that he may destroy your ignorance, but merely because such Love is possible (to you). One alone who knows how to madly Love has fulfilled the purpose of human birth; he need not be born again. The Loveless ones repeatedly come back to the stinking ocean of *samsara* to suffer more and more.

G: To everyone who comes here Bhagavan only recommends vichara.
B: *Vichara* is a means to eliminate ignorance, which obscures Love from Shining forth – for the nature of the Self is Love Itself. Love cannot be practised as a *sadhana*. All that is possible is to surrender to it. There is no such thing as preparation for Love.

Love is already there. It alone IS. All that is needed on your part is to give up thought, which makes you imagine yourself to be apart from Love, and so merge in Love. Then there is only Love, which is bliss beyond imagination. To one who has discovered the ecstatic joy of volitionless Love, *sadhana* is a laughable absurdity. To those who require justifications, we may say that such Love blossoms

only in souls which have perfected their *sadhanas* in previous births.

G: But among sadhanas vichara *is the best?*
B: Undoubtedly.

31st August 1936

40th Anniversary Event Preparation

Late in the evening today, the *sarvadhikari* [manager] requested the Master to formally oversee and approve of the preparations the ashram has made for the celebrations arranged for tomorrow. Tomorrow is the 40th anniversary of the day on which the Master is said to have attained Eternal Union with Arunachala: 1st September, 1896.

Many devotees, Indians as well as Caucasians, have gathered together here now, and the place is overflowing with people. Many items required for the day have been procured from the town in a bullock cart. The Hall has been decorated profusely with clusters of mango leaves strung together with jute yarn, and, using wet flour and red dye, decorative patterns have been drawn across the floor throughout the ashram.

Amid all the hustle and bustle, I observe Bhagavan taking the *sarvadhikari* aside and telling him seriously:

"Don't forget to consider the monkeys, the cows, and the crows in planning tomorrow's culinary arrangements."

The *sarvadhikari* merely nods meekly and says, 'Yes, Bhagavan.'

1st September 1936

The Anniversary Event

The anniversary event today went grandly. A shadow puppetry group from Madras, accompanied by a musical troupe, showed us all the different Avatars of Vishnu, which flitted by on a screen made of a simple cotton *vaetti* [cloth wrap]. The dark figures moved on the screen to the accompaniment of matching music from the instrument players. The life of each Avatar went on for around ten minutes, the performance being given in the Hall itself.

The group had come on their own from Madras – nobody had invited them. The *sarvadhikari* was highly pleased. Bhagavan also seemed to like the show. Keeping time to the music, he went on tapping the handle rings of the *kumuti* [metal stove] used to burn *sambarani* [frankincense] in the Hall. It was a great joy to watch his nimble fingers move back-and-forth, striking at the iron rings in perfect rhythm. He was being so sensitive in paying attention to the melody that according to the varying pitch of the music, different fingers were used to hit the rings.

Not once did those delicately beautiful fingers miss their mark; yet – all the while – he was looking exclusively at the *vaetti*, and never at his hands! The feat of concentration enthralled but did not surprise me. I am aware he is a proven *sahasra avadhani* [excellent poet], which is not a fact that many people know about the Master – and he, of course, would never call attention to himself. Moreover: 'With men this is impossible; but with God all things are possible.'

Chadwick (to Samuel Cohen): Mr Prendergast exhausted half his film roll yesterday on taking pictures of the anniversary celebrations. If he does not frank off the prints to the ashram soon, the sarvadhikari *will pounce on my throat and gobble me up alive, because he entrusted me with the responsibility of communicating to the fellow the rule that whatever photographs are taken here, one complete set of prints must be handed over. I told him once and reminded him twice, I think. Hope he does not let me down.*

EZ: The Mees chap from Holland who visited early this year sent in his prints of Bhagavan promptly, I remember.

C: Yes, he had a funny bellows-type machine of the olden-day variety, remember? I think it was a Tourist Multiple.

Bhagavan presently astonished the Hall by saying at this precise moment, **"Oh! No; it was a Kodak Anastigmat."** (popular 1930s camera – Ed).

All this while he had been fixedly staring into vacant space, and nobody would have guessed that he had been paying any attention to the usual trifling late-night chatter going on in the Hall! This is yet another instance which demonstrates that nothing and nobody escapes the attention of the Master, although at first appearances he might appear disconnected, aloof, or uninterested.

2nd September 1936

Samuel Cohen has Doubts

Samuel Cohen approached Sri Bhagavan and questioned him:
Co: I have just read the book, Ramakrishna, the Man-Gods and the Universal Gospel of Vivekananda: A Study of Mysticism and Action in Living India *by Mr R Roland. Its contents have disturbed me profoundly. Please let me explain why my mind has become agitated upon having read this work:*

He proceeded to read out extracts from the book. I listened with particular attention, for this book had no small impact upon my own life.

> • The Universe was extinguished. Space itself was no more. At first the shadows of ideas floated in the obscure depths of the mind. Monotonously a feeble consciousness of the ego went on ticking. Then that stopped too. Nothing remained but Existence. The soul was lost in the Self. All duality was blotted out completely. Finity and Infinity had fused themselves into the One. Beyond word, beyond thought, he had attained Realisation of the Imperishable *Brahman.*
>
> • The experience of revelation of the presence of divine consciousness in all things was the last stage in spiritual illumination so far as the ordinary man was concerned, for beyond this temporary revelation lay the Supreme Realisation, the absolute Identity, obtained in the *Nirvikalpa Samadhi* [the Highest Ecstasy] – but that was reserved for men who had achieved their mission in life. It was the ultimate and forbidden joy; for from it there is no return except in a few exceptional cases like that of Ramakrishna himself.

In spite of the prayers of his disciples, he was reluctant to let them taste of it; they had not yet won the right. He knew only too well that such 'salt dolls' would no sooner touch the first waves of that Ocean than they would be absorbed in it. He who is desirous of attaining Identity with Unique Reality only receives a return ticket by a miracle. The disciples therefore had to remain in this world at the stage before the final, wherein takes place identification of all objective reality with divine consciousness.

• During the last days of Ramakrishna's life we shall often see Naren urging the Master to allow him the highest superconscious revelation, the great ecstasy, from which there is no return, the *Nirvikalpa Samadhi*; but Ramakrishna emphatically refused him.

• Naren, while meditating, had the sensation of a light shining behind his head. Suddenly he lost consciousness and was absorbed into the Absolute. He had fallen into the depths of the terrible *Nirvikalpa Samadhi*, which he had sought for so long, and which Ramakrishna had refused to allow him. When, after a long time he returned to himself, it seemed to him that he no longer had a body, but that he was nothing but pure Subjective Consciousness, and he cried out: 'Where is my body?'

Co: Does Bhagavan now see why I have become afraid of spiritual practice on the whole? Is Samadhi *[Union with Reality] such a horrific experience then? Am I then subjecting myself with such tedious attention to the rigours of meditation, self-purification, and mental discipline only to end up in a*

state of terror, or to turn into a living corpse?
B: People who have themselves had no experience of the *Nirvikalpa* state spectate from the outside and entertain all sorts of notions about *Nirvikalpa*. Even those who have read and obtained a good intellectual grasp of all the *Upanishads*, and are thoroughly theoretically versed in the doctrine of *ajata Advaita* [the Absolute is aja, the unborn eternal non-duality], tend to have fantastic notions about *Nirvikalpa*. This being the case, would we ever be justified in blaming a Caucasian for harbouring such notions? Many Caucasian authors have produced similar material. So, why specifically point out Mr Rolland?

Co: But Nirvikalpa *has been described as a void.*
B: Some yogis – by means of practising *Kevala Kumbhaka* [breath retention] for days together deliberately – permit themselves to fall into a vacuous state far deeper than *sushupti* [deep sleep], wherein they are aware of absolutely nothing. This they glorify to be *Nirvikalpa*. Others have the opinion that once you dip into *Nirvikalpa* for a few moments even, you become an Emancipated Soul. An example for the follower of such a school is the monk Tota Puri, whom Mr Roland describes in the same work.

Still others assume that *Nirvikalpa* is attainable only through suspension of body-consciousness, in which the possibility of sensory-perception is totally eradicated, as in a swoon. But think – is there anything to be attained? What is the goal? Is it to acquire the Self or eliminate the not-Self?

All the various divergent opinions about *Nirvikalpa* arise because people who have had no experience of it, whose knowledge of it is merely intellectual, have written lengthy treatises about it and taken the trouble to publish and publicise them.

Co: Then what is the real Nirvikalpa*?*
B: *Nirvikalpa* is simply *chidakasha* [pure space of consciousness] – effortless, volitionless, pure Subjective Consciousness of Being. To the *Kritopasaka* [one who has a one-pointed mind] whose mind

is mature (in a state of advanced introversion) the experience of *Nirvikalpa* may come as a sudden inundation.

For others *sadhana* is necessary to achieve it. *Sadhana* slowly wears down the curtain of thoughts, which conceal the self-evident experience of the Beingness of the Self, and results in the eventual revelation of the screen of pure Subjective Consciousness, which is always the enduring background supporting the clouds of thought-mist that doggedly plague one.

Co: Why is it that some people have mature minds, and others have minds that are bent outward?
B: Some persons have minds that have become ripe from *sadhana* done in previous births; but this is only a seemingly plausible explanation. Next you will ask me, 'What prevented me from doing *sadhana* in my former lives?' It is like the age-old dispute, 'Which came first – the seed or the tree?' So, leave off all these theoretical disputations and seriously engage yourself in pursuit of the Truth that is here and now within you.

Co: When the topic is raised, Bhagavan often mentions one more, final state that is beyond even the Nirvikalpa.
B: Yes – that is the *Sahajastithi* [natural state] of the *jnani.*

Co: How to reach this? Does remaining in the Nirvikalpa *state for a prolonged duration of time ensure that we attain it?*
B: Granting the final state – or not – is left to God's Mercy; the *Sahajastithi* is not to be won by *sadhana.* In the course of one's *sadhana* one must have learnt to surrender to God's will.

When you have reached the stage when it no longer matters to you whether you reach this state or that, and in fact when there is nothing that matters to you anymore, then alone will God consider granting you the *Sahajastithi* or Emancipation. If you feel, even at the level of the subliminal or subconscious mind, that there is anything yet to be attained, or anything yet to be lost, *jnana* is impossible.

So long as you yearn for Liberation, it means that the ego is

alive to crave for it. Desire for Emancipation may be good insofar as it is helpful in keeping away other thoughts, but it must itself also vanish before Realisation can be had. Ask yourself, 'Whose Liberation (is it that I aspire for)?'

Co: Is Nirvikalpa *the same as the* nivritti *[inward state of mind]?*
B: Not in all cases. *Nirvikalpa* may be with or without perception of name and form. When names and forms are perceived but do not leave behind any impression on the mind, that is the *nivritti* state of mind, or *Nirvikalpa* with name and form. There is also *Kevala Nirvikalpa*, where the mind is closed to possibility of perception of name and form.

In *Kevala Nirvikalpa*, owing to physical non-perception of sensory and intellectual objects, the bliss experienced by the *sadhaka* may be more intense; also, in this state, the mind is temporarily forcibly withdrawn and retained in the Heart for the duration of the experience, and so can be said to have temporarily disappeared.

Therefore, *Kevala Nirvikalpa*, which is a temporary state of no-mind, cannot be equated with the state of *manonivritti* [mind turned inwards], in which the mind has been divested of its property or characteristic of extroversion, but nevertheless still subtly remains. However, it is unwise to try to obtain *Kevala kumbhaka* [breath retention] – the state is not conducive for destruction of *vasanas*, and is thus not desirable.

Co: What about manolayam *[state where thoughts still hazily projected] and* Kevala Kumbhaka? *Are they states inferior to* Nirvikalpa?
B: These are simply states of sleep that might be deeper than *sushupti*. They are not the same as *Samadhi*, in which awareness is perfectly maintained. These are a dangerous retardation on the spiritual path.

3rd September 1936

Kitchen Drama

It had been my observation that Sri Bhagavan had not so much as entered the kitchen for some time, a period lasting for a few days, during the last month, but he had totally avoided it. This month he was regularly attending to his self-imposed duties in the kitchen as usual. The Master was not the sort to shirk work; therefore, my curiosity was piqued as to the reason. I asked his attendants but they did not know anything about the matter. Then I asked Sri Cycle-Pillai about the matter when the Master was not in the Hall.

CP: Yes; your observation is correct indeed. Last month, the kitchen ladies offended Sri Bhagavan by not paying any attention to his explicit instructions. That is why he boycotted the kitchen for some time.

G: Why? What happened?
CP: Last month, I had purchased peerkangkai (ridge gourd) from the market for the ashram. Bhagavan told the kitchen workers that whilst the outer kernel be used as usual to prepare milagu kootu (South Indian stew), the skin outside and the flesh inside must not be wasted, but must be fried in groundnut oil and made into thuvaiyyal (chutney). His orders were not obeyed.

All the thoel and kudal (skin and intestines) of the peerkangkais were thrown away. This fact upset the Master considerably. He went there, told the kitchen workers:
"Hereafter I shall not be bothering you with my unnecessary and useless commands. Henceforth, you may do exactly as you like in this place, for having given trouble to you for so long I humbly beg you to accept my plea for forgiveness," and left the place with his eyes glimmering with tears.

CP: The workers in the kitchen did not say anything in reply, but kept quiet. Only I witnessed this sad scene as Bhagavan spoke those sorrowful words. I told nobody. Somehow, I felt that it was my responsibility to make the situation as it was before, since it was me that had purchased the peerkangkai from the market, thus triggering this unfortunate feud between Bhagavan and the kitchen workers.

So, without telling anybody, again I purchased peerkangkai from the market, and took them to the kitchen workers. I told them that it was their responsibility to make amends for their evil behaviour in the past, and that this time they must make use of the thoel and kudal also.

They were not pleased at my behaviour, but still did as I asked. The next day as soon as we sat down for food, peerkangkai-kudal thuvaiyyal was served first. A delicious smile lit up the Master's face. He twinkled at me with fun in his benign eyes. Then and there I fell at his feet and begged for forgiveness on behalf of the kitchen workers. I assured him that such negligence would never happen again. I requested him with profound earnestness to resume his usual kitchen duties. Sri Subbaramayyagaru had also noticed the Master's absence from the kitchen. He wept openly before the Master. He said that if the kitchen had a mouth, she would lament tearfully, 'Alas! I feel as though I have been widowed in my prime.'

Others also persuaded Bhagavan to pardon the kitchen workers for their mistake and take up his usual role in preparing food for the ashram. Finally, the Master agreed to our requests. Since last week, he has been going to the kitchen as usual. For this purpose, as vaendudhal *[penance] I broke twenty-seven coconuts before the Ganapati idol in the* mandapam *[a large hall] opposite to* Agni Theertham *[holy water place].*

4th September 1936

Obstacles which Hinder Realisation of the Self

Q: What are the obstacles which hinder Realisation of the Self?
B: They are habits of mind [*vasanas*].

Q: What are the aids for Realisation?
B: Introversion of mind is the one and only aid.

Q: How can I achieve the same?
B: By preventing the mind from straying out after thoughts, desires and imagined objects of sensory perception.

Q: What are *vasanas*?
B: Habits of thought, accumulated tendencies of mind, and intellectual predispositions.

Q: How does one get rid of these hindrances?
B: Seek the Self through meditation in this manner: trace every thought back to its point of origin, which is only the mind. Never allow thought to run on. If you do so, it will be unending. Take it back to its starting place: the mind's essence of pure consciousness – again and again – and thought and thinker will both die of inaction eventually.

The mind only exists by reason of thought. Stop thought and there is no mind. As each doubt or depressing thought arises, ask yourself, 'Who is it that doubts? What is it that is depressed?' Go back constantly to the question, 'Who or what is this thing called 'I'? Where is the source of the mind?' Tear everything out and go on discarding until there is nothing but the Source of all left. And then live always in That and only in it. There is no past or future, save in the mind. Only present exists. Yes, even the present is mere imagination. It IS. That is all. Ehyeh Asher Ehyeh (I am That I am).

4th September 1936

Mrs Piggot's Visit

I was told that the Maharshi had his finger on the pulse of the whole ashram, although he appeared on the face of it totally unconcerned with all mundane affairs. For instance, when in the Hall, he was supposed to know what was going on even in the kitchen – and incidentally I was surprised to find that he himself assisted in the cutting up of vegetables for the daily meal.

I was also told that he knows what is passing in the minds of people. Of this latter ability, I had a small personal experience. It was in the afternoon, and I was in the far corner of the Hall reading the translation of a collection of proverbs written in – so it appeared to me – a flowery and artificial vein. I was bored and slightly irritated.

Suddenly one of the devotees stood before me with another book in his hand – all the ashram books were bound in brown paper and looked exactly alike – and said, 'Bhagavan asks me to give you this. He thinks it will be more sympathetic to your type of mind.' It was!

How could Bhagavan know what I was reading? I was sitting far away, with many people in between us, blocking his line of vision. But I had previously noticed that many times he would answer a question in my mind whilst it was only in the process of being formulated. This happened too often to be a coincidence.

Q: Sometimes I feel thought stopping and the feeling of beingness underneath is exposed and revealed. At the same time a pulsating sensation is felt on the right-hand side of the chest. Is it right?

B: Yes. Thoughts must cease and reason disappear for 'I'-'I' to rise up and be felt. Feeling is the prime factor and not reason.

Q: Why should it be felt in the chest but not in the head?

B: Because body-consciousness is located there.

Q: When I see outside the sensation disappears. What is to be done?

B: It must be held on to incessantly.

Q: If one is active in the world whilst holding on to such sensation, will his actions be always right?
B: They ought to be. However, such a person is not concerned with the right or wrong of his actions. Such a person's actions are God's and therefore they must be right.

Q: Why then are the restrictions of food given for such persons also?
B: Your present experience is due to the influence of the physical atmosphere you presently find yourself in. Can you have it outside this atmosphere? Now in you the experience is spasmodic. Until it becomes permanent, practice is necessary. Restrictions of food are aids for such experience to be repeated. After one gets established in Truth the restrictions drop away naturally. Moreover, food influences the mind and for this reason the same must be kept pure.

Every experience has to end and the last day of my visit to the ashram arrived, and with it a great sadness filled my heart. I must go back to worries, problems and irritations. Here all was peace. Here it was comparatively easy to live in the mood of the spirit. Is this why so many holy people retire to solitude, I wondered.

I had my farewell talk with Bhagavan. He was so gentle and human. We discussed the difficulties of everyday life and mundane problems. I asked again about the relation of the body to the 'I'. He gave this simile:
B: You came up from the bungalow this morning in a cart. Yet you do not say, 'The cart came up.' You say, 'I came up.' You did not make the mistake of identifying yourself with the cart. In the same way, look upon your body as you do the cart. Treat it well, and it will be a good servant and instrument. But do not be deceived into thinking that it is 'I'.

He again stressed the necessity to see only the Self in everything.
B: Act automatically, so to speak, and let 'It' do the work. And 'It'

always will. Do not look for results. Do what is right at any given moment and leave it behind you then and there.

At the end of our talk, he quoted that wonderful saying from the Upanishad:-

> **When a man understands that he is the Self and therefore that he has himself become all things, what sorrow, what trouble can there be, to him who has once beheld this unity?**

As I went to say goodbye in the evening the ashram people clustered round in sympathy for my departure. I felt I had made and was leaving true friends. They were so simple and yet so genuine. There was a service taking place in the adjoining temple and an old Sanskrit hymn was being chanted. Just as I stepped into the cart the temple bell rang. This brought a smile of happiness on everyone's face. Apparently, to hear a temple gong in the act of departure is a wonderful omen and brings peace.

As I left Tiruvannamalai in the dawn of the next morning, I caught a last glimpse of Arunachala, the Holy Mountain, on which lives one of the saints of Earth. It was red and glowing in the rising sun. I wept with joy to behold the sight.

(This text or extracts can be found in several publications – Ed)

4th September 1936

A Miraculous New York Visit

Major Chadwick in Dialogue

EZ: I have heard that Mr Humphreys was the first Caucasian man to set eyes upon Sri Bhagavan; is that right?
B: Yes.

EZ: Was Mrs Piggot the first Caucasian woman to set eyes upon Sri Bhagavan?
B: No.

Chadwick: Then who came before her?
B: A Caucasian woman came here many years back. She was from the United States. She was a young woman, but had a deep scholarly interest in *Vedanta*.

C: What was her name?
B: I do not recall the name with perfect accuracy, although I remember her well. I think the name was a Mademoiselle Marie Barkös.

C: I find this piece of information to be hugely fascinating. Exactly when did she arrive here?
B: Around the time of the major Wall Street crash which took place in 1929.

C: How had she come to know about Bhagavan? Paul Brunton's Secret India *was not published then.*
B: She had read about me in the *International Psychic Gazette*, but that article had not motivated her visit. Reading that article, she had become briefly fascinated with the 'Hindu saint' described there;

later on, she forgot all about him. One day, she seems to have heard a knock on the door of her apartment, situated near Stonewall Inn in Manhattan. On opening it, who should be standing there but Sri Ramana Maharshi himself! (laughing)

Apparently, I told her to come visit me here. I fortunately remembered to ask her whether the Manhattan-based Ramana Maharshi also was clad only in a loincloth or whether he was wearing anything more! Do you know what the response was?

'Oh! No, Sir. You were, I remember, wearing a cobalt-violet coloured double-breasted shawl-lapelled smoking jacket, with three large brass buttons; also, you had on your head a homburg hat of the same colour.' Then I thought to myself, see, at least the Manhattan-based Ramana Maharshi has some amount of decent dressing-sense! (shaking with laughter)

C: (smiling) After this vision, did she come to India straight away?

B: She told her Guru, a Japanese Buddhist monk named Sri Chokkaiyyan, about the matter. He suggested to her that she must go at once. The Manhattan-based Ramana Maharshi had told her in detail how to reach this place! Upon arriving, she was greatly surprised to find the same person she had met in Manhattan. The Manhattan-based Ramana Maharshi had not introduced himself as being Ramana Maharshi, apparently.

He had merely told her to go to a certain ashram in Southern India, where she would find a great spiritual master who would guide her towards God; then he had told her how to reach Ramana Ashram – where to change trains, and so on. Thereafter he had abruptly turned around and left, leaving her baffled. After coming here, the woman asked me why I had not introduced myself when I had visited her in Manhattan.

What to say? Then those in the Hall explained to her that what she had seen was a miracle, because 'this' was neither in the habit of leaving Tiruvannamalai nor in the habit of donning smoking jackets and hats! She brought presents for the ashram: a big box filled with 'hardtack biscuits', and a few loaves of baguette

bread, baked thrice to endure the long journey from the United States to this place by steamer. Actually, prior to her visit I had no idea that bread was baked in the world that was shaped in this manner. So, when she arrived, I initially wondered why she was wandering about carrying long sticks of firewood with her.

Then she told me that these stout branch-like contrivances were in fact edible bread loaves. The people here would not eat bread if given to them directly. So, I ensured that the same was sliced and put in the sambhar (stew) as naan (Indian bread). For a week we had nothing to eat but rice and sambhar with bread-pieces in it as nan.

In those days the cooking arrangements at the ashram were not so elaborate. People happily ate the sambhar that was served. Other than a few who watched whilst I was working in the kitchen, the rest thought it was pooshinikkai-thaan (pumpkin dish), and ate it happily.

If given to them to eat straight away, they would not eat it; they would say that it was polluted food, having been brought from another country (overseas). I did not want to waste what this poor girl had brought with so much sincerity from such a long distance. As for the biscuits, 'this' and a few others finished it off in a few weeks. The breads were fragrant; they were flavoured with marjoram spice on the outside; she must have taken a lot of effort to prepare them and bring them all the way here.

Apart from the bread and the biscuits, she also brought a personal gift for me: a large kaleidoscope. It was an interesting experience to look into it. It was here for several years until one day Sahib brought his son here. The small boy started playing with the instrument, and became quite attached to it. So, the device was gifted away to him.

Q: A friend of mine has an apartment in Manhattan. I can take it on rent from him if I wish; he would oblige me anytime. Shall I move there? Will Bhagavan please come visit me there every day? I can arrange for plant-

based food to be served to Bhagavan. Please come to visit me also.
B: (kindly) There was and can be no volition on my part that I must visit this person or the other. These things happen automatically. All events in one's life are preordained by *Ishwara* [The supreme Being]; we have no say in them.

Let us turn the mind inward and obtain for ourselves unlimited happiness; that is the only thing in our control. You say that you would like Bhagavan to visit you every day. There is no need for Bhagavan to visit you. He is with you always. Can you be apart from Him? Impossible. Realise Him as the Self of yourself. Then there can be no question of parting from Him.

Q: But I am attached to Bhagavan's mortal frame. Will such attachment obstruct my attempts to Realise the Self?
B: Any attachment is an obstacle. However, mentally sticking with one attachment to the exclusion of every other attachment ripens the mind rapidly for Realisation. In the end, of course, even that one single attachment must be given up before Realisation can dawn.

Q: I am attached to the mortal frame or physical image of Jesus. Is it a help for Realisation or an obstacle?
B: It is a help.

Q: Does such attachment count as abhyasa *[practice]?*
B: In the preliminary stages of practice, yes. Finally, the aspirant is expected to move irrevocably towards *nirgunopasana* [meditation on the formless Brahman].

5th September 1936

Meditation

Q: I am unable to Realise the Self by means of meditation.
B: Where are you now? Are you in the Self or out of it? Can there be anything apart from the Self?

Q: I understand that the Self is non-dual. Yet ignorance prevents me from realising the non-dual Self.
B: Who is ignorant of what? Are there then two selves, so that one of them can be ignorant of the other?

Q: I am only a limited being and not the unlimited Self.
B: Limitation is only a mental concept; it is only an idea in the mind. What is your state in deep sleep? You exist in deep sleep. You also exist now. It is the same you. But the feeling of limitation does not arise in deep sleep. Why?

Q: Because now my mind is active. In sushupti *[deep sleep] the mind was asleep.*
B: There was no mind in sleep. But YOU were there. So, mind comes and goes, but there is no change in That which is actually YOU. YOU, the Self, remain always. The Self remains unaffected whether mind is present or absent.

Q: I understand all these concepts theoretically. But I am unable to realise my true Self.
B: Introvert the mind gradually and you will see one day what you really are.

Q: Is the dawn of Realisation gradual or sudden?
B: Introversion of mind, which is an essential condition for Realisation, is usually gradual. Realisation is always sudden.

Q: Meditation is with mind only. That being so, how can it kill the mind itself?

B: Meditation means sticking to one thought to the exclusion of every other. One particular thought keeps away all others. A distracted mind is weak and filled with numerous thoughts. A strong mind is focused on one particular thought only. Constant meditation transforms the weak mind into the strong mind. The mind is a layer of thought obstructing the Real Self. By constantly sticking with one thought, that one thought also eventually disappears and the enduring background is revealed; this is free from all thought; the background upon which the mind is superimposed is the Beingness of the Self.

Mind in its purity is the same as the Beingness of the Self. The Beingness of the Self is not the same as the Self, in the same way as the rays of the sun are not the sun himself. The feeling of beingness felt by you is only an experience of reflected consciousness. Supposing you stare at a reflection of the sun in a pool of muddy water; this cannot compare with the experience of being the sun himself. To reach that state, one's bodily and mental identifications must be given up. The ignorant man believes that his self is confined to the body only, whereas the *jnani's* experience is that the body and world cannot remain apart from the Self. The Self of the *jnani* is infinite and includes the body also. The blissful peace of the Self is your true nature.

Contrary ideas are only illusory superimpositions. Peace is not to be obtained or procured from somewhere far away through practice. Peace is already there. It is not to be freshly obtained. Then what is the use of practice? It is to give up all your wrong notions; that is all. Your true nature encompasses the three states and extends beyond them. You are really the formless Self. The Self or Heart is all that exists.

The Heart is neither within nor without. It simply IS. It has no second. The mind is the *shakti* [primordial energy] aspect of the Self. After the emergence of the mind, the universe appears and the body is seen to be contained in it. The body and the rest of the

cosmos are only an appearance in the imperishable Self. The body and the world are all contained in the Self only and they cannot exist apart from the Self.

The Self is the same always and remains unaffected whether the cosmos or mind appears in it or not. Self can and does exist without mind. Mind exists only because of the Self and only in the Self. There can be no mind apart from the Self. Realisation means non-recognition of the mind as being apart from the Self.

Q: But how to practise meditation, practically speaking?
B: What is meditation? It is *Atmanishtai* [your true nature]. When thoughts present themselves, trace them back to their source and thus continue to remain indistinguishable from the fundamental state of Beingness that serves as the substratum of the mind; the effort involved in doing so is termed as meditation. *Atmanishtai* is your actual nature. Remain as you are. There is no aim or goal to be reached. In the absence of mind, you are THAT always.

Q: Thoughts present themselves to the mind without invitation. Is our effort only meant to eliminate thoughts?
B: Meditation being on a single thought, all other thoughts are kept away. Meditation is simply negative in effect inasmuch as thoughts are kept at bay.

Q: How to fix the mind in the Self?
B: Not by thinking of the Self, for the Self cannot be comprehended or conceived of by the mind.

8th September 1936

Self-Enquiry, Vichara

Kunja Swami: How is it that without a mind, Bhagavan is able to conduct rational conversations with us and engage in many other tasks and functions besides?

B: Causality is unknown to the *jnani*; the Emancipated Soul's actions therefore are always without motive, purpose, or volition. Bhagavan does not act at all. Action is alien to the Self; He is Life Itself, but yet absolutely motionless. He is simply AWARE.

Other than fullness of Being-consciousness, which he abides as, he does not know anything. The body may act in the world or remain idle; he cannot know. The faculties of sensory perception may remain inactive or function so as to take cognisance of objects in the world; he cannot know.

Being the Self, the *jnani* is totally ignorant of anything and everything but the Self. He is referred to as the Witness-consciousness transcending space, time, and causality; but that is exclusively from the point of view of objects with name, form, and shape that take their origin in Him, subsist in Him, and dissolve back into Him, being merely appearances in Him, of Him, and by reason of Him; he Himself has nothing to witness or see.

The body might be working day and night like a steam-engine, but no *karma* can touch Him. His sensory organs might be caressingly assailed by the greatest of pleasures, but he enjoys nothing. His body might be racked with debilitating pain, but he does not make the foolish mistake of coming under the influence of the notion that the one undergoing experience of pain is he. No matter what manner of work the body might be engaged in doing, he never does anything.

K: Bhagavan, please clarify this one thing for me: are you, or are you not, now talking to us?

B: No. 'I' am not talking to you.

K: (reflectively) That's right. Bhagavan is not doing any talking. Bhagavan simply IS.

Chadwick: I am sometimes given to wondering how a jnani's *awareness of the Self could formerly have been obscured or obstructed by prior ignorance. Was there ever ignorance for a* jnani?
B: No.

C: Are jnanis *born* jnanis *then?*
B: One's idea that one took birth is merely mental information. When mind is annihilated, there is nothing to falsely inform the *jnani* that he was born. Therefore, the Emancipated Soul abides in perpetuity as the Unborn, to which time, space, and any other firmament of transformation or possibility of measurement is wholly alien.

We point to the body of the Emancipated Soul and give it the name *'jnani'*, thinking that such person must have awareness of the Self. But what is the fact? Is there anybody who can both stand apart from the Self and yet know the Self? The only way to know the Self is to BE It. So, the *jnani* is truly *jnana* and nothing but *jnana*. There are no *jnanis*. *Jnana* IS, *jnana* alone IS, and *jnana* alone could ever BE.

K: (in an over-awed intonation of voice) Bhagavan, you inspire me. I also want to become great like you; I want to attain your same greatness; I want to become as great as you. I consider it my life's mission to take after you. You are my idol, my super-hero. Please tell me what I should do to attain the same greatness that you have attained: you the incomparably great Bhagavan.

C: Impossible and inconceivable. How could anybody become our Bhagavan? He is God Absolute.
B: (smiling) What is there in it? Only remain still – *summa iru*.

K: Bhagavan I would like to know how I shall get rid of all my sin.
B: Original sin and original ignorance are all one and the same

thing. To get rid of the one is to get rid of the other, and the other the one. One certain effect of pursuing the investigation Who am I? all the way to its successful culmination in Realisation is the total erasing of all your sin.

K: Is the investigation Who am I? easy or difficult?
B: It is the easiest thing there can be. If attending to other things is readily possible for you, imagine how much easier should be attending to yourself, and attending to yourself exclusively!

K: Some say that it is exceedingly difficult.
B: Pay no attention to their words. Do you trust Bhagavan or not?

K: Implicitly and absolutely.
B: Then never mind what others are saying. Regard only what is said here. Bhagavan (tapping right cheek with palm multiple times rapidly and then pointing to own face) says *vichara* is easy. Will you practise it or not?

K: (eyes swimming in barely suppressed tears, voice choked, and face convulsed with emotion) Yes, Bhagavan.
B: (smiling) Good.

Q: I have been investigating Who am I? for several years. I see no result. What is the reason? Where am I going wrong? What am I doing wrong? Please help me.
B: What is meant by *vichara*? Is it to intellectually analyse one's Self along the lines of the question, Who am I?

Q: Isn't that it?
B: No. *Vichara* means effort to trace thought back to its source, culmination of which effort is discovery of such source as being the Shining of the self-resplendent Heart that is the Beingness of the Self. The penultimate triumph in *vichara* has come about when

effort is needed in order to leave the Shining of the Heart rather than in order to plunge and merge into It.

If you incessantly hold on to the source of thought, there will come a time when emergence from such source becomes altogether impossible; the embodiment of this state is what *vichara sadhana* seeks to achieve. *Vichara* means hunting for the source of thought so that we might abide exclusively and permanently there as and there in. To practise *vichara* is simply this: seek where within yourself it is that thought arises; having found such source, stay there once and for all.

Q: Since the ego is said to emerge from the right-hand side of the chest, can we say that this is the source of thought? Shall I therefore concentrate on the right-hand side of the chest?

B: Trace back thought subjectively, not conceptually. Do you need a mirror to enable you to ascertain that you exist?

Q: I don't understand.

B: Any sort of concentration of mind, be it upon the right-hand side of the chest or otherwise, is mental activity which cannot take you beyond mind. There is only one way to get rid of mind: that is to transcend or by-pass it. If you catch hold of the 'I'-'I' consciousness (that treats itself as real itself) when the mind remains submerged in its source, and hold on to the same indefinitely, the mind will fade away of its own accord. This alone is the way to earn the undying state of *Sahajastithi* from which there is no return possible. No amount of concentration of mind or other mental activity can result in Revelation of the Self.

Q: How shall I search for the origin of the ego? Please explain to me in such a way that I shall be able to understand.

B: Whenever you find the mind wandering, pull it back by asking yourself Who am I? and fix it in pure Subjective Consciousness. Who am I? is like a mongoose patiently but vigilantly waiting outside the termite mound, so that when the snake should emerge,

the animal can spring upon it, break its neck, and eat it.

If the mongoose is resolutely determined to feast upon the snake, can anybody save the snake from certain annihilation? If it remains inside, fearing for its life, it eventually dies out of starvation; if it emerges from the termite-mound to look for prey, it itself becomes prey and dies. This analogy becomes splendidly appropriate when the mongoose happens to be an aged creature. He would not have the stamina to kill a living snake. So, whenever the snake's head pops up, he hisses ferociously and the terrified snake beats a hasty retreat back inside.

Eventually the snake, living in perpetual terror of being devoured, gives up the attempt to go outside and perishes inside the termite-mound out of starvation. Then the mongoose, sensing that the snake has given up its life, breaks open the mound and gleefully consumes his dead prey.

Likewise, the mongoose known as Who am I? cannot by itself kill the snake known as *ahamvritti. Vichara* is a watchman. When the villain shows himself, he drives him back inside, so that he eventually perishes on account of a lack of food to feed on (thoughts to think about or concepts to ruminate upon).

Immediately when a thought presents itself, arrest its further progress by means of asking yourself 'To whom has this thought presented itself?' and then and there return your attention to being aware of the one who is having the thought (that is, to pure-subjective-consciousness sustained effortlessly and volitionlessly). This is how *vichara abhyasa* should be deployed. (Smiling) Is it clear now?

Q: Yes. But without thinking thoughts is it possible to run the household or attend to office duties? Our day-to-day activities require usage of the mind.
B: Do not speak from theoretical presumption. Try it and see. Do you know what your observation will be? In the absence of thought, work is found to go on even more efficaciously and efficiently than before.

Q: They say a Guru is needed to Realise the Self. There is no Order of monks in this ashram. Where shall I go?
B: Where is the need to go anywhere? BE as you ARE.

Q: Without Guru's Grace there cannot be success on the quest.
B: True. But such Grace is automatically granted to him – and him alone – who sincerely goes on with his *abhyasa*. There is no need to separately look out for a Guru. Go on practising and the Guru will come to you. His form and shape would depend upon your mental predilections and predispositions. He may or may not be in the human form. It is unnecessary to worry over not being able to find a Guru. You go on with your practice – steadfastly and incessantly. See if the Guru comes in search of you or not one day.

Q: Does the world exist or not?
B: What is your experience concerning the matter?

Q: I see a world around me. But what is the truth? I heard that Bhagavan has said, ***'The world and mind arise and set together as one.'*** *But what about the minds of other people? Is it a question of my own mind only? This world is home to countless people. What about these others?*
B: When you are dreaming, are you the only person in the dream?

Q: No. But if the world is a dream, why the same dream every day? Each night upon going to sleep, we dream a different dream. Here the world is the same day after day. What is the explanation?
B: '*Swapna* is short', '*Jagrat* is long': these are arbitrary mental conceptualisations or modifications. In other words, merely mental notions. So far as the Absolute is concerned, they have no meaning. Have you pondered over the question of what the measuring scale is that you are using to judge the quantum of time which has passed?

What is time? These are all mental ideas: nothing more. The mind creates something it recognises as being time; the same mind which created time measures what it calls time. The same is true for concepts involving space also. Space and time are myths.

Q: Some practise vichara *for a short while and succeed in Realising. Others try for decades; their efforts are rewarded only with failure. What is the explanation?*

B: What matters is extent of intensity of introversion of mind. There must be desperation to Realise the Self. The thirst to discover Reality, the yearning, the longing must burn brightly in the mind, burn with enough force to reduce the mind into ashes. Half-baked and half-hearted efforts are not going to get you anywhere.

Once you know that all this is fiction, can you remain content until and unless Reality is gained? The more actually unacceptable the mundane Existence is, as opposed to the mere intellectual understanding or conceptual notion that Existence in the form of the body is undesirable to you, the greater your chances are of Realising the Absolute Existence. Perfection in *vairagyam* [renunciation] automatically brings about *jnana* in its wake.

9th September 1936

Consciousness

Q: After investigating Who am I? I find that blankness prevails. What do I do?

B: Did you exist or not whilst the blankness mentioned by you prevailed? It is only because you existed then that you now are able to recollect having experienced something at that time. Is that correct?

Q: Yes.

B: So, blanknesses come and go, but YOU always ARE. For YOU there is neither coming nor going. YOU ARE now as YOU always WERE and YOU will BE always as YOU ARE now. Is there any change in YOU, who are one and identical with the light of beingness of the Self? No. So, hold on to that YOU and do not be swayed by transitory, fleeting visitors. Phenomena come and go. Do not bother about what has an origin and an end. Hold on to that which is changeless and absolute even in all that is changing and relative. Simply put, remain as That-which-IS and all your problems are over.

Q: It needs effort to remain without thinking.

B: In the beginning, yes. But as you practise more and more you will find the thought-free state to be the natural state and the state in which there are thoughts to be the alien state. Whatever it is that we practise, that becomes the *svabhava* [inherent existence] of the mind. It is we who determine what the mind's *svabhava* should be.

Q: But everything is said to be pre-destined.

B: Free will holds the field in association with individuality and is as real as the ego. Whilst the ego lasts, so does free will.

Q: What is the relationship between body-consciousness and 'I'- consciousness?

B: What IS, is only consciousness. Since consciousness is not different from subjective awareness, it is known as 'I'-consciousness. Consciousness + *upadhis* [limitation] = qualified or conditioned consciousness. For example, consciousness + *dehatma-buddhi* [I-am-the-body] = body-consciousness.

In consciousness alone there is no variation. Changes take place in *upadhis* only. Red-hot iron can be hammered into any shape you want. What changes? Is there any change in the fire that imparts plasticity to the iron? One more example which can be given is that of actors performing on a stage. There is a lantern which illumines the stage for the audience to see; without the light from the lantern no play can be seen at all; light from the lantern shines before the play commences, and continues during and after it. Many plays are performed in succession, but nothing happens to the lantern; it goes on shining light.

Q: What am I? An actor in the play or the lantern?
B: Why ask me? Find out!

Q: How to get rid of attachment toward the body?
B: Reflect on the inevitable fact that it will perish one day. Why at all harbour attachment towards this body which is made of potentially rotting substances? The body is not you. You are That-which-IS.

Q: Then how did I get this body – and why?
B: The insentient body is altogether innocent. He is not the culprit. Does he say, 'Here I am! I am your body; I am you'? Did he even once say so? No. It is we who confound ourselves with the body. We take ourselves to be the body and think we suffer when it feels pain. Pain and pleasure are both imaginary. The body is already a dead body. Can it say, 'I am experiencing pain' or 'I am experiencing pleasure'? The 'I'-sense is not even remotely connected to anything physical. Being of the nature of consciousness, it emanates from the Self only. So, really there is no body but for the mind.

9th September 1936

Renunciation, Vairagya

Q: How does viveka *[discernment] differ from* vairagya *[renunciation]?*
B: Mere intellectual discernment of the real from the unreal is not of any great use. The unreal must be totally shunned. That is to say, the mind must be divested of any inclination to pursue it. One's *vasanas* [tendencies of mind] must be burned to the point of complete annihilation in the fire of *vairagya*; otherwise, rebirth cannot be successfully avoided. *Viveka* may stop with intellectualisation and mental contemplation of the truth. But without *vairagya jnana* cannot be achieved.

Q: Summayirutthal *[naturally being still] or the investigation Who am I? Which is the quickest and most efficacious route leading to Realisation of the Self?*
B: As and when thoughts arise, or whenever you feel, unhurried, ask yourself Who am I? so that you can return to the state of *summayirutthal*; otherwise remain as you are: that is, *summayiru*. *Summayirutthal* is the goal of all our effort to remain without any effort.

When *summayirutthal* has become permanent and natural, the resultant state of mind – in which there is effortlessly maintained, thought-free, and languor-free Subjective Consciousness – matures automatically into *jnana*.

What does it mean to say that one is in the state of *summayirutthal*? When the mind is completely submerged in the Shining of the Heart, one is said to be in the state of *summayirutthal*. When it is no longer possible for the mind to emerge from or leave the Heart, the person is said to have attained Self-Realisation.

When the *jiva's* [individual soul] latent *vishayavasanas* [tendencies after objects] and *poorvasamskaras* [habits] have not yet been totally destroyed, Realisation is not possible. In the case of such *jivas*, when the mind submerges itself in the Shining of the

Heart it is invariably bound to eventually forsake this position; such temporary or reversible submergence is known as *ahamsphoorti* or *vrittijnana* [temporarily merged in the Absolute].

Submergence, never to rise again, is Emancipation or *sahajajnana* [always the same as from the beginning]. *Sahajajnana* cannot exist side-by-side with *vasanas*. The state of *summayirutthal* is granted in both *vrittijnana* and *sahajajnana*. What then is the difference? In both, the mind is sucked in so as to result in total submergence in the Heart, but in *vrittijnana* the mind's distinctive identity is kept unimpaired and not harmed. Whereas in *sahajajnana* the mind is totally ruined and destroyed. For this reason, in the case of one whose *vasanas* still lie dormant in the cover of the Heart, after some time the experience of *vrittijnana* is lost and one's mind starts wandering and meandering again; whereas in the case of one who has altogether relinquished all his *vasanas*, *vrittijnana* goes on to mature into *sahajajnana*.

The investigation Who am I? is a tool with which to retire into the state of *summayirutthal*. To shake off thoughts and keep lethergy away: these are essential if one wants to get rid of the mind. For this purpose, *vichara* is suggested. *Vichara* is a gentle, safe, and effective tool for coaxing the mind back into its nativistic state of *summayirutthal*. *Summayirutthal* is the way to *jnana*. *Vichara* is the way to *summayirutthal*.

Q: What is swapnasakshatkara *[a mystical experience beyond mind]? I heard Bhagavan talking about it last week but could not understand what he was saying.*

B: Some deceive both themselves and others into believing that they are *jnanis*. They falsely imagine themselves to be *jnanis* – so much so that they themselves honestly believe that they are *jnanis*. The actual *jnani* can never say, 'I am a *jnani*.' For what is left in him to make that claim? To believe yourself to be this or that implies the continued Existence of the 'you' in whom that belief is harboured. Those who think arrogantly, 'I am *Brahman*, and therefore am entitled to do precisely as I please,' have already

wandered far, far away from the path of illumination. A mind that has remained cosseted in the darkness of self-conceit for a long time will actively resist attempts to bring it to the path leading to redemption. Have you not heard of the proverb: Somebody who is pretending to be asleep can never be woken up.

Q: Is it wrong to believe that I am the Self?

B: Is it the Self who believes Himself to be the Self? If not, who is the impostor who, not being the Self, falsely pretends to be the Self or imagines himself to be the Self or believes that he is the Self? The Self is the Impersonal Absolute. There is no question of Him believing or disbelieving in anything. So, the Self never does any believing or imagining or asserting. For this reason, that which believes in anything cannot be the Self.

You say that you believe that you are the Self. This proves that the 'you' who is engaged in the act of believing is not the Self. So, who are you who believe yourself falsely to be the Self? *Aham Brahmasmi* [I am Brahman] does not mean that the ego is the Self. It only means that so far as the *jnani* is concerned, the Self is the same as *Parabrahman* [the Supreme Reality]. The *mahavakyas*, 'the great sayings' of the *Upanishads*, can practically hold good only after the ego-self has been fully removed. The meaning of the *mahavakyas* could only ever be 'potential-truth' as far as the *ajnani* is concerned.

***Aham Brahmasmi* means that the true 'I' is *Parabrahman* and nothing but *Parabrahman*. The *mahavakyas* must be understood in the correct spirit. Their intention is not for the ego to claim the stature of *Parabrahman*, but to remind man that there is a Self available for experience beyond the petty ego, and that this is the same as *Parabrahman* or Absolute Reality.**

The ultimate goal of all the *srutis* [sacred books] is to facilitate the aspirant to trace his mind back into its source, the Heart. What is the aim of life? *Mukti* [liberation]. What is *Mukti*? It is to irrevocably merge the mind in the Heart, irretrievably leaving it there to perish once and for all.

Q: I am swayed frequently by the many tempting distractions this world has to offer.
B: The world is nothing but information manufactured – and not sensed or discerned – by one's sensory perceptiveness. Sensory information does not have an external origin. The cosmos is projected by and from your own mind only.

Q: What is Bhagavan's motto that he likes to give to spiritual aspirants?
The Master remained silent, but somebody shouted from the back of the Hall, *"I think it is 'Stop smoking, Keep walking.' Isn't that so, Bhagavan?"*
The Master laughed shortly but did not otherwise respond.

Q: Is that so?
B: Tobacco is an insidious poison. It is better to give it up and make do without it.

Q: What about walking?
B: Yes. Keep walking around this Hill. It brings about all sorts of benefits.

Q: I have enough worldly wealth and have no craving for more. Please tell me whether going around the Hill will bring me peace of mind.
B: Yes.

Q: In caricatures of Lord Shiva, *we see that he has been depicted as being an anthropomorphic person with three eyes, all of which happen to be in the opened position. Does it mean that if man also opens his third eye, he would merge into or become one with, or the same as,* Lord Shiva *Himself?*
B: Yes.

Q: The third eye is the ajna-chakra. *Am I correct in saying so?*
B: The third eye is that source which beams that light which illumines the other two eyes and facilitates them to see. Light from the Heart is caught or reflected by one's *vishayavasanas* [desire after

the sense objects] and *poorvasamskaras* [habits] giving rise to the phenomenon of reflection that is referred to as 'mind'.

The air that flows through a flute is the same, but the instrument produces many mutually distinguishable sounds based on which holes are covered and which left uncovered. Likewise, such phenomenon of reflection as just mentioned is capable of producing multiple personalities depending upon the nature of those impurities that catch the light of *mahat* and so cause reflection.

***Mahat* itself is pure subjective awareness and nothing but that; its source is the Self-resplendent Heart. If one were to suppose that the Self could be compared to the sun, *mahat* might be compared to a ray of light proceeding from there. The third eye is the infinitesimally minuscule point at which the light of *mahat* is caught by the individual's mental traits of personality, leading to emergence of that which is known by us as 'mind'.**

While it is true that this point has no spatial or temporal manifestation on the relativistic plane, it draws attention to itself when the mind is in the state of *Sphurana* [Realisation], and one perceives it then to be on the right-hand side of the chest, two digits to the right of the median. However, all this is true only from one's present vantage point. When mind is dissolved and washed away in the all-consuming fire of *jnana*, the body is also irretrievably lost; then the question of the third eye's location cannot possibly arise.

Q: How to open this third eye?

B: Clearing consciousness of all its contents and making it shine by itself and of itself is identical to opening of one's third eye.

Q: How is that to be done?

B: By eradicating all the mind's *vrittis*. Other *vrittis* are only modifications of the *ahamvritti*. If the *ahamvritti* is killed, our work is finished.

Q: How to kill the ahamvritti*?*
B: By means of it discovering (not intellectually or conceptually, but actually) that itself, the discoverer, has no Existence.

Q: Practically, what am I to do?
B: Investigate Who am I?

Q: What is the way leading to Emancipation?
B: Total, permanent, effortless, and volitionless submergence of mind in the Shining of the Heart.

Q: What is Emancipation?
B: From the present standpoint, one may say that it is deliverance from *samsara*. But the fact is that there is no such thing as bondage or liberation. What is, is and continues always to be. That which is not never could be. The truth was beautifully summarised by *Sri Krishna* when he said "*...nasathovidhyathaebhavo nabhavovidhyathaesataha* [...of the transient there is no endurance, and of the eternal there is no cessation]."

Q: But can it be denied that samsara *or* ajnana *[false apprehension of reality] appears real to those who are experiencing it?*
B: First and foremost, ask yourself who the experiencer is. After finding out the answer to this question, let us raise other questions if need be.

15th September 1936

Only the Self, No God

Q: What is the difference between jivanmukta *[liberated being, released while living] and* videhamukti *[liberation after death]?*

B: There is no difference. They say that the *jivanmukta* attains *videhamukti* when the body dies. But think, can there be anything which he has yet to attain? Such differences are exclusively from the point of view of the onlooker. They do not exist from the *jnani's* point of view. There is no change in the *jnani's* state before or after abandoning the body.

Q: Can presence of body-consciousness not be inferred from the fact that the body is alive? Can we say that one with body-consciousness has attained Emancipation?

B: Who told you that the *jnani* has body-consciousness? When the knot between the sentient and the insentient is sundered, body-consciousness is irrevocably lost.

Q: Can the body be alive without body-consciousness?

B: Why not? The body is only an inert mass of organic chemicals. It has no 'I'-sense about it. Do you think the word 'Life' refers to or suggests one's bodily or biological Existence? 'Life' means 'Consciousness'. Consciousness or one's awareness 'I-AM' is never lost in all the three states.

I am. I always am. Let the derivatory-consciousness assume any form it likes. The parent-consciousness 'I-AM' is always there. It is known as *mahat* in Vedantic language. If that is steadfastly held on to it is discovered that the body is only an appearance in and of the Self. Only then does the idea that it is the body that is responsible for harbouring one's Life fade away and die out completely.

Q: If everything is an illusion, is God at least Real?
B: Are you aware of God in your deep sleep?

Q: No.
B: What is the inevitable inference?

Q: So, God also is just a myth, as is the case with the world – is that right?
B: God is real only if and until mind or ego remains.

Q: What about the Impersonal Absolute, which Bhagavan calls 'the Self'?
B: In his case who do you think is available to raise this or any other question?

Q: What about the not-Self?
B: What is meant by 'not-Self'?

Q: That which is not the Self.
B: Impossible. There cannot be anything apart from the Self.

Q: What about the ego?
B: Whose ego?

Q: So really the ego does not exist at all?
B: No. Mind or ego is fictitious. The moment 'I' tries earnestly to know itself, it finds itself to be the Self. But this cannot happen whilst any *vishayavasana* [tendencies after objects], *poorvasamskarara* [habits], or other *chittavritti* [thoughts that clutter the mind] lie latent in the mind. That is why the practice of *vichara*, which steadily destroys all *chittavrittis* of mind, is advocated. *Vichara* succeeds only if it is deployed continuously and incessantly.

Q: How then is worldly work to be carried on?
B: Both *vichara* and worldly work can be carried on at the same time.

Q: Vichara *aims at a state of mind where there is no movement of thought waves.*
B: Correct.

Q: On the other hand, worldly work requires me to think thoughts.
B: Not correct.

Q: I am an architectural engineer. While drawing up plans, do I think Who am I? or do I think, 'What measure of length shall this facade extend up to?'
B: That is the mistake.

Q: What?
B: You are under the impression that performance of *vichara* merely involves asking yourself Who am I? That is just the first step. As you yourself, *vichara* aims at a state of mind where there is no movement of thought waves. This cannot be brought about just by asking yourself Who am I?

The question Who am I? is only meant to arrest further progress of the thought that you currently happen to be thinking. After the present thought has been curtailed, take the mind back to its source, which is the primordial state of subjective awareness sustained effortlessly and volitionlessly.

When you are in this state, neither the thought Who am I? nor any other thought should disturb you; if it does, ask yourself Who am I? and come back immediately to such state. Who am I? is an axe with which to chop down thoughts as and when they occur, at once. After the current thought has been struck down, the mind must retreat into its natural state. The question itself is only a tool to help you move from the realm of thought to the realm of effortless and volitionless stillness of mind. A still mind is a mind that is exclusively subjectively aware.

When, by means of and as a result of having extensively practised in this manner, you are able to remain effortlessly and volitionlessly still, all the work that it is the body's *prarabdha* [destiny that effects our life] to carry out will go on of its own accord like

clockwork. You will then be surprised at the success and efficiency achieved by you, although you never in fact did anything! So, whilst drawing up plans for constructing buildings, think neither Who am I? nor think any other thought, but keep your mind still. Then the work will go on of its own accord.

Q: Is this natural state of mind mentioned by Bhagavan the same as the Parabrahman *mentioned in the* Upanishads*?*
B: No. He is the Beyond.

Q: How then shall I know Parabrahman*, which is the final goal of human birth according to the* shastras *[sacred scriptures, precepts]?*
B: The natural state of mind to which thought, desire, aspiration, volition or effort are altogether alien, will of its own accord take you there. But you cannot have It overnight. Sustained practice is necessary to uproot all your ancient *vasanas* and other *chittavrittis*.

Q: If mind must be destroyed before there can be possibility of Realisation, the question arises: How did the mind arise, and why?
B: There is already no mind. Searching for the mind, we arrive at the Self. Mind can never be found. How to find something that is not there at all? What never could be, never was. What cannot be is not. What IS, is only that which IS, and That is the Self. Speaking from the point of view of mind, it certainly will not be possible for you to deny the Existence of mind. The only way to genuinely discover the mind's non-Existence is to Realise the Self and vice versa.

Q: Bhagvan's words make a powerful impact on me. But will I remember them?
B: There is no need to force yourself to remember anything. The words of Sages are not meant to be memorised verbatim. You may practise *vichara* when you remember me, but don't try to 'do' anything else with whatever you have listened to here. Let the words sink deep within your mind. When the time comes, they will do their work. Birds drop their seed containing excreta on all sorts of terrain.

In some terrain the sprouting is immediate. In others it takes time because favourable conditions have to arrive before germination can take place. There will come a time when you cannot rest content until you have Realised the Self. The longing to wake up or discover Reality grows slowly in the mind of the novice. In due course of time, it kills all other thoughts and emerges as the one sole thought or concern supremely dominating or exclusively occupying the mind.

That is the stage when the aspirant is ready to plunge the mind in the Heart so that it stands annihilated there once and for all. The thirst for *jnana* must be permitted to wax undisturbed in the mind. It is like the harmful water hyacinth weed irrevocably choking the entire ecological system of a water body to death. The weed drifts in upon the pond as a tiny seed. In due course it multiplies itself rapidly and shuts off access to sunlight to the other living organisms inhabiting the pond. How? It covers the entire surface of the pond. Nothing in the pond can survive.

Likewise, if Guru's Grace is available, the seed of *jnana* planted by the Sage multiplies into the great destroyer [*mahaviksheenaka*] of illusion which chokes the mind to death. How? It covers the entire surface of the mind with the blazing fire of *vairagya*, that is revulsion towards *samsara*.

Q: So, until then I just have to wait?

B: No; go on with your effort in investigating Who am I? But only when the present, mundane bodily Existence has become completely, intolerably unacceptable will the effort bear fruit.

19th September 1936

Vinayakar Chaturthi Celebrations and Mr Knowles

Today *Vinayakar Chaturthi* [Celebrating the birthday of Ganesh] celebrations are observed at the ashram. When I entered in the morning, a small motley crowd consisting of yellow, white, and brown faces was standing near Sri Bhagavan's mother's *Samadhi*. A large clay idol of Vinayakar has been installed near the *Samadhi*.

As I moved closer, I was somewhat astonished to see the Master himself standing in the midst; he did not usually attend the *puja* [worship ritual] performed every day at the spot of the sarcophagus. Not being interested in the ceremonies of ritualistic worship, I tried to move on towards the Hall as usual and scurried forwards; but a hand caught hold of my right arm: it was Sri Bhagavan himself!

I turned and stood facing him speechless; the exhilarating thrill of the divine touch of his sacred flesh can be known only by those who have experienced it for themselves. The Master's flesh was soft and loose – almost unwilling to be stuck to the bone; it was tender and cool to the touch.

"Where are you going? Without you, how can we celebrate *Vinayakar Chaturthi*?" he joked.

The *sarvadhikari*, who was standing nearby, laughed and said: *"Bhagavan refused to allow the* puja *to be started without you having arrived."*

So I was made to stand near the clay idol. Every time the priests finished one line of their incantation I was asked to throw some flowers upon *Vinayakar's* idol. After some time *Naivaedya* [ritual food offering] was offered to *Vinayakar* and *prasadam* [sacred food] distributed.

A widow known as Yechammazl, who is apparently an old devotee of the Master and has been coming to see him every day since the time when Bhagavan used to stay in the Virupaksha cave, has come well before day-break today with a young boy I took to be her grandson, bringing kozhakattais (sweet dumplings) for all to eat. But (incorrectly) assuming her to be of not-Aryan (one belonging to the *Panchamabandham*) race, the priests silently kept her dilapidated tin vessel aside. Her offering was not included in the *Naivaedya.*

When *prasadam* was first given to the Master, he sat like a stone, completely ignoring the priests who were attempting to hand it over to him. Soon the reason was discovered and *Naivaedya* was performed for a second time, now together with the food the lady had brought.

This time the Master accepted and ate what was placed in his hands; the first thing he put into his mouth was a Kozhakattai made by Yechammazl. The old woman's eyes glistened with tears of joy at the sight. Bhagavan smiled kindly at her. Later I heard that the boy with her was not her own grandchild, but an adopted one.

Interestingly, this boy's name is Venkataraman, but everybody calls him Ramana! This boy and I distributed *prasadam* to everyone assembled. Chadwick seems to love Kozhakattais (sweet dumplings) and asked me how they were made; I grinned at him and told him candidly that I had no idea. The young Ramana somehow understood these lines of conversation and made an extremely wise comment: "To eat it is easier than to make it; let us therefore confine ourselves to the former." Everyone laughed.

Mr Knowles was greatly interested in the *ezhaik kolam* patterns [traditional designs drawn on auspicious days and festivals] drawn on the floor for the occasion. Bent over, he was attempting to copy down the designs in his notebook. He received a tap on the shoulder and turned to see the Master standing behind him.

"Not like that..." he said and squatting on the floor by the side of the astounded Mr Knowles, took the pencil and notebook from him. Competently his hand traced the pattern correctly over Mr Knowles incompetent scribbling, and he handed them back saying,

"Like this...now let us see you try the next one."
But Mr Knowles could not get it right. So Bhagavan moved closer to

him, caught hold of his hand, and guided the pencil effortlessly over the notebook. For some time, the blessed contact remained. Then the Maharshi laughed and went away. The crowd dispersed.

But one person was not moving. Mr Knowles had become paralysed with some strange, catatonic ecstasy. He was smiling in peculiar fashion, like an infant; his eyes, and, I am sure, his attention, were not focused on anything. The notebook and pencil lay abandoned on the floor. Every few moments or so, the man twitched with a small spasm evidently motivated by some inner compulsion. Samuel Cohen tried to rouse him, but Chadwick restrained him, convincing him that the experience given by the Master ought to run its course.

Only some hours later did Mr Knowles come into the Hall and prostrate himself before the Master. One might easily deem him a chatty man, but I did not ever observe him taking up this experience afforded him for discussion in the Hall.

22nd September 1936

Illusion and the Body

Q: Bhagavan asserts that 'awareness' is the real nature of 'I'. But what exactly is this awareness? Awareness of what?
B: Do you exist or do you not?

Q: Yes.
B: How do you know?

Q: I don't understand what Bhagavan is trying to tell me.
B: Do you need a mirror to be placed in front of your eyes in

order to enable you to infer that you have eyes? You see, therefore you can tell that you have eyes which are functioning. Likewise, awareness of the world or bodily awareness is not necessary for ascertaining your own Existence.

You know that you exist because of the awareness 'I-AM'. This awareness is nothing but Subjective Consciousness of being. This consciousness is always there whether you are asleep, dreaming or supposedly awake. It is unchanged and unaffected always. Recognise it as your own being.

Man thinks he is made of flesh and blood. But this attitude is a mistake. You are pure consciousness. Whatever is physical comes afterward and its disappearance or destruction cannot affect you, who are non-physical and eternal as the One Self. All phenomena have a beginning and an end. What is born dies and what is created is destroyed. Were you ever born? If you take yourself to be the body, yes. But are you the body?

Q: What is the proof that I am not this body?

B: The fact that the body, which you now erroneously believe to be identical with yourself, is lost in the states of dream and deep sleep is the proof. Yet on waking you find yourself in the same body. This is continuity of memory and nothing more. What proof do you have that you are this physical body made of flesh and bone?

Q: All my memories pertain to this body only. I have no memory of occupying any other body.

B: The experience of occupying a body is only a mental phenomenon, which is super-imposed on top of pure consciousness. Suppose you are riding a bicycle, and seriously thinking about something all along the way. After a time, you find yourself at the intended destination. But you have no recollection or memory of having made the journey because your faculty of concentration was fixed in its entirety upon the problem you were trying to solve inside your head whilst you were busily pedalling all the while. Even with your attention elsewhere, your hands and feet have carried you to

your destination involuntarily.

What does it show? We super-impose the sense of doer-ship upon ourselves; in fact, all activities only take place spontaneously. The body has a pre-destined script of its own that it carries out automatically. If we concentrate on being the Self, our responsibilities in life will be smoothly performed by the body without need for the slightest intervention on our part. You say you remember occupying this body only. Even in dreams we occupy so many bodies. Does that mean we are any of those dream bodies? In our dreams, bodies came and went, but our Self, the dreamer, remained unaffected.

So also, many are the bodies that you have found yourself in over the ages – but none of them is YOU. You are, I repeat, the bodiless Self.

Q: Why did I then come to mistake myself for this body?

B: In dreams you have many strange experiences. It is only after waking up that you ascertain that the experiences in your dreams never actually happened but were all imaginary only. Likewise, here. Our Real Nature is that we are and always were the bodiless, formless and indestructible Self. But we imagine that we are trapped within a body and are making strenuous attempts to become free from the illusion of being tied down to the experience of carrying around a body, while we in fact are all the time free.

This fact will be understood only when we reach that stage. We will be surprised that we were desperately trying to attain something which we have always been and ever are. An illustration will make this clear: A man goes to sleep in this Hall. He dreams he has gone on a world tour, is roaming over hill and dale, forest and country, desert and sea, across various continents and, after many years of weary and strenuous travel, returns to this country, reaches Tiruvannamalai, enters the ashram and walks into the Hall.

Just at that moment he wakes up and finds he has not moved an inch but was sleeping where he lay down. He has not returned to the Hall after great efforts but is and always has been in the Hall.

It is exactly like that. If it is asked why being the formless Self, we imagine we are tied down to a body, I answer, why being in the Hall did you imagine you were on a world adventure, crossing hill and dale, desert and sea? It is all mind or *maya*.

Q: What is meant by maya*? I understand that it is a Sanskrit word which translates into 'illusion'.*

B: When mind pays attention to anything other than itself, we say that it is under the influence of *maya*. When mind pays attention to itself exclusively, it discovers itself to be the Self, and there is then no *maya*. Illusion means that we have mistaken ourselves to be the body or mind or intellect or anything else. That is, we have taken ourselves to be what we are not.

If, on the other hand, we remain as we truly are, we stand liberated from illusion. Freedom from identification is immortality. We imagine or think that we are the perishable body and thus delude ourselves into believing that we are mortal creatures. If this false identification with body and mind drops away, we Realise ourselves to be the immortal Self.

Q: How can I convince myself that I am the Self?

B: There is no need to do so. Give up the thought that you are the not-Self and only the Self is left as the reminder. That will do. That is all there is to be done. The Self does not affirm Itself to be the Self. It merely remains as the Self. No purpose is served by telling yourself, 'I am the Self.' What meaning is there in doing so? Does a man go on repeating, 'I am a man, I am a man...'? If a doubt arises in your mind that you might be a cow or a dog then you might go on assuring yourself that you are indeed a man.

Only in such a case should one be continuously reminding oneself 'I am a man.' But does this ever happen? We know that we are neither cows nor dogs but men and women. Likewise, being always the imperishable Self, we need not dwell on the immortality of the Self. It suffices if we abide as pure consciousness which is not perturbed by thoughts.

Q: If I want to Realise the Self, should I close my eyes to the world?

B: It is enough if the mind be made insensitive to the goings-on of the world. It is like exposing photographic film to light; the more exposed the film becomes, the less apparent is the image formed upon it. If the film is left exposed to bright light for a long time, thereafter no image can be discerned from it.

Likewise here. If the mind continuously and exclusively exists permanently and inseparably in the light of consciousness for a long time, it loses the capacity to register objects or think about the things of the world. Then it remains in its own native state, the state of pure consciousness.

Q: Will a person whose mind is fixed in pure consciousness lose the capacity to function normally in the world? Does he become a mere vegetative form of life, like one who has slipped into the state of comatose?

B: No. The activities destined to be carried on by the body go on of their own accord without any intervention from you.

Q: That means I would no longer have any control over what my body does! Is this not a dangerous situation?

B: Once we have surrendered to the Higher Power, he automatically takes care that only the right thing is done at any given point in time. He knows what to do and when and how. Leave everything entirely to Him. But you should not try and judge him. Even if what he does is not to your liking or preference, do not interfere. If you have surrendered, it means that you must totally accept God's will as being the supreme guiding force of your life, and that the exclusive consideration or priority in your life is to not permit your own ideas for your life to come into conflict with God's.

After perfect self-surrender, only complete acceptance remains. There can be no room for making any complaint about one's perceived defects and deficiencies if surrender to God has been genuinely unconditional or without reserve.

Q: Meaning that we must blindly trust God? But that obviously requires a huge leap of faith!

B: The explanation relating to surrendering to God was given to you since you wanted reassurance that things would go on in a friendly way even after your mind ceased to pay attention to the world. But the fact is, one who is truly desperately interested in Realising the Self will not bother about whether life in the world proceeds positively or not; if it did not, yet he would not bother about the matter. When the mind becomes introverted owing to the investigation Who am I? and remains merged in the Heart, the conditions of outer life automatically continue as destined, owing to the force of *prarabdha*.

Do not worry about how life in the world would come to be affected if you dedicate your mind to the quest; it may even be that there might be no change in the outer life at all. If you calmly focus on remaining as the beingness of the Self, the upheavals and disorder of the outer world will gradually begin to fade out or distance themselves from you and you will rest in the *shanti* [peace] of the Self while the body's activities and your roles as a person will be automatically fulfilled by the Higher Power.

This is a matter for experience, and you will understand only when you sink yourself deeper and deeper into the bliss of the Self, by means of holding the mind steadily in that state where there is alert consciousness of being but neither thoughts nor sleepiness.

Q: If the world disappears, is that not a bad thing? Were we not born into this world in order so that we might live in it and experience it?

B: You are asking this question because you are under the impression that you are the body. Imagining yourself to be the body, you ask me whether you were not born into the world in order so that you might experience the same. Was there ever any birth for you? Know that you, the changeless Self, were never born. What was born was only the body. What do you have to do with the body? You are not the body.

In dreams you take up one body after another but after

waking up do any of them ever remain with you? Likewise here. The body and the world it is experiencing are super-impositions over your nature of pure consciousness. When you Realise your Self, the world disappears as an objective Reality and is seen to be what it really is – merely an appearance in the Self.

According to you, you are a finite subject, made of physical matter, living in and spectating a permanently existing, objectively real world. This attitude must go. You are pure Spirit. Appearance of gross matter is a delusion. There is nothing physical at all. What IS, is only Spirit.

Q: But we are able to touch and feel solid matter.

B: That is the beauty of *maya*. You think you touch and feel solid matter. All sensory perceptions that we feel, including bodily sensations such as hunger, cold, pain, et cetera, together are like a strip of film-reel permitted to run in front of the light from a projector's light bulb. The projector is the Self and the light emitted is pure consciousness. In a cinema show, when the film starts running, pre-recorded images are projected on the screen, but the light that gives life to the pictures remains unchanged.

Likewise, pure consciousness remains unaffected always. In our unwisdom, we identify ourselves with one of the characters seen on the screen and complain that we are mere perishable mortals. You are that unseen force of content-less consciousness that gives life to the body and also to the world that is apparently the body's environment. The body, together with all the rest of this cosmos, is only an appearance in the pure consciousness of the Self.

Q: But how to know this is a direct experience? I am able to understand your words only at the level of the intellect. How shall I have the practical experience that the world is only an appearance in me?

B: Such experience comes naturally to those who have Realised their Self.

Q: So, if I completely cease to regard the world as being real, shall I be able to Realise my true Self?

B: Yes, that is it. The mind can either diversify itself into the cosmos or it can stay fixed or still in the Heart; in the latter case it quickly stands transformed into the Self.

Q: Can you please tell me what exactly is this Self that you are talking about?

B: It is that unlimited expanse of consciousness which has nothing to do with and is in no way capable of being limited by temporal or spatial considerations, which are merely mental constructs or ideas. It is different from your feeling of subjective awareness, which, owing to your perverse imagination 'I am the body', finds itself to be locked into a particular body and therefore is inevitably bound by time and space.

Q: What prevents me, then, from being aware of my true Self?

B: Each and every person in the world styles himself as 'I', taking himself to be the physical body which was born. But nobody investigates into what 'I' means. If the investigation is seriously pursued, no such thing called 'I' is ever found and then only the Self remains.

What prevents Self-awareness? 'I' is the culprit. It is 'I' that is known as *maya* or illusion. 'I', which is nothing but the ego or mind, cannot remain in isolation; it always latches itself onto, or associates itself with, something.

In the *jagrat* state, it takes itself to be the gross body made of flesh and blood, in dreams a dream body, and so on. These adjuncts or unwarranted outgrowths are manufactured by the mind because the mind does not want to sink down into the Self and become one with it. If the mind's tendency to associate itself with objects is killed, the mind stands destroyed. In the state of absence of association with thoughts, objects and mental concepts, the mind's actual nature can be discovered to be pure consciousness in which there is not the slightest ripple of unease.

In order to recover our original nature of freedom from

false limitations, we must search continuously and incessantly for the source of the mind. Then the mind subsides, and we remain as our true Self. Continuous search for the mind or what the mind is results in its disappearance.

Q: I am frightened to imagine a state without mind.
B: How are you in the state of deep dreamless sleep?

Q: In deep sleep there was no awareness of anything.
B: You say so now, but did you say this or anything else in the state of sleep itself?

Q: No.
B: The state of sleep is considered to be emptiness or blankness from the perspective of the *jagrat* state. The mind cannot remember what it was to be like without mind. How can something recollect its own absence? In sleep there was no mind. Therefore, anything the mind says about sleep is necessarily false. Taking the mind's testimony in relation to the state of sleep is meaningless, because the mind was not there then to witness anything.

Mind cannot know no-mind, because no-mind implies total absence of mind. The fact is that sleep is a state of Unity. We are quite happy in sleep because we are entirely free from thought or imagination. We say we have woken up when 'I' comes into play again. But what is the fact? Are you awake now? No. You are fast asleep – to your true Self.

The same Unity that existed in the state of deep sleep exists now also; there can be no break in it. The present diversity perceived in the cosmos is the handiwork of the mind. If mind is transcended, only unqualified Bliss, which is your true nature, remains.

Q: But how to do this?
B: No special efforts are needed to realise the Self. Only remain or BE as you ARE.

Q: I don't understand what you are trying to say.
B: Awareness of the Self need not be cultivated, because it is always existing. The only thing, which needs to be done is to give up awareness of the not-Self. Then only the Self is left as the eternal residue. Man's mind is crowded with attachments, desires and thoughts of all sorts; if all these are discarded, only the mind's essence, which is pure consciousness, is left as the underlying, undying substratum.

Suppose you want to make space inside a room filled with useless junk. Do you bring or import additional space from outside? No. You simply throw out everything that is in the room and the room is found to have become perfectly spacious. Likewise, relinquish or abandon all of the mind's contents. Thereafter we need not do anything further – the Self, stands automatically Realised. Realisation of the Self, only means and is only possible through abandonment of the not-Self.

Q: But if I am really the formless Self, why do I have this body?
B: It was explained to you that the body is nothing more than a mental phenomenon. Owing to the fact that you pay attention to it and mistake it to be yourself, the body appears real. The world, not excluding the body, is nothing more than the impression in your mind that something called 'world' exists.

What people call 'world' is only a mere concept in their minds. So, if you pay attention to your Self exclusively, you will soon discover that you never did have anybody at all, and that you always have been the bodiless and formless Self, the one perfect Reality underlying the myriad variety of names and forms you see around you.

Q: So, I am only imagining that I have a body, whereas in fact I already have no body?
B: That is so.

Q: But the bodily sensations such as pain seem very real to me. I am unable to dismiss them or explain them away as being mere mental creations or imagination.
B: It was explained to you that all sensory perceptions and impressions – including those related to bodily awareness – are super-impositions of ideas on top of pure consciousness. You mentally identify yourself with bodily sensations instead of remaining as pure consciousness; therein lies the mischief.

Q: But when we feel pain, cold, etc. in our body, these sensations are not the result of our thoughts; they have a physical reality quite apart from our mind or its thoughts.
B: The pain does not occur to you as the body; the pain occurs in you as the Self. When there is pain, you become miserable because, thinking that you are the body, you imagine that pain is being inflicted upon you. But is there anything apart from you, from yourself? The pain is you, the body is you, everything is truly yourself and there is nothing apart from YOU.

You are not the body or mind you imagine yourself to be. You are that complete, unbridled expanse of pure consciousness that knows no limitation whatsoever. But to remain as pure consciousness, without spilling over into the entanglement-like realm of thought, requires continuous, sustained practice.

Arunachala Mountain in Tiruvannamalai. On the left Arunachalesvara Temple

Bhagavan walking towards Ramana Ashram

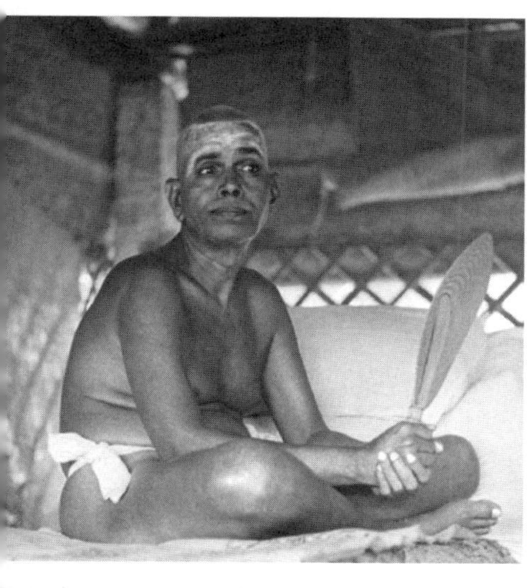

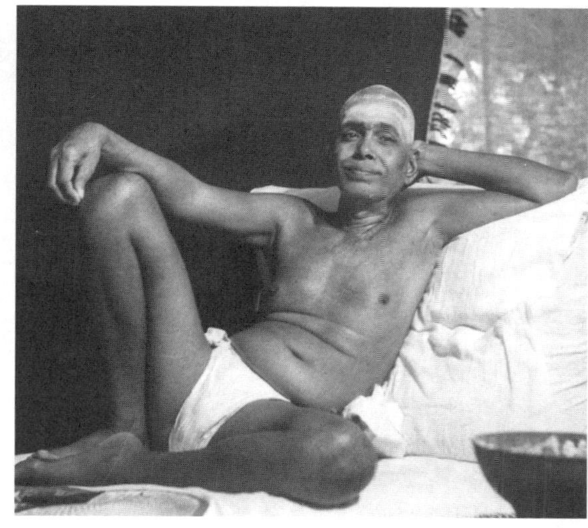

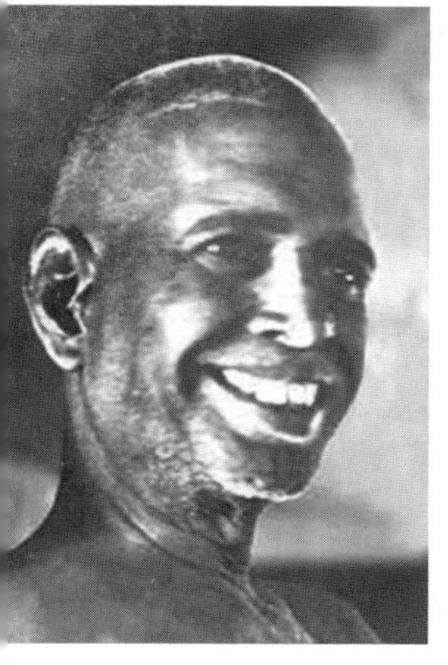

Bhagavan with Muruganar (on the right)

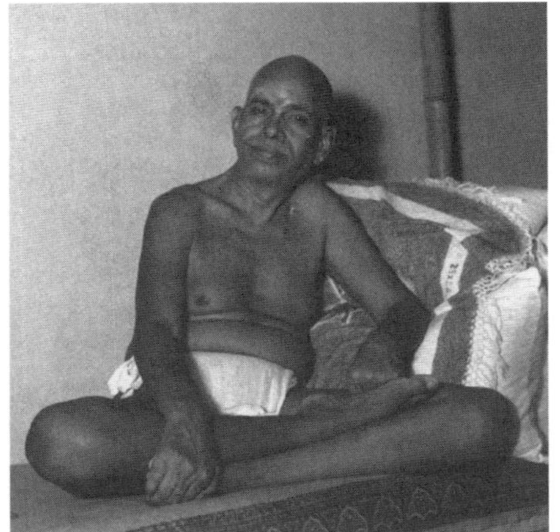

Major Chadwick with Bhagav

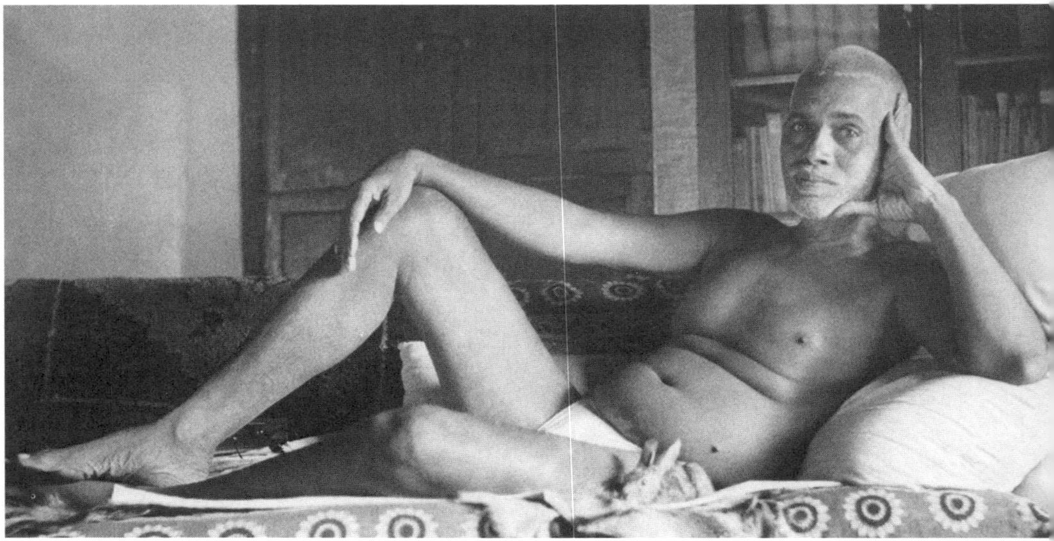

23rd September 1936

A Small Wise Boy

A small Iyyengar boy, whose family has come to visit Sri Bhagavan from the neighbouring village of Nedungunam, and who has accompanied his parents and relatives to the ashram, had brought along a *pambaram* [spinning top] and was playing with it in the Hall. The attendant felt that it would be a disturbance to those who were meditating in the Hall and tried to seize away the boy's toy. The boy understood why the attendant was moving towards him and cried out, "I shall not play with it afterwards, but please let it finish spinning of its own accord; pray do not stop it!"

His childish voice rang out with these words in so shrilly earnest a fashion that everybody smiled, including Sri Bhagavan. The boy's father apologised to the Hall, came forward and grabbed the *pambaram* off the floor, and thrust it into a pocket of his khadarjibba (cotton shirt).

Then he roughly lifted his son off the floor by the arm and deposited him in his mother's lap. The boy started whimpering, but was swiftly lulled into sleep by his mother, who rocked him up and down and uttered soothing words in his ear.

The Master cheerfully remarked to the boy's father, **"See, your son has answered your query."**

Q: I don't understand what Bhagavan is trying to tell me; it is hoped fervently by me that he will kindly pardon my ignorant son for having made a disturbance.

B: Yesterday you asked a question about the *jnani's prarabdha*. Do you remember?

Q: Yes; if the jnani *has transcended all* prarabdha, *how come there yet remains a body for him, is my doubt; but Sri Bhagavan silenced me by saying, "Why bother about* jnanis? *Attend to yourself first and foremost. If the truth about one's Self is discovered, all doubts stand resolved."*

B: Did you notice what your son said? What was his request? He would stop playing with his *pambaram*, but the present session of rotation must come to a close naturally. You, of course, paid no attention to his imploration, but stopped the *pambaram* then and there.

However, *Ishwara* is not like this. The *prarabdha* which is attached to the *jnani's* body will have to exhaust itself inevitably. It has to be remembered that this explanation does not hold good as far as the *jnani* is concerned; from his point of view he already has no body at all. It is only the onlooker who thinks that the *jnani* is the body; the *jnani* Himself does not make that mistake. The body, being insentient, is not capable of saying, 'Look here, I am you; you must take good care of me, who am yourself.' It is you who imagine, 'I am the body.' Put an end to such imaginary identification and all will be well.

23rd September

Absolute Surrender

Q: I have heard that Bhagavan once spoke highly of Schopenhauer.

B: He has discovered that the world is an inherently and helplessly unhappy place; he has also discovered that man's true purpose is happiness; furthermore, he states correctly that eradication of one's personal will leads to Emancipation. However, what seems to be missing is practical technique. How shall the ego, which is the cause for all suffering, be defeated and annihilated? Will cannot be conquered by will. Mind cannot kill mind. Only absolute surrender can result in ruination of the ego.

EZ: Schopenhauer is said to have been extremely impressed by the Upanishads.

Q: Schopenhauer is also said to have been a follower of the Buddha's teachings; he likewise contended that desire alone is the cause for all sorrow in life. This is evident from his writings.
A long text in German was read out ending: '...thus almost all old faces wear the expression, which in English is called, disappointment.'

B: Yes – and by that time it is usually too late to do anything. If one's *vasanas* [tendencies of the mind] are to be destroyed and Realisation achieved, perfect *vairagya* [detachment] is necessary. *Vairagya* is not the petty frustration that develops toward the world when one has failed in all of one's pursuits and is left with no successful standing to speak of in the world; *vairagya* is the matured conviction that *samsara* is futile, pointless, and inherently devoid of meaning or purpose; it is the former that Herr Schopenhauer is referring to when he mentions that some elderly people seem to have expressions on their faces that could indicate presence of disappointment within the mind.

This mood of despondence, disappointment, or frustration is not *vairagya* and it is certainly not enough to check one's *vasanas*; it is merely a transitory inclination of mind that soon passes off without having left behind any noteworthy consequence; *vairagya* is not like this. *Vairagya* scorches the mind. Repeated failures and frustrations in life might lead to mental bitterness, which does harm but not good; but if such adverse experiences in life must result in or blossom into *vairagya*, which does good but not harm, Guru's Grace is absolutely necessary.

Q: How to get Guru's Grace?
B: By surrendering yourself unconditionally.

Q: Whom shall I surrender to?
B: Absolute surrender cannot involve surrendering 'to' anything.

Surrendering to God can at best be called partial surrender. To totally surrender is simply to LET GO altogether. If everything is given up including, the renouncer or relinquisher, only Reality remains, and that alone is the true Self. Asking "Whom shall I surrender to?" is the same as asking "If I am to let go, who will catch me as I fall?" You want to be 'caught' again; that is why this question arises. Mature souls want to fall; they do not want to be caught at all. What is the point of letting go if you would only be caught again? So, the *paripakvi* [fully ripe person] does not surrender 'to'; he simply surrenders.

Q: And thereafter?
B: There is no thereafter.

Q: I meant, what is the state after surrendering perfectly?
B: Is the one that surrendered perfectly asking this question? Can he?

Q: No, but I am asking.
B: The only way to truly know is to yourself do it and see. There cannot be anything to witness the Self.

23rd September 1936

A Dialogue with a Mature Visitor

Monsieur Greenleaves (GL) introduced himself to the Master, and Bhagavan smiled kindly at him. He handed over a note to the interpreter. As was sometimes done, especially in cases of practice-related doubt raised by Caucasians through a notepaper scribble, for the benefit of all attendees the contents were read out to the Hall, so that the Master's (presently anticipated) reply (to the extent any came) could be comprehended in the light of enhanced contextual clarity by all present.

GL: *One experiences sometimes a flash of cosmic consciousness whose locus seems to be without the normal self. Given that the seeker is not interested in burdening himself with philosophical concepts, and so seeks an explanation that would be pragmatically useful, how would Bhagavan advise him to work towards (a) obtaining, (b) retaining, and (c) extending such flashes? In order as to be eligible to invoke such flashes at will, should one retire from worldly life?*

B: You say that what you experienced was felt to be outside you. But think – can there be any experience in the absence of the experiencer? All his experiences are vested in the experiencer only. So, there cannot be anything which, being outside you, is yet within the horizon of your perceptivity or experience.

Outside or inside whom? Whose, outside and whose inside? The one who forms the subject matter of the split 'inside' and 'outside' – who is he? Investigate. You will find that the ideas of inside and outside are relevant only if and exclusively insofar as there is a subject and object. Since the perceiver of objects and experiencer of experiences is vested only in the subject, upon introspection it is discovered that all objects and experiences resolve themselves into the subject only.

But who is this subject? Investigate Who am I? or tracing the *ahamvritti* [pure 'I am'-feeling] to its source is the practice. Investigating yourself, the subject, you are drawn into the realm of

pure Subjective Consciousness, which is beyond the subject. You talk of a normal self. What, according to you, is this normal self?

GL: The mind.
B: Yes. Mind is only a notion. Have you ever investigated into what it actually is?

GL: No. I seem to have taken its Existence for granted so long.
B: That is the mistake. The mind is accepted as being the Self. The Self is always – whereas the mind appears and disappears. Is there any mind in deep slumber? But your Self is always there. The mind, which has deluded itself into imagining that it is a mortal with a physical form living in an objectively real world as its perceiver, is beset with limitations. On the other hand, pure Subjective Consciousness knows no limitation.

GL: How do I reach this pure Subjective Consciousness?
B: By the investigation Who am I?

(a) You talk of obtaining consciousness. Consciousness is always there. Only we attend to other things: then we allow ourselves to be tormented by the pointless question of how consciousness may be reached. Consciousness is self-evident; it seems hidden only because our attention happens to be extroverted. Remove the veil of thought concealing Revelation of consciousness and consciousness is Revealed.

(b) You talk of retaining consciousness. If and when consciousness is realised as being the changeless substratum underlying the egotistical notion of 'I', it forms the subject matter of your direct and immediate experience, and can never be lost.

(c) There can be no question of extending consciousness because it is an *akhandakaravritti* [unbroken experience] it always remains as it ever IS, without contraction or expansion.

(d) You talk of retiring from worldly life. Retiring from the world of thought – that is, abidance in the Beingness of the Self is the only genuine solitude. Can there be anything alien to the Self? Retirement can only be from one place or state to another. There is neither the one nor the other apart from the Self. All being the Self, retirement is impossible and inconceivable.

GL: If the Self always stands Revealed of Its own accord, where is the need for practice?
B: *Abhyasa* [consistent practice] only means prevention of disturbance to one's inherent nature of undying Peace. As the substratum underlying the mind, you always remain in the natural state whether you do *abhyasa* or not...to remain as you ARE, without question or doubt, is your natural state.

GL: In that case we may say that everybody is Self-realised!
B: The natural state remains unimpeded and unchanged whether you abide in it or not. Even in thinking, you are functioning only within a modification of the natural state. The natural state is simple beingness; when thoughts appear in it, you become the mind. People are merely pretending that they are not Realised.

Everybody says 'I'. How then can he be ignorant of the Self? Only, he is confounding the not-Self – such as body and mind – with the Self. If this evil habit is put an end to, simple beingness alone prevails. From our present standpoint we call the state of effortless-and-volitionless thoughtlessness as Realisation; but in fact, the thought-free state is the natural state and everything else – collectively known as 'mind' – is needless accumulation.

If these unwanted accumulations are eliminated what remains is the Beingness of the Self.

GL: How shall I destroy my ignorance of the Self?
B: Ignorance may be understood to mean either unconsciousness of the Self or the evil habit of paying attention to that which is not-Self, which obstructs knowledge of the Self. All our effort is

directed only at destruction of the habit of thinking. Thoughts are remanifestations of latent predispositions remaining in seed form; they give rise to mental diversity, which is the root cause of all trouble.

According to the *Vedanta* system, effort may be divided into *sravana* [the knowledge acquired by study], *manana* [stabilised by reflection], and *nidhidhyasana* [steady contemplation].

In case of the *kritopasaka* [one who has a one-pointed mind], the effect of *sravana* is immediate, and the *sadhaka* [disciple] abides in the Beingness of the Self at once.

On the other hand, the *akritopasaka* [one who has not a one-pointed mind] may feel that he is unable to abide as simple beingness, even after repeatedly hearing the truth that the mind's tendency to move away from its source must be wiped out if the natural state of bliss is to be regained. Why? It is on account of the three-fold impurity: ignorance (imagining the world to be objectively real and one self to be contained within it, whereas the fact is that the world is not different from the mind that perceives it), doubt (wondering whether the teachings articulated by *Vedanta* might be wrong) and wrong identity (imagining the not-Self to be the Self).

GL: How shall I uproot these impurities?

B: (a) To remove ignorance at the level of the intellect, the *sadhaka* has to hear the truth repeatedly, until theoretically his knowledge of the subject of *ajata Advaita* [unborn, non-duality] becomes perfect.

(b) To remove doubts, he must go on reflecting upon the truth of *ajata Advaita* until his confidence in the truth of the doctrine is free from misgivings of any sort.

(c) To remove the wrong identity of the Self with the not-Self (such as the body, its sensory perceptivities, the mind, the intellect, and so on and so forth), his mind must become one-pointed. *Chittaikagratha* [one-pointedness] of mind is the preliminary practical or applied dimension involved in our effort to reach the state of *ajata Advaita*.

These criteria accomplished, obstacles are at an end and permanent peace reigns. There is no need to aspire for any new state. Give up your existing thoughts, and that will do. Without perfect introversion of mind, where the mind is reduced to a single infinitesimally miniscule point, can we achieve Realisation.

GL: In my day-to-day experience, I find my mind crowded with thought even when I am making no conscious effort to think or be without thought.
B: It means that extroversion has become the natural state. Practice is necessary before perfect stillness can be attained. What is the practice? It is *sravana* [knowledge from the teacher], *manana* [stabilised by reflection], and *nidhidhyasana* [living the truth], as explained to you just now.

These steps are not executed by means of reading books or engaging in discussions on philosophy. Incessant practice to keep the mind withdrawn from the tendencies for sensory perceptivities is necessary.

Introversion or stillness of mind is not to be achieved in a day. Keep on practising until the practice becomes as natural and easy as breathing. The practice of withdrawal or introversion of mind should be kept up until extroversion is possible no more.

GL: Some seem to Realise the Self with no effort at all. Others make efforts but do not succeed. Why?
B: The *sadhaka* may be *kritopasaka* or *akritopasaka*. The former is fit to Realise the Self, even with the slightest stimulus: a few slender doubts may stand in his way, but they are easily removed if he hears the truth but once from the Guru: immediately he reaches the *sashwatamanonivritti* [mind always turned inwards] state.

In case of *akritopasakas* all manners of aid are necessary; for him doubts cause disturbance even after repeatedly hearing the truth from the Guru; therefore, he must not give up contemplation on the words of the Guru until he gains the gains the *sashwatamanonivritti* state.

In *sravana*, *manana*, and *nidhidhyasana*, the first two

are intellectual activities, whilst the last one involves a practice – the practice is introversion of mind: it is carried out by means of *vichara*.

GL: Does Bhagavan support the theory of rebirth or reincarnation?
B: Birth and death are spurious mental experiences, not fact. On the other hand, one's subjective Existence is an incontrovertible fact. Concern yourself with fact, not fiction. If you are born now, you may always be born later also. But consider – are you born now?

GL: Meaning that the actual Self has neither birth nor death?
B: Yes. Do not disturb yourself over needless questions. What is born will take care of itself and finally fade away as it came. What IS remains always. There is no end to the diversity or variety of mental phenomena. Ignore the contents of the mind and sink yourself into the Heart: this is the way to Peace from which no return is possible.

GL: Will Bhagavan kindly tell me how the mind arose – how did the mind part or get separated from the Self?
B: Any answer you receive to this question can only be at the level of the intellect or mind itself. Can such an answer be a genuine answer? The only true answer to this question is to yourself Realise the Self.

Realise the Self and see for yourself whether there ever could be anything called mind: then you will see that mind never arose. Theoretical explanations cannot convey the truth.

GL: If everything is predestined, is my Realisation – my discovery of my true, eternal nature – also predestined? What if I am destined to not Realise the Self?
B: Don't bother about the question but go on with your effort. Before settling down to eat dinner, do you ask yourself, "Anyway, one day I am going to die; that being the case what is the use in feeding this body, which is doomed to inevitably perish one day?" Or do you sit down to eat with relish after an exhausting day at work?

GL: The latter – especially if the food is good!
B: (laughing) Likewise, go on with the investigation Who am I? Incessant, earnest, persistent, determined effort cannot fail. Success is bound to result!

24th September 1936

A Former Classmate Visits Bhagavan

Mr Abdul Wahab, a former classmate of Sri Bhagavan's at the American Mission High School, Madurai, has paid a visit to the ashram. The Master is beaming with delight to see him. Then both the Master and his former classmate shared with the Hall their reminiscences about each other.

B: In those days I would be exceedingly fond of playing football. Sahib (for that was how Sri Bhagavan addressed the Moslem gentleman) **would take particular care that he always played on the same side as myself. Once whilst playing I happened to injure my right leg, which then became inflamed and swollen. Sahib took me to a nearby hospital and ensured that some medicine was applied over the affected area. Only after the swelling had subsided somewhat could I return home; otherwise, I would be scolded by my elders, who did not approve in the slightest of me participating in games of any sort.**

AW: I feel disturbed to ponder over the fact that I used to call Bhagavan familiarly by name for so many years, not recognising or realising his greatness. Venkateswaram Aiyyer was the name given to Sri Bhagavan at birth, since the kuladheivam *[family deity] of their family was Thirupathi Venkatachalapathy; however, at the time of enrolling him in school it was, for some reason, changed to Venkataraman.*

Sri Bhagavan used to take me to the Thirupparangundram Murugar Kovil [colourful temple outside Madurai] often on Saturdays; he would insist that together with himself I also should visit the shrines of the various gods and come about in circumambulation around the temple. I would protest saying that I belonged to the Islamic faith, where idol-worship would be considered disobedience and heresy; but he would always overrule my objections, saying that these differences were not inherent in God but had merely been created by man.

Bhagavan would also occasionally take me to Thirucchuzhi; he went there periodically to see his family. Bhagavan's mother was an orthodox Brahmin, *but still she would serve me food whenever she saw me. On occasions when I declined to accompany him, he would meet me the next day and hand over a tiffin-box, saying, "Mother has asked me to give you this food." Such was the kindness of Bhagavan's mother!*

Both the Moslem and Sri Bhagavan had moist eyes at this point, and the Master suddenly looked away from the Hall and at the window, remaining so for some time. At the time of taking leave, the Moslem presented the Master with a small quantity of *Shankha Bhasma* [ayurvedic medicine, a gold-based herbal mixture], saying, *"I have procured it especially for Sri Bhagavan since I know that he is an asthmatic."*

B: This cannot be accepted. There are so many asthmatics around the world. If all of them start clamoring for *Shankha Bhasma*, will the quantity of gold left on the earth suffice? Moreover, why all these fancy things for me? Can I afford such things? I am a *daridranarayanan* [in service to the poor] who must make do with whatever is available. Such exotic items are for those who have a taste for them and are able to afford them. What can I afford? Nothing. Even the *koupeenam* [loin cloth] I am wearing is given by somebody else, and not earned by me. What right have I got to partake of these fanciful indulgences? Some leftovers with a small quantity of buttermilk to go along with it will do for me.

AW: (piteously) Still, for my sake will Bhagavan not change his mind and accept my presentation?
A voice near the Sofa said: "It is given as a token of the gentleman's love and affection for Bhagavan; Bhagavan must kindly accept it for our sake if not for his own." Yet the Master would not be persuaded.

B: Why all these fancy items? You yourself have family members who are suffering from asthma: Is that not so? Is this body more important than or in any way superior to those bodies? How is it that ignoring them you have brought this medicine over to me? If you give this to those who truly need it, they will feel happy. I have no use for such things. I cannot think "Oh! we are taking medicine for our good health," and feel elated.

Smiling, in demure fashion saying, **"I hope you are not angry with me!"** The old school-friends both laughed heartily. Presently the Moslem gentleman prostrated in front of the Master and departed from the Hall.

30th September 1936

Destiny

Q. Is it true that Bhagavan has said that if a man is destined not to Realise the Self, no matter what manner of aid or assistance is offered to him or stands available so as to be plunged into ready deployment by him, he will not Realise the Self. On the other hand, if a man is destined to Realise the Self, no matter what manner of hindrance or obstacle is placed across his path or is forced to be encountered by him, he will Realise the Self?
B: The statement is correct.

Q: Then what is the use of making efforts to Realise the Self?
B: What gives you the luxury of entitling yourself to believe that you will not Realise the Self?

Q: Only the commonplace belief that unlikely things are unlikely to happen.
B: On the other hand, they happen all the time.

Q: If the Atman *[Self] has already decided not to permit me to Realise the Self notwithstanding my best, sincere efforts in that direction, what is the point of me making any efforts at all to Realise the Self?*
B: Did the *Atman* come and tell you that he has made this decision? It is your own ego which dangerously formulates such pointless non-issues and then bombards your mind with them, so that you are distracted and thwarted from making efforts to Realise the Self.

In order so that it may safely retain itself from getting destroyed, the ego might manufacture all sorts of excuses to keep you away from *abhyasa*; do not believe these deceptive ideas fabricated by the ego. Incessantly go on with perseverance and determination in your efforts to Realise and one day the Self shall Reveal Himself.

Never feel discouraged with lack of progress. The Self – although here and now – cannot be Realised overnight. Rome was not built in a day.

Q: I have many problems in my office and home. They will not allow me to focus on the quest to Realise the Self.
B: Perception of the problem is the only problem. Since you go on thinking about the problem, the problem grows bigger and bigger. Eventually it becomes unmanageable and drives you mad. Why? Because you keep paying attention to it, because you go on worrying about it.

Q: Ignoring a problem is no way to solve it.
B: Neither is thinking about it.

Q: What Bhagavan is saying makes no sense to me. If a problem has to be

solved, a solution must be found. Without thinking, without analysing the problem, how can I devise a solution to it?
B: Carefully study the problem, in accompaniment with the associated circumstances. That done, keep the mind quiescent in the Shining of the Heart. The solution springs forth or flashes upon mind in an instant – uninvited, of its own accord.

Q: Is Bhagavan serious?
B: Try it and see. Such a phenomenon cannot be explained or understood using any theoretical parameters – it has to be experienced.

Q: Will this, pardon me, crazy approach to solving problems work for all people and all problems?
B: It works no matter what the problem might happen to be. But it needs a mind which is completely submerged in the Heart and which feels no inclination at all to leave the Heart.

Q: Then it might not work for the ordinary man.
B: All their lives people wander about trying to 'do' something. One who has seen the futility of the 'doing' approach alone recognises the value of the 'non-doing' approach; until then he thinks that 'doing' is virtuous and righteous and 'non-doing' indolent and unnecessary. It would be erroneous to assume that non-doing is the same as devotion to luxury and pleasure.

There is a difference between not doing anything and there not being anybody to do anything. For the Emancipated Soul effort is impossible and so is volition, although you may see his body moving about and doing things.

Q: Is simply remaining idle the solution to the question of Realisation?
B: Remaining idle is not the same as keeping the body idle and permitting thought to run riot. The mind must remain without thinking and without falling asleep, but neither effort nor volition must aid it to remain in such state. This alone is actually remaining idle *[summayitutthal]*.

Q: I cannot even imagine such a state.

B: The state of *summayirutthal* cannot be conceived of, or imagined or visualised by the mind. All that is possible is to BE it. By means of expenditure of effort or pursuit of desire you cannot reach it; rather, total absence of effort and of volition reveals that you were never different from it. All our effort is only to become perfectly effortless.

Q: It is said that unselfish, platonic love for fellow man leads to Emancipation from samsara. *Is this true?*

B: Action performed without harbouring the idea of being the doer of the action helps in effecting purification of mind.

30th September 1936

Good and Evil

Q: Why does God permit evil-minded persons and evil doers to exist in the world? He is omnipotent, is he not? Should he not get rid of such persons by means of a single wave of the hand?

B: Good and evil are relative terms.

Q: I am aware of this familiar argument; it is used by philosophers all the time to answer the question of why God permits evil to live on in the world. But some persons in this world are downright wicked. Will Bhagavan deny the fact?

B: Let God take care of His creation. You bother about yourself first and foremost. Only evil could ever see evil. Are you perfect? That which is Itself perfect sees perfection and perfection alone everywhere. That which sees imperfection sees so exclusively because

it is Itself imperfect.

Swami Vivekananda said, "How can you see evil outside, unless it is within you?" To the *jnani*, the world is overflowing with perfection everywhere; all he can possibly see is perfection only. Therefore, know this, everywhere, in everything, and always: ALL IS WELL.

Q: What is the purpose of life?

B: It is to raise this question to oneself and find out the answer for oneself.

Q: But what is the answer to the question? I acknowledge my inability to understand out the answer for myself by myself. Thus, I am asking for your help.

B: The idea that there is a 'one' who is experiencing what he calls a 'life' is illusory, false, and wrong. Life, which is Absolute Awareness, does not and cannot question the reason for its own Existence. There is nothing apart from Life so that such separate component can raise this question. So, really the question does not arise at all.

What is actually Life does not and cannot have such a thing as purpose or objective; it is effortless and volitionless Bliss. But what you evidently mean by 'life' is your life. You are asking me the reason for your bodily Existence, imagining that the body is yourself.

In effect, thinking that you are identical with the body and thus that you were born, you are asking me why you were born. But is the body 'I'? Does it ask, "Excuse me, kind Sir, could you please tell me why I happen to exist and why I was born?" No. Who raises the question then?

Q: Bhagavan has cleverly transformed my original query into his usual Who am I? question!

B: Any question, if thought about deeply enough, reduces itself into that one single question. You are asking for the purpose of life because you are under the wrong impression that your bodily Existence is real. Your question about life pertains to mundane life

or the bodily Existence because with reference to Absolute Existence the question can never arise: who would be there to ask anything?

So, in asking what the purpose of your life is, you are without doubt asking the reason for your birth. You say to me: "I was born. Tell me why." I say to you: "You were never born. You are the Unborn. Realise It." Only if your birth actually did take place do we have to ask why it took place.

Q: But this body here was born! That is a fact! How can it be denied?!
B: The body and 'I' are not one and the same thing. The body was born and it will perish. 'I' was never born, never changes, and never perishes.

Q: What is the proof that I am not this body? When I am walking under the hot sun, I feel the heat on my skin – not on anybody else's. When I swim in a river, I feel the fluidity and coldness of the water on my skin – not on anybody else's. How then can I say that this body is not me? Does it not sound silly to say such a thing?
B: You may have similar sensations in your dreams also. Does that mean your dreams are real?

Q: Is the world a mere dream, then?
B: Undoubtedly.

Q: But you are here! Are we both dreaming the same dream, then? Is it not too much of a coincidence that so many people in this world should be dreaming up the same world precisely – same sun, same moon, same Tiruvannamalai, same Bhagavan, et cetera, et cetera?
B: Everything, including the other people you mention, is your own mental creation. This is your own dream, through and through.

Q: Bhagavan who happens to be telling me this now?
B: Absolutely.

Q: What proof is available so that I may believe in this explanation?

B: Were you asked to believe in anything? Keep an open mind. Admitting that it is possible for everything to be unreal or a dream is sufficient to eventually make you see Truth. It needs expenditure of mental effort to even see a world. When all possibility for such expenditure has faded away entirely, there will not remain any world (to exist, see, or be seen). That is when the Self is Realised.

30th September 1936

The World is a Dream

Q: Does Bhagavan have the ability to make his body invisible?
B: It is already so.

Q: Nonsense. I see Bhagavan on the Sofa as usual.
B: I was referring to my own point of view.

Q: Do Bhagavan's eyes not see the body sitting on this Sofa here?
B: These eyes cannot see Bhagavan. Bhagavan is the Deep Beyond.

Q: I heard that Siddhapurushas *[Self-realised beings] possess the ability to make their bodies invisible. Why won't Bhagavan admit the fact?*
B: The *jnana siddha* has no body. That is his experience.

Q: But I can see Bhagavan having a body, it is sitting right in front of me, here on this Sofa.
B: That is the onlooker's point of view.

Q: What does Bhagavan's intellect tell him when his eyes see his body?
B: These eyes may be open. They do not see anything.

Q: Is it owing to some defect of vision?
B: No. It is owing to perfection of vision.

Q: How can a man with healthy eyes have them open and yet not see anything?
B: The *jnani* is like a new-born infant. Its eyes are open. Yet it does not see anything. It moves about its hands and legs and smiles, but everything is done unknowingly.

Q: An adult like that would be diagnosed with serious mental retardation.
B: The *jnani* is worse than mentally retarded: He is mentally not present.

Q: But how then is Bhagavan able to have this conversation with me? To formulate intelligible words and speak them requires a mind.
B: Some power seems to animate this body and get done whatever job it is that needs to be done. The *jnani* himself would not know anything about it. Relative knowledge needs a mind; that is, to understand or process relative knowledge, a mind is required.

Q: So, Bhagavan does not know that this conversation is taking place between us?
B: There is no Bhagavan independent of the Self to attend to or know anything.

Q: I do not understand what is said.
B: The world and its goings-on are the Self Itself. Therefore, the question of the Self being aware of them or unaware cannot arise.

Q: But usually Bhagavan says that the world is a dream.
B: From the point of view of the ordinary man, certainly the world is a dream. But from the *jnani's* point of view there can be no such thing as non-Reality. To Him everything is Real: exclusively because he is truly everything.

Q: Despite the presence of the intellectual understanding that the world is a dream, the mind refuses to stop taking interest in it. Why?

In response to this question, Bhagavan asked Mr TKS to read out to the Hall the following passage from a book written by Swami Vivekananda:

> Once upon a time, Indra was, as usual, flying through the sky seated on his heavenly chariot. As he was surveying the earth, he caught sight of a few domesticated pigs wallowing in human excreta; some of them were feeding upon it. Indra was nauseated with revulsion upon having beheld the sight. He asked Narada, who was by his side, why the pigs could not be reformed and taught to behave better.
>
> Narada replied that it was in the determined nature of a pig to behave so. Indra, however, was not convinced. He asked, "Do you mean, then, to say that if I were to take birth as a pig, I would behave like this?" Narada merely smiled and did not say anything. However, not liking the mischievous glint in Narada's eyes when that smile was in attendance upon his lips, Indra said, "Very well. I shall demonstrate to you my greatness. Presently I am going to transform into a pig, and you shall see for yourself how elegantly dignified my behavior shall be..."
>
> Narada tried to dissuade him, but could not succeed in trying to stop him. Indra descended on the earth, and asked Narada to see for himself what was going to happen. Indra was now in the shape of a hefty pig. He went here and there and tried to keep a distance from the other pigs roaming about the region, which were spattered with human ordure whilst remaining engrossed in the act of consuming it with relish. Indra felt the experience of being a pig to be so relaxing that he dismissed the chariot and told Narada he would like to stay in this form for a few more hours. Laughing, since

he guessed what was about to happen, Narada bade Indra farewell and departed to his own realm.

Indra was now captivated by the sight of a female pig, which was covered with excreta all over. He tried to make love to the pig, but she would not consent to be approached, because he looked and smelled different from the other pigs. Indra was wondering what to do. A few hours passed, and he felt hungry and absent-mindedly chewed at something that was lying near his feet; after swallowing it with relish, the thought dimly occurred to him that he had just consumed a particularly foul-smelling turd.

Vaguely he recollected that the act of pigs consuming excreta was something he had once borne an aversion to. Now that he was smeared with excreta, the female pig, finding him an acclimatised sight, was more interested in reciprocating his lustful advances. The pigs made passionate love to each other, and they happily rolled about the slushy ground in the frenzied ecstasy of coital exhilaration, covered all over with the faeces of humans and animals. In the days of frolicsome, aggressive love-making that followed, Indra had completely forgotten who he was. Soon the she-pig was pregnant, and a lot of baby pigs were born; and the couple was very happy.

Then some gods saw his unfortunate situation, and came to him, and told him, "You are the king of the gods, you have all the gods under your command. Why are you here?" But Indra said, "Never mind; I am all right here; I do not care for heaven, while I have this sow and these little pigs." The poor gods were at their wits' end. After a time, they decided to slay all the baby pigs

> one after another. When all were dead, Indra began to weep and mourn.
>
> Then the gods ripped his pig-body open and he came out of it. He began to laugh when he realised what a hideous, nightmarish experience he had had – he, the king of the gods, to have become a pig, and to have deluded himself into believing that that pig-life was the only life; and not only that but also to have wanted the whole universe to come into the pig-life!

What is the moral of the story?
The *Purusha* [pure consciousness], when it identifies itself with *Prakriti* [the material world], forgets that it is pure and infinite. The *Purusha* does not love, It is love itself; it does not exist, It is Existence itself; it does not know, It is knowledge itself. It is a mistake to say the *Atman* [the Self] loves, exists, or knows.

Love, Existence, and Knowledge are not the qualities of the *Purusha*, but its essence. When the *Purusha* associates with *Prakriti*, the resultant ego is characterised by the appearance of having become so degenerate that if you approach it to communicate to it: 'You are not a pig; your true nature is one of Infinite and Eternal Glory,' it begins to aggressively squeal and bite.

B: Mere intellectual understanding of the precepts articulated by the doctrine of *ajata Advaita* is not of any great use. Practise of mental introversion is necessary to scorch the *vasanas* and eventually destroy them altogether. Complete destruction of *vasanas* is the same as Realisation.

30th September 1936

Realise the Self

Q: Is surrender a means to overcome and vanquish the vasanas, *thus resulting in Realisation?*
B: Yes, provided it is unconditional, surrender is a fool proof way to Realise the Self.

Q: What is the guarantee that I shall Realise the Self if I surrender?
B: You are missing the point of surrender.

Q: How so?
B: To surrender is to let go of everything without anticipating or expecting anything in return. Letting go of everything also encompasses abandoning the aspiration to Realise the Self. Suppose you are holding a red-hot iron ball. Your hand is quivering in unbearable pain. Somebody suggests to you that you let go.

If your response is 'What benefit will I obtain if I let go?' will not the other person wonder 'Poor fellow! The pain of holding that dreadful thing in his hand – has it confused his brains?'

That is how it is to me having now listened to your question. *Samsara* is intolerably painful. Why look for reasons to let go of it? If *samsara* still appears as being acceptable to one – no matter however remotely or infinitesimally so – can he Realise the Self? One who does not see *samsara* as actually being the horribly excruciating misery that it indeed really is – will he Realise the Self?

Q: Suppose I surrender yet fail to Realise the Self – what then?
B: Yes, that possibility is always there from the ego's point of view.

Q: But just now you said: "Surrender is a fool proof way to Realise the Self."
B: What did the preceding words say? Surrender works only if it is unconditional. That means your mind must be genuinely reconciled to the possibility that anything can happen or not

happen, including one's failure to Realise the Self.

Q: So, success in Realising the Self is made possible only if I wholeheartedly accept the possibility that I may fail to Realise the Self?
B: Such acceptance must be natural or genuine. For instance, it must not be self-imposed so that realisation to be made possible, the mind ought to stand reconciled to the possibility that anything can happen or not happen, including one's failure to realise the Self.

Q: The idea sounds complicated.
B: On the other hand, it is so utterly simple that trying to communicate it emphatically leads us into a hopeless swamp of complicated-sounding ideas. TOTALLY LET GO and the Self stands Realised: that is all there is to Realisation.

Q: Siddhis *such as making the body invisible, making it levitate high up in the air or fly, making it impervious to fire, and so on, do they come to the* jnani *automatically?*
B: If such be his *prarabdha*, not otherwise.

Q: *Bhagavan is omnipotent. Shall he not use his unlimited powers to help the suffering masses of humanity? Shall he not take up an active role in guiding mankind along the proper path to follow – both spiritually and otherwise?*
B: How do you know that I am not doing it?

Q: But Bhagavan never left Tiruvannamalai since 1896. Other spiritual heavy weights in India such as J. Krishnamurti and Meher Baba travel around the world attempting to enlighten people.

TKS: Those people go around from place to place, but seated at this one corner of the world Bhagavan draws here people from all nooks and crannies of the globe!

The Master smiled but did not say anything.

Mr Snead wanted to know "*How shall I become a disciple of Bhagavan?*"
B: If you continue in my word, then are you my disciple indeed; and you shall know the truth, and the truth shall make you free. Sincerely follow Bhagavan's teachings and you are Bhagavan's devotee.

Q: So, those who diligently follow his teachings are deemed to be counted as being amongst Bhagavan's disciples. May we proclaim to all that Bhagavan has said so?
B: (smiling) Yes.

Q: How to escape from sin that I have already perpetrated, which causes a series of painful rebirths according to Hindu philosophy?
B: 'For the law of the Spirit of life in Christ Jesus hath made me free from the law of sin and death.'

Q: Will faith in Jesus suffice to save me from sin?
B: All that is necessary is to Love him with all your heart. Your Love is its own reward; you need crave none other.

Q: There are times when depression grows over me like an ominous, thick cloud. I feel as though an inky blackness were steadily enveloping me, about to carry me away to my doom. I am so petrified with terror on these occasions that it does not even occur to me to introduce a comforting counter-thought which might have the effect of doing away with the fear.

I have, countless times, reminded myself that on these occasions I ought to try asking myself, "Who becomes aware of this unpleasant sensation?" But it is of no avail – every time this paralysing terror overtakes me, I am unable to think of anything else. Please provide me with a useful technique that I would be able to follow whenever I am besieged with such horrific mental states.
B: When such a thing happens, stop trying to fight with it; instead, observe it with diligent calmness until it has dissipated. The feeling as though one is suffocating arises because one is trying to protect oneself from harm. But so long as there remains a 'you' who desires not to be harmed, that long will it remain possible for

you to become threatened with harm.

Give up the idea that you are precious to yourself; and give up the idea that you ought to stay free from harm. After all, what is it that can be harmed? Only the perishable body and mind, which are doomed to disappear one day. Knowing that there remains a Self – available for Realisation by you that is indestructible and undisturbed – why should you become terrified at the prospect of the body and mind coming under harm? Whatever it is that the environmental or mental circumstances might happen to inflict on you, remain evenly balanced in mind, knowing that it is all transitory and unreal.

Q: How to deny the reality of the world whilst yet remaining in it?
B: As you go on with your *sadhana* to introvert the mind, pure Subjective Consciousness alone captures your attention and information obtained through sensory perceptivities (the world) begins to gradually fade out from your mental view.

Q: In that case, the worldly life can be expected to become impossible.
B: No. If the burden is thrown on the Higher Power, the body's destined actions, as decided by *prarabdha*, are found to go on automatically. It is the experience of the mind, that has unreservedly surrendered itself, that the faculty of intuition has wholly taken charge of the intellect and directs its functioning on a moment-to-moment basis.

Q: Can a cowardly wretch like me ever find the courage to surrender everything and utterly throw myself at the feet of the Almighty without a second thought?
B: The state of absolute surrender, being not different from *jnana*, is impossible for the ordinary man to straightaway resign himself to; that is why *vichara* is suggested as a tool with which to gradually turn the mind inwards.

Q: The objective of vichara *is to destroy the ego. Am I correct?*

B: What does not exist cannot be destroyed. What really exists cannot be destroyed because it is immutable and imperishable. So, where is the question of destroying anything? Experience of mind is a self-contained illusion; all that is necessary in order to dissolve it is that you look properly at it: then you find out that it was never there.

At twilight, a lamp post situated in a corner of the road may trick you into believing that some crook is standing there, waiting to spring upon you and attack. Hurrying to run away from the spot will not help, because at every corner you turn you will meet with the same disturbance. There is only one way to overcome the problem: stand still and face it.

Look at the crook closely. Then you discover that there never was any crook – that all along only an innocent and harmless lamp post had been standing there. Did the crook disappear? No: he never existed. All along he was there only in your imagination. Likewise is it with the ego. It is a non-existent opponent who gives us so much trouble. Look continuously at the mind and it will disappear, never to have existed. Continuous search for the mind results in its disappearance.

30th September 1936

The Heart

Q: Will chanting "A-HAM" mentally lead to Realisation of the Self?

B: Whilst doing it, fix your attention at the source of the *japam* [meditative repetition of a mantra] in you. That is, investigate from where within yourself the *japam* arises and retain your faculty of attention exclusively at such source.

Q: Bhagavan means the right-hand side of the chest. Am I correct?
B: Trace back the feeling of 'I' or the *japam* until it merges back there. Concentrating on that spot in the body may result in freedom from thoughts for the time being. If you are seeking Realisation the mind must be traced back into the Heart. Fixing one's attention or concentration on anything is mental activity. Only subsidence or cessation of mental activity Reveals the Heart.

When you are asked to merge back into the Heart, from where you have come, it does not mean this is to be accomplished by means of 'doing'. To 'do' is to use the mind or permit it to function – that is, to encourage it to drift away from the Heart. Not to 'do' is to not stand in the way of the mind becoming permanently overwhelmed in the Shining of the Heart. You need not try to assist the mind to reach the Heart.

Anything you try to do in facilitating the mind to sink into the Heart will only drive the mind farther away from the Heart. There is only one way to truly reach the Heart, and that is relinquishment of the realm of doing once and for all. Abandon trying to do anything with the mind. Keep the mind perfectly awake and alert but perfectly motionless and still.

Effort made or volition entertained to remain motionless is also movement. If the mind is indefinitely kept up in *jagrat-sushupti* [wakeful sleep]**, it sinks into the Heart automatically and is dissolved there once and for all like a salt doll thrown into the ocean. So, rather than concentrating on the right-hand side of the chest, seek the source of the mind and in consequence practically discover it to be on the right-hand side of the chest.**

People ask what *sadhana* should be done to keep the mind still. What reply is to be given to this query? Stillness is one's natural state. We ruin it by permitting thoughts to arise. Stop thinking and the mind is still. It is as simple as that.

Q: I am trying to stop the flow of thought. I am not meeting with any success.
B: Why? Because you try to counter thought with thought. The thought 'I must not think thoughts' cannot kill thought. Only

stillness can extinguish thought.

Q: How can I cultivate this stillness?
B: By giving up *vrittis* of mind.

Q: How is that to be done?
B: Who am I? is the way.

Q: Is effort a hindrance to Realisation of the Self?
B: Yes.

Q: Then why does Bhagavan exhort us to put in effort to Realise the Self?
B: Effort is necessary until it has become unnecessary.

Q: I don't understand what Bhagavan is telling me.
B: Until the mind has become reduced into the primordial state of pure Subjective Consciousness to which possibility of expenditure of effort and accommodation of volition are altogether alien, effort is necessary to gain such natural state.

Once this state is reached, further effort returns one to the predicament of 'doing'. So, make effort until it has become impossible to make any more effort – that is, until the *sashwatamanonivritti* [mind always turned inwards] state is reached. This will not happen in a day. It needs relentless practice over a prolonged period of time.

Q: *But Bhagavan realised in twenty-seven minutes of practice in Madurai!*
B: Not all are born the same. At the time of birth some people have minds that are more introverted than those of others whose birth has just taken place.

Q: Why this disparity?
B: It is unnecessary and pointless to go into it. Work with what you have.

30th September 1936

The Best Preparation for Vichara is Vichara

Q: How to acquire the siddhi *of at will manifesting objects desired by one? Is there any particular meditation practice which can be followed for it?*
B: There are other places where such things may be learnt.

Q: Where?
B: This does not know anything relevant to such matters.

Q: There are said to be herbs growing on this Hill which can transmute base metals into gold. You have lived for three decades on this Hill. You must know – please tell me where they grow. You are said to be Sarvagnar [one who knows everything]. *Don't say you don't know. I shall be highly disappointed.*
B: This Hill itself is the philosopher's stone which converts the base mind into the Self, which, like gold, cannot be contaminated.

Q: You are an Enlightened Soul. Why not show some siddhis *to entertain the public? What is the point in sitting idly and uselessly like this?*
B: (smiles but does not say anything)

Q: What is the use of jnana*?*
B: What is the use of quinine (malaria medicine)?

Q: It is used to treat those diagnosed with malaria.
B: Likewise, *jnana* is used to treat those afflicted with *samsara*.

Q: Only those affected by disease swallow medicine.
B: Yes. Only those to whom *samsara* has become entirely unacceptable (could ever) take up seriously the quest for *jnana*. There are some who are horrified by the idea of being confined to their bodily Existence. Naturally the vigour with which they pursue the search for their Real Nature will be vastly greater than that possessed by a casual seeker, who is attempting to Realise the

Self merely out of curiosity or inquisitiveness.

Q: So fear of one's own mortality is a good motivator perpetually reminding man of the need to embark on the quest to discover his immortal Self.
B: Exactly.

Q: When he was here, Sri Narasimha Swamigazl seems to have begun to formulate a conversational version of Sri Ramana Gita. *But it appears he abandoned the work halfway through. I was reading the manuscript yesterday and observed that there is a purported conversation in which Sri Bhagavan has been caricatured as saying that certain qualifications are necessary for those intending to successfully pursue* vichara. *Will Bhagavan please explain those qualifications?*
B: It is enough to intuitively recognise that the three states are passing phenomena not having any reality. But again, consequent to steadfast and unintermittent practise of *vichara*, such intuition dawns unbidden. So, there is really no need, prior to commencing practice, to sit down and endlessly reflect whether you are competent enough to pursue the practice so as to result in the outcome of success. If you find that it attracts you, you can certainly go on to practising *vichara*.

Q: Before taking up vichara, *is it necessary to first qualify myself or prepare myself using preliminary practices such as breathing techniques or visualisations of pleasant mental imagery? Or can I plunge into vichara straightaway?*
B: The best preparation for *vichara* is *vichara*. The other practices are for those to whom *vichara* – for some reason – does not appeal favourably.

Q: For the past week, I have been delighting myself in listening to Bhagavan's soothing spiritual discourses in the Hall. I also have been meaning to ask Bhagavan the same doubt for all these days. I am a man who is utterly new to spiritual practice. Should I begin with vichara? *Or should I begin with an easier method, such as watching the breath, for instance, and move on to* vichara *once my mind has acquired sufficient maturity?*

B: No method is by itself easy or difficult. Depending upon one's temperament, what one finds easy the next man finds difficult. The thing to do is to stick to what fascinates you. Never mind which method is best. Which method appeals to you?

Q: When thoughts occur, I should revert my attention back to pure Subjective Consciousness. That is the point of vichara. *Is that right?*
B: What you mention is without doubt *vichara*. But there is more to it [*vichara*].

Q: Please explain.
B: Once the practise of *vichara* has brought about a sufficient degree of ripeness (that is, maturity or steadiness in introversion), the mind is reluctant to think thoughts and is now content to remain merged in the Beingness of the Self.

Even then, however, there is the subtle 'I' who spectates the fact of the mind remaining so merged. Catch hold of him and incessantly investigate him – and when he vanishes, *jnana* alone remains.

Q: Has Bhagavan said that the meditation 'I am Brahman*' is counterproductive?*
B: Yes.

Q: Why so?
B: Rather than meaninglessly attempting to concentrate on the Absolute Self, which is beyond the pale of understanding or perception by mind or through mental faculty, work with what you have. See what the ego is. What is this 'me'? That is the investigation needed. There can be no investigation into the Absolute. Work not with what is unknown but with what you readily have: the ego 'I'.

The 'rabies terror' which apparently is spreading through the town has left its mark upon the ashram also. This afternoon, a puny, pygmy-like resident of the ashram was bodily carried into the Master's presence by three persons; he seemed to be in a semi-conscious state. Allegedly last night a rabid dog had bitten him. Fearing that he may give birth to rabid puppies at any time, the *sarvadhikari* [manager] and other office-bearers had allegedly tied him up by an ankle to a pillar in the dilapidated mandapam opposite the ashram and left him quarantined there with some plantain fruits for company.

When the Master heard about it, he seems to have ordered that the man be brought before him at once. This was done despite protests from several quarters highlighting the dangers involved in permitting such persons to immediately return to civil society. The small man was restored in Bhagavan's presence. At length he stopped moaning and groaning. He looked at Bhagavan and tears began to stream out of his eyes. He gulped down some water offered by the attendant.

A doctor from town has been summoned to the ashram. He is still awaited. The *sarvadhikari* has ordered the attendants to keep a close eye on him and report to him immediately should he start behaving or barking like a dog or foaming at the mouth. Nobody at the ashram has had the courage to dress the man's wounds, lest they fall victim themselves to the dreaded malady. The poor, trembling creature is sitting in a corner of the Hall, and the attendants have their eyes glued on him. The wounded man's only comfort seems to be Bhagavan, who occasionally glances and smiles at him, as though attempting to bolster up his spirits.

Late in the evening today, Mr Knowles tearfully took leave of the Master. Before his departure, he presented to the Master as a gift to the ashram from out of his rucksack the enormous book in six volumes, *An Exposition of the Old and New Testament* by Matthew Henry. He told Bhagavan, *'Since Maharshi quotes often from the Bible whilst explaining his teachings to attendees in the Hall, I thought this might be useful for him.'* The Master accepted the volumes with a smile. Mr Knowles prostrated on the floor, his eyes still moist, gazed once more into the Master's fathomless eyes, and then turned around and exited from the Hall. I never saw him again.

Unpublished Notebook Fragments

Winter 1936

Notebook A – Self-Enquiry

Notebook B – Illusion

Notebook C – Theosophist Visit

Notebook D – Tendencies of the Mind

Summer 1936

Four Original Notebook Pages

Unpublished Notebook Fragments

Winter 1936

The Open Sky Press Team has been sent four unpublished notebooks from Blutkeim, who has published the original unformatted manuscript.
We scanned and transcribed them. They have not been included in the previously published manuscript.

The notebooks are fragments and so the texts also are incomplete. Most likely this material is from winter 1936, most of which seems to be lost. Their content appears similar to most other dialogues in the published manuscript from the summer of 1936.

The four notebook fragments are from October, November and December 1936 and have not yet been published anywhere. These may be all that remain from the so-called 'Manuscript Part Two'. However, for devotees of Bhagavan they are included for the fine quality of the teachings.

Summer 1936

Blutkeim also sent us four pages from the notebooks described as original from summer 1936 (published in the manuscript).

Paper Testing

We have been encouraged to have the paper from the notebooks analysed. The report from CICS, Institute of Conservation Sciences, T. H. Cologne, Germany, says it can be assumed that it originates from the 1930s. There are date entries from 1936. The paper is from after 1929 as at that time the technique of paper production changed.

Four Unpublished Notebook Fragments
Winter 1936

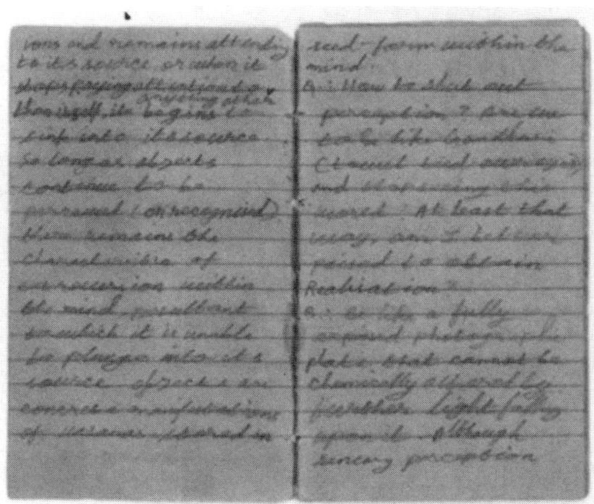

Four Original Published Notebook Pages
Summary 1936

(see Gajapathi taking notebooks to Bhagavan – page 7 – Ed)

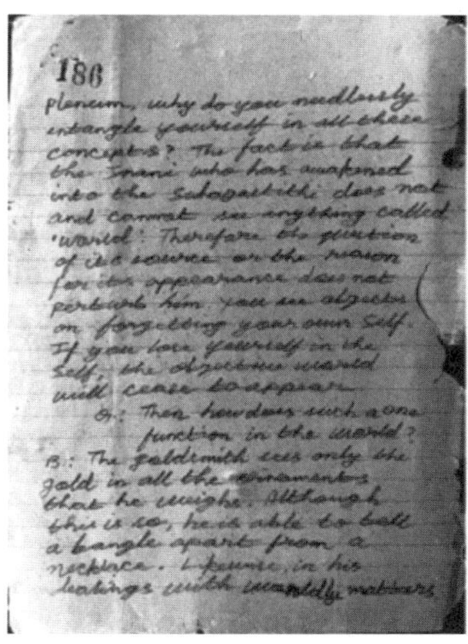

186

plenum, why do you needlessly entangle yourself in all these concepts? The fact is that the Jnani who has awakened into the Sahajasthiti does not and cannot see anything called 'world'. Therefore the question of its source or the reason for its appearance does not perturb him. You see objects on forgetting your own Self. If you lose yourself in the Self, the objective world will cease to appear.

Q.: Then how does such a one function in the world?

B.: The goldsmith sees only the gold in all the ornaments that he weighs. Although this is so, he is able to tell a bangle apart from a necklace. Likewise, in his dealings with worldly matters

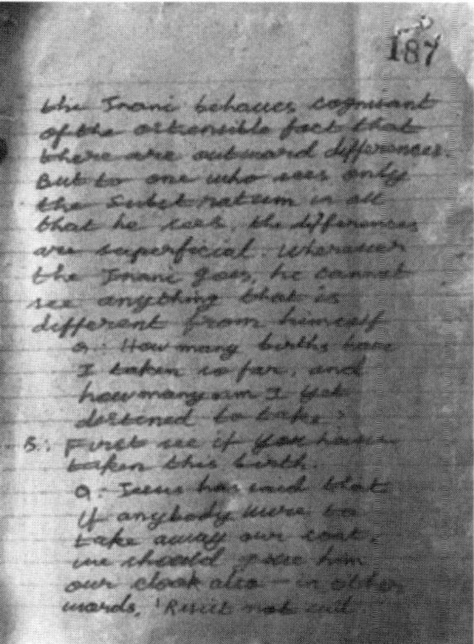

187

the Jnani behaves cognisant of the ostensible fact that there are outward differences. But to one who sees only the Substratum in all that he sees, the differences are superficial. Wherever the Jnani goes, he cannot see anything that is different from himself.

Q.: How many births have I taken so far, and how many am I yet destined to take?

B.: First see if you have taken this birth.

Q.: Jesus has said that if anybody were to take away our coat, we should give him our cloak also – in other words, 'Resist not evil'

Unpublished Notebook A
Self-Enquiry

Q: When thoughts arise, I need to ask myself Who am I? and that is all there is to vichara. *Am I right?*

B: No. That is only the preliminary phase of *vichara*; the actual *vichara* takes place when the mind sinks into the Heart. Remaining permanently submerged in the Heart alone deserves to be called as *vichara*.

Q: So, when I am deflecting or warding away thoughts with the question Who am I? being used as a counter-thought, I cannot meaningfully call it vichara *– is that right?*

B: Yes. The real *vichara* is to keep the mind retained in the Heart.

Q: But the mind does not sink into the Heart when the question Who am I? is raised. I am pursuing Who am I? adamantly, but while I find it a moderately useful mechanism with which to eliminate thoughts, the question does not sink the mind in its source. What is the reason? Where am I going wrong?

B: When thoughts arise, you counter them with the opposing thought Who am I? and the distracting thought retreats. But that is not enough. After the distracting thoughts have vanished, attentively see yourself or see the 'I'. Go on using the entirety of mind to scrutinise the 'I' until 'I' stands transformed into 'I'-'I'. The investigation Who am I? thus encompasses two aspects, which are related: the mechanism of thought-deflection, and also the mechanism through which 'I' incessantly attends to nothing but that very same 'I'. When you stop at the first of these, you are merely skimming the surface of *vichara*, and fail to make full use of the technique.

Q: What is this 'I'- 'I'? How does it differ from 'I'?

B: 'I' is the conceptualising power of the mind that identifies itself

with this or that (I am a doctor; I am the father of these children; et cetera). 'I'-'I' is when the mind abides in its own essence – which is the Beingness of the Self. 'I'-'I' blossoms when 'I' has begun to fade. Inasmuch as the *sadhaka* [disciple] has won the Grace of the Guru, there comes a time when the apparent perfection of the ego gets broken; and the ego feels the futility of its own puny, helpless Existence. This prompts it towards an internal attitude of surrender.

It is then that the dormant power manifests itself. Surrender is not a positive act. Not rising up arrogantly as 'I' in opposition to the actual Self is known as surrender. Surrender does not come easily, merely pursuant to a whim. It requires repeated attempts to cajole the mind to cease to take any interest in things other than itself. There can be no Realisation in the absence of perfect surrender, and for perfect surrender to be achieved, there must be a burning, all-consuming eagerness to discard everything you have cherished for the sake of Truth.

Q: Schopenhauer has observed:

> *Truth is not a whore who throws herself at those who do not desire her. Rather, she is such a brittle beauty that even whoever sacrifices everything to her can still be assured of her favour.*

So, how can we be sure that sacrificing everything for Truth will result in Revelation of Truth? My sacrifice might go in vain if my pre-screened destiny has decided beforehand that Realisation is not for me in this lifetime.

B: (smiling) The desire or ambition to obtain Realisation is also required to be sacrificed. Once that is also done, there can be no worries as to whether one's sacrifice might lead to a positive result or not. Sincerity, and not a calculative mentality, is required for Realisation. This is not a swap transaction, where you go to a shop, hand over a few annas (coins), and buy all the salt, tamarind, and asafoetida (spice) you need.

If you still want something in return for surrendering, then

you never surrendered. The doorway leading into Realisation is indeed open to all, but the lintel is fixed very low. If you want to get inside, you have to crawl. That is the Almighty's design. If you want him, you have to give up yourself.

Q: What is the basis for saying that there is something called the Impersonal Absolute, out of which all of manifestation is said to arise?
B: It is not necessary for you to believe in any such thing. After having been told that investigating the 'I' is the one direct method to awaken into your identity with the Formless and Limitless Space, why do you needlessly entangle yourself in all these concepts?

The fact is that the *jnani* [the Self-realised sage] who has awakened into the *sahajastithi* [natural state] does not and cannot see anything called 'world'. Therefore, the question of its source or the reason for its appearance does not perturb him. You see objects on forgetting your own Self. If you lose yourself in the Self, the objective world will cease to appear.

Q: Then how does such a one function in the world?
B: The goldsmith sees only the gold in all the ornaments that he weighs. Although this is so, he is able to tell a bangle apart from a necklace. Likewise, in his dealings with worldly matters, the *jnani* behaves cognisant of the ostensible fact that there are outward differences.

But to one who sees only the substratum in all that he sees, these differences are superficial. Wherever the *jnani* goes, he cannot see anything that is different from himself.

Q: How many births have I taken so far, and how many am I yet destined to take?
B: First see if you have taken this birth.

Q: Jesus has said that if anybody were to take away our coat, we should give him our cloak also – in other words, 'Resist not evil.' Is this pragmatic advice?
B: For those in whom the doubt is sustained as to its pragmatism, it cannot be pragmatic.

Q: Since the ultimate Truth is supposed to be the same; why should different teachers recommend different paths?
B: The different paths are meant for seekers with varying grades of spiritual maturity.

Q: Why should it be acknowledged that vichara *alone is the efficacious means to bring about Emancipation?*
B: The other methods are done by retaining the subject, and so reinforce the false notion of its Existence. But *vichara* undermines the apparent Existence of the subject. Transcending the 'I' that is doing the *vichara* is the objective of *vichara.*

***Vichara* is not done by retaining the subject as the instrument by which to perform the practice; it is done by the subject questioning, or rather self-examining, the Existence of the subject. Seeing 'I' with the eye of 'I' is *vichara* – and not repeating like a parrot, Who am I? Who am I?**

Q: Is a Guru necessary to guide us along the path?
B: Absolutely.

Q: How can we find him?
B: As you go on introverting the mind, the day will come when you are drawn into his Presence automatically.

Q: How can we ascertain for ourselves whether a particular person is competent to be a Guru?
B: If, when you are in the vicinity, inexplicably your mind stops functioning and you are swept away in a current of ineffable Love, there is no need to look further.

Q: But nowadays many charlatans seem to be posing as Guru to cheat the gullible public and make money. What does Bhagavan think about it?
B: Bhagavan does not think about it.

Q: Sri Bhagavan has told Sri Sivaprakasam Pillai (from Nan Yar*) that if one goes on investigating the nature of the mind, the mind will disappear of its own accord. What is the nature of this investigation? I have been trying to reason what the 'I' is, but there is no indication apparent to me that I am succeeding.*

B: *Vichara* is not intellectual. There are no two minds that one might study the characteristics of the other. What is called mind is only the thought 'I'. Seek this without ceasing and it will vanish.

Your difficulty is that you are so used to objective knowledge that when asked to probe into the mind, you create a conceptual fabrication called 'mind' within your own mind and then study that intellectually. But *vichara* does not involve any conceptual analysis; reject all conceptual knowledge and see what 'I' is. Then the 'I'-'I' shines forth.

Q: I do not understand what I am to do. I beseech you to lead me aright. Your Grace is needed to lead me to God-Realisation.

B: The Grace you seek is already leading you onwards.

Q: But I feel frustrated in my efforts to attain Realisation. Possibly I am too weak to obtain Realisation.

B: This thought of imagining one Self to be this or that is an impediment. Why hold on to it?

Q: Is it good to qualify myself with preliminary practices before I take up vichara*, since there is an opinion among a section of Bhagavan's devotees that it is suitable only for the most advanced amongst aspirants?*

B: Curiosity about the 'I' [*atmajignasa*] will automatically lead you up to *vichara*. It is enough to hold on to the current of introversion incessantly.

Q: What exactly is this curiosity [atmajignasa]*?*

B: The curiosity about one's self that prompts (an aspirant to undertake for himself) *vichara* involves inward-pointedness or introversion of mind. It is not intellectual curiosity. It is exploration

of the apparent self, and it results in the Revelation of the Shining of the Real Self.

Mr Snead interjected at this point in the conversation, remarking: *I have heard that the Hindu scriptures say that this curiosity descends upon all minds that recognise the futility of mundane living and thus seek, or actively crave, to transcend manifestation.*

Q: And what is to be the fate of those who are not blessed with any such curiosity? Until I am visited or seized by such a curiosity, are my efforts at vichara *doomed to meet with failure only?*
B: The intellectual curiosity about 'I', provided it is unintermittent and prolonged, will lead you up to the curiosity that is actually *atmajignasa*.

Q: But please mention a preparatory practice that I can make use of while I am yet unripe for vichara.
B: Hold on to the one thought 'I' to the exclusion of all other thoughts. In time, this will plunge you into *vichara* when the time is ripe.

Q: So, observing the thought 'I' cannot amount to vichara. *Is that right?*
B: Yes. Keeping the mind permanently submerged in the Heart alone deserves to be legitimately known as *vichara*.

Q: What exactly is this submergence of mind in the Heart?
B: It is a state in which the mind is temporarily sunk in the Heart, but wherein, owing to the continued concealing influence of the *vasanas*, its destruction is not yet rendered possible.

Q: What are the steps that I should take to ensure that the mind remains attending to the vichara sadhana *always?*
B: Prevent this thought at this moment!

Q: So, then, repeated and continuous practice is the only way?
B: Yes.

Q: What can be done in the case of those whose minds are particularly prone to giving in to indulging in their perverse fantasies, especially those relating to intimacy and other forms of excess?
B: The remedy for all ills is to turn the mind inwards and plunge it into the Heart.

Q: But the urges are often uncontrollable.
B: Yes, that will happen. As often the mind tries to remain established in its source, something will seemingly stir it up and make it rise again.

Q: The more I try to concentrate my mind on my favourite image of God, namely Sri Krishna *surrounded by the* Gopis, *the more other thoughts rise to tear me away from the object of my concentration. What is the remedy?*
B: Let the distractions come and go, but you hold on to *Sri Krishna* without wavering. If you remember that the distractions are appearing only in *Sri Krishna*, and that you are also only in him, they will not perturb you.

Q: But the mind has to be prevented from wavering!
B: So long as there is imperfection in your surrender there will be wavering. Has he not said, quite unequivocally, "*mam ekam sharanam vraja* [surrender all personal beliefs to me]"? Then why continue to be swayed by the tantrums of the personality?

Q: If I leave everything in his hands, will he guide me towards jnana*?*
B: In *Bhagavad Gita* 10:10, he has said "To those whose minds are always united with Me in loving devotion, I give the divine knowledge by which they can attain Me."

Unpublished Notebook B
Illusion

Q: "…Self will not shine." So, why is it said that in order for Realisation to dawn, it is necessary to lose one's foothold over objective knowledge?

B: Knowledge of objects is the means by which the ego avoids looking at itself. Extroversion and object perception (or object recognition) are all one and the same thing. When the mind ceases to know its own mental creations and remains attending to its source, or when it stops paying attention to anything other than itself, it begins to sink into its source.

So long as objects continue to be perceived (or recognised), there remains the characteristic of extroversion within the mind, resultant to which it is unable to plunge into its source. Objects are concrete manifestations of *vasanas* stored in seed-form within the mind.

Q: How to shut out perception? Are we to be like the blind (towels tied over eyes) and stop seeing this world? At least that way, am I better poised to obtain Realisation?

B: Be like a fully exposed photographic plate that cannot be chemically altered by further light falling upon it. Although sensory perception goes on as usual, the *sadhaka* who has given up his mind is not affected by the information conveyed by the senses. He is like an oil lamp that is placed in an alcove, sheltered from the elements.

Q: If I go on watching the thought 'I', can I call this exercise vichara *[Self-enquiry]?*

B: No. This is a stepping stone to *vichara* itself. *Vichara* does not involve one 'I' looking for another. 'I' seeing itself is *vichara*. When you say that you are watching the thought 'I', what you are really doing is dividing your attention into two. There is the one who imagines that he is looking at something called 'I' and then there is the thing called 'I' which he thinks he is looking at.

This is a subtle mental activity. But *vichara* does not allow mind to conceptualise. *Vichara* makes mind cease its extroversion (or diverts it from its faculty of extroversion) at least for the time being. Seeing 'I' with that very same 'I': this is *vichara* – and not mind paying attention to a mental concept known as 'I'.

Q: In Aksharamanamalai, *Bhagavan says that Arunachala gave him the* upadesham *[teaching, instruction],* 'Thirumbi agandhanai dhinam agakkannkaan *[drawing your mind from external material matters].'*
B: Quite so.

Q: I have resorted to the method of going on watching the 'I'. Will it suffice for Realisation?
B: When mind is ripe enough, the present method will of its own accord metamorphose into *vichara*.

Q: *Unless the false knowledge of snake goes away, true knowledge of rope will not dawn. So also, unless illusory perception of the world goes away, darshan of* Adhishtana Swarupa *[substratum of truth] will not be caused.*

I understand that physical world-perception is not referred to here. But even when the world is physically right in front of me, I am supposed to mentally ignore it – is this not what Bhagavan is trying to say?
B: No effort need be undertaken especially (or particularly) for eliminating world-perception. If you keep on attending to yourself, the day will come when the world has disappeared as an object of perception. When we say that world-knowledge (or world-perception) must cease, we mean that the mind's objectifying tendency must die a definitive death in order to facilitate Realisation to become possible.

Objectification is the same as extroversion. The point is to give up your fascination for anything that is not 'I'. Use the mind to attend to 'I' and don't give scope for any other mental pursuit.

Q: But just now Bhagavan said that vichara *is different from holding on to the thought 'I'.*

B: Yes. When I say that you should attend to 'I', what I mean is that 'I' should gravitate towards itself, and then embrace itself. Now your 'I' is preoccupied with thoughts of things that are not itself.

By the investigation Who am I? 'I' is reduced into its most primordial form, a form where it is not attached to knowledge of objects (or knowledge of name and form). When it is in this form, the mind cannot sustain, and begins to sink into the Heart.

Q: How long does the quietened mind stay put in the Heart?
B: The period extends by practice.

Q: But once made to sink into the Heart, why should the mind re-emerge from there?
B: Because the eradication of *vasanas* is not complete.

Q: I find this line from Bhagavan's essay most interesting. Does it mean that I should keep on hunting for 'I'?
B: It means that every time your attention is captured by anything other than yourself, pull the mind back and fix it again on the search for 'I'. But you should not make the mistake of creating a mental concept called 'I' and looking at it. Seek 'I' without harbouring presumptions as to its Existence or non-Existence.

When asked to seek 'I', it does not mean there is actually such an entity and that your endeavour lies in locating or seizing hold of it. See if there is anything called 'I'. Instead of looking at objects, see yourself – that is, see the subject ('I'-'I'). Mind depends on objects for its survival. In the absence of objects to concern itself with, it remains merely in its essence, which is the Beingness of the Self.

Mind in which there is not the slightest object of contemplation holding the field (for the time being) cannot be called mind; in that state it has already started its descent into the Heart, and can be experienced as 'I'-'I'.

Q: Why does Bhagavan use the word 'idam' *[position] here? The* hridayam *[heart] cannot be localised to any spatial location; how then can contemplating*

along the lines of 'I'-'I' lead to the Heart as a place, rather than as the fruit of Realisation? Is not the Heart the Unmanifest parabrahma*?*
B: Yes. But with reference to your bodily Existence, there is a locus where the ray of Consciousness from the Absolute makes contact with the sum total of *vasanas* that constitute your psyche (or personality). This source can be clearly felt; and this experience is known as *Aham Sphurana* ['I'-pulsation].

Q: Is the difference between jagrat *[state of being awake] and* swapna *[dream] only imaginary?*
B: (smiling) Yes, that is so.

Q: Am I then now dreaming this conversation that I am having with Bhagavan?
B: Yes.

Q: Have I then invented Bhagavan in my dreams, so that he may wake me up from these same dreams?
B: Yes.

Q: It seems too fantastic to believe.
B: What is wrong with the sense of reality you have while dreaming? So long as the dream continues the dream sensations also go on, and their reality is on a par with the reality of the state within the confines of which they occur. These objects you see around you appear solid and permanent because the ego is firmly – and wrongly! – convinced that it is a transient subject living in and witnessing an objectively real world that is believed to exist irrespective of perception.

But can there be anything more permanent than you? The fact is that you remain as you are, while these scenes shift all around you. How can anything that is perceived be real? Perception and imagination are not different.

Q: In a dream there is no logical connectivity between sequential events and circumstances. But in this physical world, we do observe rigid cause-

consequence relationships.

B: These ideas about how the dream and waking worlds ought to be are all merely arbitrary mental conceptualisations. Speaking as you are now from within a dream, in what way is it meaningful for you to discuss what waking ought to be like?

The fact is, the mind, which has so long been feeding on forms generated by virtue of the power of its own delusion, is not easily convinced of the fact that the seen is not apart from the seer. Nevertheless, perception springs only from the perceiver and is therefore indistinguishable from him.

Q: Please tell me how I can overcome the miserable curse of having to be born over and over again. The stain of rebirth must stop. What shall I do for it?

B: Birth and death are for the body. We have taken ourselves to be the body and so made ourselves one with it. In sleep you remain free from the taint of carrying around a body. Now a body has appeared. Be it so: that is the body's *karma*, not yours. You be as you are: pristine and unaffected.

Q: When the body suffers injury, I am the one who is burdened with the pain.

B: No. You are forcing pain upon yourself. It is the wrong identity with the body again. Give it up and be happy.

Q: Maybe my karma *is not allowing it.*

B: The *karma* is his who thinks of it as being his.

Q: I do not know what action I should participate in and what action I should stay away from.

B: There is no need to devote thought to the matter. If you are destined to perform a certain action, you will find yourself forced to engage in it. Likewise, your destiny will not allow you to perform actions which do not form part of your scripted destiny [*prarabdha*].

Q: Is the action mine or is it motivated and caused exclusively by the Higher Power?

B: The actor is concerned about the outcomes of his actions. Irrespective of the condition of the body, the surrendered mind is always actionless.

Q: In what way is vichara *superior to other methods – such as* japa *[meditative repetition of a mantra], for instance?*

B: In the other methods, mind requires to be retained as the instrument through which the *abhyasa* [practice] might be carried out – and thus, the notion of there being something known as mind is reinforced. But *vichara* investigates whether there exists anything known as mind, and in discovering that no such thing could ever possibly exist, shatters the illusion of mind.

This is the only way to put an end to the mind. Otherwise, if mind is taken to exist and one seeks to extinguish it, it would be like chasing one's own shadow with the sun behind one: there would be no end to the quest.

Q: But what is really the answer to the question, Who am I?

B: The disappearance of the questioner is the one and only answer.

Q: Is not the clear perception of Brahman *the outcome of the quest, Who am I?*

B: In *Brahman*, who is there to perceive anything? And, without there being clarity about your own identity, why do you bother about *Brahman*? We do not know anything about *Brahman*. He might be close by or far away. But you are in the immediate proximity of yourself. In you there is operative a sense of 'I' or 'I'-ness.

What is this 'I', and whence does it arise? 'I' is not to be seen in sleep. Immediately on waking, it rushes out and identifies itself with this, that and the other. What then, is this 'I'? This is the quest, and not thinking about merging into *Brahman*. Find the 'I' in 'me' and then there will be time enough to think of *Brahman*.

Q: Is it true that if one were to remain fixed in the beingness of the Self, one's worldly duties would be discharged automatically by the Higher Power?
B: It requires you to remain steadily in the surrendered state. Also, such a one would not concern himself with the outcomes of his actions.

Q: But is it not better to give up action altogether, so that we can be free from the taint of karma*?*
B: Who are we to act or refrain from acting? Is it in our control to determine what the destiny of the body ought to be? The only thing in our power is to abandon the sense of doer ship. That done, everything is left to the mercy of the Higher Power, and you are relieved of your burden.

Q: Then there is no need to take responsibility for the actions committed by the body?
B: Once the personal 'I' has been diminished to the point where it does not appropriate to itself doer ship for the body's actions, this question will not arise.

Q: Bhagavan says, "Swarupa-dhyanatthai vidappidiyai" *[relentlessly meditating on the real form]. But is relentless pursuit of* vichara *compatible with the effort-free surrendered state?*
B: The effort-free surrendered state is the outcome of having practised *vichara* successfully. In Realisation, only perfect surrender remains.

Q: My surrender to the Higher Power is only my mental commitment to be resigned to the Will of the Almighty. How can the same be equated with the exalted state of Atmasakshathkaram *[Self-realisation]?*
B: The commonplace understanding of the term surrender might be the line of thought indicated by you. However, what I mean by surrender is the absence of the 'I'-thought. Complete surrender is another name for *jnana* or Emancipation.

However, until you are able to reduce yourself into the state of unequivocal surrender, you may go on trying to surrender yourself. Surrender appears easy because people think that they can touch the feet of the Guru, loudly proclaim that they have surrendered to him, and thereafter do as they please.

But in genuine surrender there is no scope for 'I' to arise. To surrender without reserve is not easy. As often as the attempt is made, the ego raises its head, and one has to try and suppress it. It is only by the merciful Grace of the *Satguru* [true Master] that complete surrender is granted to him alone who has tirelessly toiled along the path to Freedom.

Q: In Who am I? does 'I' refer to the ego or to the Absolute Self, namely Parabrahman*?*

B: There is no possibility for investigation into the *Atman* [the Self]. Investigation can only be into the *Anatman* [non-Self]. Once the *Anatman* is realised to not exist, Existence of the *Atman* becomes spontaneously evident. The question is not one of Realising the Self, but rather one of unrealising the not-Self. Our effort is not directed at acquisition of knowledge, but at annihilation of illusory ignorance.

Q: How long is effort necessary?

B: Effort is necessary right up to the state of Realisation. All effort has as its *lakshya* [destination] only the state of perfect effortlessness, where the Realisation of the Self is spontaneously self-evident.

Q: Are the various experiences encountered by us in the world merely forms assumed by thoughts?

B: That is so.

Q: It seems too fantastic to believe. Supposing that my hand is cut and bleeding, is this only a mental experience, on par with the thought that my hand might undergo injury?

B: Yes. The physical world that you believe yourself to be living in

is nothing but an outgrowth of the mind. The world and the mind arise and set together as one. It is the mind that illumines the world.

Q: What is the difference between deep sleep and Samadhi *[union with reality]?*
B: When the mind is merged in perfect darkness, the individual is said to be asleep. When mind is merged in perfect illumination, the individual is said to be in *Samadhi*. World perception is possible in neither of these.

World is perceived owing to the mind having become entangled in a combination of light and darkness. World is seen because mind is aware, but trapped in the misery-inducing web of *avidya-maya* [illusion caused by ignorance], which makes one perceive non-existent diversity in That which is perfect unity.

Q: Can the life of action go on when the mind remains plunged in the bliss of Samadhi*?*
B: In *Samadhi* it is not possible to retain any sense of doer ship over the body's actions. The one in *Samadhi* is asleep in the Self: thus, he is awake to the Self and asleep to everything else.

November 1936
Unpublished Notebook C
Theosophist Visit

Q: The Hall that 'I' did not see is clearly perceptible.
B: When objects of the world are clearly perceptible to you, how can your own Self remain obscured from your vision? The Self is That Entity, which is the most intimate, while objects are far away.

Q: But the universal experience seems to be the reverse!
B: Because of *avarana* [covering], it appears as though the Self is hidden behind a curtain of ignorance. However, that curtain of ignorance is not something that is imposed on you from outside. Your own unwillingness to turn your mind towards its source and plunge it into that source, leaving it to remain merged there once and for all, is what your supposed ignorance actually is. You are conscious of your Existence because you are experiencing the Beingness of the Self all the time. On investigating who it is who is experiencing the Beingness of the Self, the intermediary 'I', which is now claiming to be that experiencer, will collapse, exposing the substratum of pure subjective consciousness shining underneath as 'I'-'I'. This truly is *Samadhi*. The 'I'-'I' consciousness is the gateway or doorway into *jnana*.

Q: I question myself Who am I? but thereafter am unable to proceed further. Please guide me and help me Realise jnana.
B: Ask the question once and thereafter keenly focus on the sense of 'I'. It is not necessary that you should go on repeating the question to yourself, like a parrot that has been trained to talk. The point of the question is to siphon away your attention from other matters and fix it on the quest for the source of your beingness. If you go on concentrating on the concept 'I', 'I' will eventually and gradually begin to subside into its source, leaving behind the experience of

being alone in the presence of peace. Who am I? means that 'I' should concentrate on the subject, namely itself. *Vichara* is nothing but the subject's quest for the subject. Do not expect the answer to the quest to come from outside. The disappearance of the questioner is the only answer, because *vichara* does not seek to supply the ego with answers, but rather to undermine its illusory Existence. The point of the process is to make the idea 'I' that is active in you to subside.

Mr TKS was asked by a visitor from Thindukkal why, for the past six months, the ashram was suddenly being flooded with an unusual number of Caucasian visitors. Nowadays, almost twenty Caucasians could be spotted in the Hall every day, and four or five new Caucasian faces were making their appearance every month almost.

Mr TKS said that since April of this year, it had been so. These Caucasians seemed to arrive punctually at 8am every day, and they would generally leave before five in the evening. It was not clear whether they had taken up lodgings in the town, perhaps near the Big Temple.
B: No, no. These are followers of Sri Aurobindo's teachings. They are coming from and returning to Pondy every day. Apparently, they find the idea of staying here unattractive.

Chadwick: How did they manage to hear of Sri Bhagavan's existence?
B: These are mainly Theosophists from America and Europe. They are interested in transcending the physical or body-based Existence, and in awakening into knowledge of *Brahman* [the universal Self]. While staying in Pondy and trying to practise Sri Aurobindo's teachings, they have come across a copy of Mr Brunton's *A Search in Secret India*. First a handful came out of curiosity, and after that they have started coming in large numbers.

But they never consent to stay in Tiruvannamalai overnight, nor do they eat anything at the ashram, preferring to bring something from their lodgings in Pondy for their afternoon snacks and evening meals, every day on their visit. But they have been informed that they ought to bring only vegetarian stuff, and that those bringing meat foods will not be allowed to enter the ashram.

C: These people seem to be interested in talking only about vichara, *and I have observed that they don't participate in other discussions.*
B: Yes, that is the purpose for which they have come. But after listening to my suggestion, they are staying behind for the *Veda Parayana* [*Vedic* chanting in Ramana Ashram].

In the evening, there was a slight drizzle and a soothing atmosphere prevailed in the Hall; the pleasant smell of moist earth permeated into the cosy little space, and, what with the little charcoal fire blazing by his side as usual, Bhagavan resembled *Indra*, Lord of the Heavens, holding court. Just then Mr TKS arrived in the Hall, prostrated in front of Bhagavan as was customary with him, and then handed over a telegram to the Master. One of Bhagavan's relatives on his father's side, living in Erode, had passed away the day prior. With a smile and addressing nobody in particular, Bhagavan said: **'The dead are indeed happy. Only the ones left behind are shaken. Why should we feel disturbed at the prospect of death? Let that which dies mourn over its inevitable death. You are always deathless.'**

After the ashram dinner was over, an educated *Brahmin* youth questioned Bhagavan as to whether the various gods and deities of Hinduism and their respective *lokas* [realms in Hindu cosmology] were real.
B: They are as real as you are in this body.

Q: Does Ishwara *[the Supreme Being] exist? Or is he imaginary?*
B: So long as your ego exists, He is real too. There is no point pondering over the Reality of *Ishwara* when we are yet to discover our own Reality.

Q: Does God have a form? Does he have attributes?
B: If you choose to worship God with form, he is found to be with form. He chooses to wear name and form so that the devotee's mind may find it easier to contemplate him. As for his attributes, they are what you might, through the power of your concentration, imagine them to be.

Q: But what is his actual nature?
B: He is the Self that shines once your ego has been burnt up in the fire of self-investigation.

Q: How can I get rid of maya *[illusion]?*
B: What is *maya*?

Q: Attachment towards the various objects we see in the world.
B: If that attachment were your actual nature, it should have persisted in deep sleep also. Since it is not to be found in sleep, it is merely an accretion, and therefore unreal or illusory. The illusion can be shaken off by regaining as the primal consciousness, which is fully aware yet totally free from the concealing influence of thought. You are the same one as the one who was in sleep. In sleep there was happiness – absolute and unqualified. But the present state is a mixture of pleasure and pain. Why should this transition have come about? What is the change that has taken place to lead you from the happy state of sleep to the present state of misery? It is the rise of the mind. Mind is the cause of your misery. If mind be traced back to its source, only Joy – without rhyme or reason, without beginning or end – will be the sole remainder.

Q: But is not sleep a state of ignorance?
B: Is the present state then one of *jnana*?

Q: But there was no awareness in sleep.
B: What you mean to say is that the awareness that persisted in deep sleep was not one that you are able now to mentally recollect. The Self in deep sleep is the Self remaining by Itself, in the absence of mind. Now the mind is passing judgements over the state prevailing in deep sleep. How can the mind be competent to reach conclusions in relation to a state in which it did not exist? The state of deep sleep is beyond the mind. The Self prevailing in the state of deep sleep is the unqualified Self – in which mind does not make its appearance.

Q: Such Self is even in a cadaver.
B: The cadaver is at peace, because it has no afflictions, raises no doubts, and does not seek anything. But your mind is always trapping you in the torturous net of wants and desires. You are confined with so many questions now. But in deep sleep these questions did not torment you. Why? Did you not exist in deep sleep? You did. Why the was there no sense of imperfection or feeling of want when you were asleep? It is because the Self then remains uncontaminated by anything called mind. The pure Self is Absolute Awareness. It does not cognise any objects. The objects that appear in your consciousness now are the handiwork of *avidya-maya* [illusion caused by ignorance]. What you now understand to be waking consciousness in the present state is associated consciousness. It requires brain, body, mind, intellect, et cetera, to function. But in deep sleep consciousness persisted without these equipments, which, therefore, is your real state (or true nature) – associated absolute consciousness.

Q: But I am unable to recollect the absolute consciousness which was prevailing in my deep sleep.
B: I have just said that the state of deep sleep is beyond the mind. To become established in the thought-free consciousness effort is necessary. Every time the mind strays away from its essence of beingness, take it back to its source and merge it there – this is the practice.

18th November 1936

Q: Is it better to gain Realisation by doing service to the Guru, or by vichara*?*
B: As the mind goes on getting introverted pursuant to practise of *vichara*, an intuition will arise which will automatically direct you along the right path. It will keep you away from events and circumstances that would entice your mind away from the path of

introversion leading into the Self. It will keep on directing your attention inwards. This intuition is your Guru. It is said, *'Ishwara Gururatmaethi'* [God, Guru and Self are one]. So, *Ishwara*, the Guru and the substratum underlying the world are merely different facets of the same imperishable, unmanifest Absolute Self.

An arrogant elephant can be awakened from its dream only by a ferocious lion that appears in the same dream. The lion is merely part of the elephant's own dream, but it does cause the elephant to awaken from the dream, crushing its arrogance and bringing the creature to the point of complete surrender. Likewise does the Guru appear in the dream of *samsara* [cycle of birth and death dictated by karma], in order to pull you out of it. Up until the moment of Realisation, the Guru appears to be separate from you. Upon Realisation, He is found to be identical with your Self.

Q: Since the Self is shining always, what prevents me from being aware of it right this moment?

B: It is because of the relative knowledge arising from the ego, which allows scope for concepts and ideas to taint and blacken the mind. Believing in concepts, the mind loses its foothold over its own essence of beingness. 'I am this or that' is conceptual knowledge. 'I am that I am' is of the nature of absolute knowledge. Conceptual knowledge encompasses a subject and an object; whereas in the Shining of the Heart, there is nothing to know, but only to BE. Because we have strayed away so far from our real nature, it appears as though beingness is required to be attended with effort; when all distractions have finally been conquered, there will not remain anything apart from beingness for you to meander away to. That will be the culmination of your practice.

Q: What happens to the ego when the body dies?

B: The ego is nothing but the notion 'I'. In the subtle form it is only a mental concept; in the gross form, it encompasses the mind, the sensory perceptivities, the body and the individual's agglomeration of memories and other thought-forms. Ego is only an appearance –

a transitory, momentary appearance – in the Self. Its appearance we call birth. Its disappearance we call death. Conceptual knowledge is merely a component of mind and therefore illusory, because the mind, the framework in which such knowledge is gained, is an unreal phenomenon.

Q: Your teachings are elegant and beautiful; I find them awe-inspiring. Why don't you preach to the public at large?
B: What gave you the impression that I am not doing it? Silence is the most effective method of preaching.

Q: Exhaustion forces us into slumber, and after refreshing itself, the body wakes up yet again. Why cannot we remain in deep sleep for precisely as long as we like?
B: *Sushupti* [deep sleep] continues in the present state also. Consciously Realising *sushupti* is *jagrat-sushupti* [waking deep sleep] or *Samadhi*. To be plunged in *Samadhi* is to keep the mind idle or asleep in the Beingness of the Self – effortlessly and volitionlessly so. The ordinary man cannot indefinitely remain in this state because his *vasanas* would force him out of it. By constantly maintaining our *lakhshya* [aim, perception] on the source of the ego, which is nothing but the Shining of the Heart, the ego is dissolved in the Heart like a doll made of salt thrown into the ocean. The ego sustains itself by identifying with an object simultaneously with its arising – it cannot remain in the absence of association with objects. This tendency of association is the same as the ignorance that you are trying to eliminate. When the idea of the world being an objectively real entity is destroyed from the mind, the mind's objectifying tendency dies; the result is that it merges into its source.

The fact of your identity being the same as pure beingness is revealed to you in those infinitesimal moments when the ego is out of contact with thoughts and objects. The rise of the ego is the appearance of everything; the subsidence (or quiescence) of the ego is the disappearance of everything. The present state is not different from *sushupti*. In *sushupti*, there is simple nescience (ignorance);

whereas in *jagrat/swapna* [awake/dream], the nescience is diversified into multiplicity, since objects and their perceiver arise simultaneously. In the Fullness of Realisation, the mind is bathed in perfect light, whereas in *sushupti*, it is bathed in perfect darkness. Objects can appear neither in perfect darkness nor in perfect light.

Q: What is the test by which I can discover for myself whether I am competent to Realise the Self in my current lifetime?
B: Complete absence of attachment – or in other words, complete renunciation – is the index of fitness. It is necessary to sacrifice everything for Truth, and *jnana* is for those alone who are able to do so.

19th November 1936

This morning, a visitor from Guntur went on complaining to the Master that although he was putting in his best efforts to concentrate his mind on the quest and gain Realisation, the distractions preventing him from doing so were proving to be too strong, since God seemed to be unwilling to extend any mercy towards him.

B: How can we find fault with God for our shortcomings? Do you now recall the old saying, that if you take one step towards God, he takes nine steps towards you?

Bhagavan then asked Mr TKS to read out aloud in the Hall Sri Manikkavacakar's *Neethal Vinnappam*. The same was translated verse-by-verse for the benefit of the visitor, who seemed unfamiliar with Tamil. Merely moments into the recitation, Bhagavan's eyes, I observed, had become moist with emotion:

> I am a wretched person, but owing to your boundless compassion, you have made me yours.

Free me from my agonies and do not abandon me. I am exhausted. Please take care of me.

The seductive glances of women with red mouths and mature breasts that collide with each other torment me without interruption. I have not done you any good deed, and I am a thorough scoundrel. Even so, you have been gracious enough to make me yours. I can only wonder why.

My senses are continually drawn towards the attractive eyes of pretty women, as though I were a hapless sapling sprouting on the edge of a river, swept away in the fury of its overflow. Oh! You who shares a body with his wife! Nourish me and do not abandon me!

You extended your compassion to me, but I drifted away from you, wishing to enjoy the sensuous pleasures available in this world that is overflowing with sultry temptations. Oh! Lord with hair decorated by the moon! Rescue me from my troubles and do not abandon me.

Oh! Lord whose hair is decorated with fresh flowers that bees wish to swarm around always! Like the firefly that wishes to be roasted in fire, I have been wanting to fall into the tight embrace of women whose mouths produce sweet words. Even when you offered me your nectar, I refused to…

December 1936
Unpublished Notebook D
Tendencies of the Mind

Q: Throbbing 'I'-'I' scintillating within me. This is an intensely peaceful state and I wish I could remain in it forever. Alas – unfortunately, the experience lasts for only a few seconds before fading away. Can I please know the reason from Bhagavan?

B: It means that the tendencies which cause extroversion are still dormant within the mind. It is necessary to go on, unabatedly practising keeping the mind submerged in the Heart until all of the latent tendencies are wiped out without trace.

Q: How shall we kill the mind?

B: Is it the mind that wants to kill the mind? The mind cannot kill the mind. Anything that you endeavour to 'do' with the mind will only reinforce and perpetuate the notion of mind. Rather than pointlessly wondering, "How shall I eradicate the mind?", go on seeking the mind. Incessant search for what mind is results in its disappearance.

The thing to do is to completely ignore the objects that appear by the reflected light of the mind, and instead seek the source of the mind's illumination. If the source of the mind is continuously sought for, it begins to subside.

The point of *vichara* [Self-enquiry] is to continuously hold on to the subject. No matter what the experiences might be that present themselves, pay no attention and continue to remain focused on the subject. The subject is your notion of 'I'. Go on examining this notion until it disappears.

Q: Self-doubts haunt and taunt me often. I wonder if I shall ultimately succeed in the quest for Realisation, piteous weakling that I am. I catch myself in this gloomy train of thought often and become despondent. What

does Bhagavan advise that I do?
B: Doubts might keep on coming but nobody can deny the Existence of the doubter. Hold on firmly to the doubter and doubts will cease to cause affliction.

Q: Will repeating 'I am Brahman*' mentally help in bringing about a state of mind that is conducive for Realisation?*
B: No. On the other hand, it strengthens your erroneous impression that there is an 'I' who styles himself as *'Brahman'*. That which is truly *Brahman* does not even say 'I'. Mental bubbles are not competent to discover *Brahman.* It can be done only by overcoming the illusion of mind.

Mind carries with it the seed of its own destruction. The extroverted or thinking mind presents itself as the world, whereas the whole introverted mind is absorbed into the Heart. The tyrannical grip of the ego can be broken only through persistent effort over a prolonged period of time.

Q: Please explain to us the purpose of manifestation. We are aware that according to the Vedantic *standpoint, the entity known as* Brahman *or* Purusha *[Self] remained as Unity. Thereafter, he got contaminated with unknowingness, giving rise to diversity in the form of the objective world that we see around us. But how and why did this stain of diversity come to take place?*
B: This is not a correct understanding. *Brahman* knows no ignorance. Ignorance is for the one who experiences a sensation that he is bound by ignorance. The one complaining of ignorance is the only ignorance troubling him and there can be no other. You are yourself the ignorance that you are investigating. Ignorance and ego are one and the same thing.

Q: I crave for the experience of Nirvikalpa Samadhi *[the highest ecstasy], but am unable to obtain it, although I am pursuing* vichara *with painstaking detailed care. Please illuminate me. I wish to find out where I am going wrong.*

B: It is enough for the mind to become resolved into its source. You have evidently understood *Samadhi* to mean the same as absence of body consciousness. It need not be so. *Samadhi* refers to that state in which mind abides as one and identical with the Beingness of the Self. In sleep and when fainted, there is no body consciousness. Is sleep, or when fainted, the same as *Samadhi*? The point of *abhyasa* [practice] is not to shake off or eliminate body-consciousness, but to trace the thought 'I' back to its source and leave it there to be destroyed.

Destruction of the false entity known as 'I' is the objective underlying all our effort. If, for some time, the body becomes inert like a stone and remains without breathing, how will that bring about your Deliverance? Liberation is only in that state in which 'I' is unequivocally destroyed.

Q: In his essay Who am I? *I find the following fascinating utterances from Bhagavan:* **"Oruvan nirandhara swaroopa smaranaiyai kaipattruvanayin, adhu ondre podhum."** *[If one follows permanent essence contemplation continuously, that only is enough.]*
And **"Sadhakalamum manadhai Atmavil vaitthiruppadharkkudhan Atmavicharam endru peya."** *[Always keeping the mind in* atma *is called* atmavichara.*]*

What exactly is Bhagavan implying in making these statements? And how do we follow these instructions? What do the terms 'feeling-recollection of one's true form' and 'keeping the mind in the Atman *[the Self]' actually mean?*

And how can we ascertain for ourselves whether we are following these instructions correctly?

B: Both the terms are referring to the requirement to keep the mind incessantly merged in its source. There are three distinct possibilities. The first is the disorderly mind, which takes pleasure in enjoying objects of sensory perception and intellectual conceptualisation. This is the extroverted state of mind that is commonly observed among people in the world.

The second is the introverted or still mind, about which you

are asking. Keeping the mind in the *Atman* or practising feeling-recollection of the Beingness of the Self is only this: that you go on seeing mind with mind. Instead of using mind towards thinking thoughts or analysing objects (rendered available for perception through sensory input), use mind to search precisely that same mind. *Vichara* is nothing but seeing mind with mind.

The third is the *jnani's* state of destroyed mind. The third cannot be brought about through our effort. The state of a still mind, where the mind abides as one and identical with the Beingness of the Self, if persistently and unintermittently inherent, automatically results in the Realisation of *jnana*, provided one has surrendered without reserve.

Thus, so long as there remains the one who desires *jnana*, *jnana* cannot be had. You asked how you can find out whether you are correctly following my instructions on *vichara*. When the entirety of mind stands reduced into the quest for the source of the mind – or when the mind is no longer interested in seeking anything other than itself – the 'I' becomes transformed into 'I'-'I'.

In *Vedantic* parlance, the 'I'-'I' is known as *Aham Sphurana* or *spandabhraja* [absorption in divine bliss] This is the state preceding the *sahajastithi* of the *jnani*. For it to blossom into *jnana*, complete destruction of the *vasanas* [tendencies of the mind] is necessary. If this *Sphurana* [pulsation] has been awakened in you, then you are correctly practising *vichara*. However, owing to the perverse, influence of the *vasanas*, the *Sphurana* is extinguished in due course and the old habits extroverting the mind assume command once again. If the *Sphurana* is to become permanent, practise is necessary.

As and when you find the mind slipping away from 'I'-'I', pull it back and fix it on the quest of *vichara* again. When the *Sphurana* has become the effort-free, natural state of mind, that will be the crown of your achievement. Another aspect required to be taken into consideration is the extent up to which the world has receded from view, so to speak. So long as there remains in the mind the erroneous impression that the world is an entity that is objectively

real in itself, so long will it be impossible for *jnana* to dawn.

The world is the means or defense or point-of-anchor, using which it becomes possible for the mind to keep away from plunging into its source. Once the mind ceases to pay the world any attention, its eventual descent into the Heart would be a natural consequence. What is the world, after all? *Lokyate iti lokah* ["the world is nothing but that which is perceived"].

Consider the position of your Self in comparison to the world that is seen. The world requires perception in order for its apparent Existence to be made clear to you. There cannot be a world in the absence of a 'You' to perceive it. The world becomes evident to you as a result of a succession of causative factors – there has to be physical light to illuminate objects, that light from the source has to make its way toward the object and then be reflected in the direction of your eyes, your eyes need to take in the light and finally your brain recognises the object.

It is through this process that the world and the objects contained in it announce their Existence to you. But Self-knowledge is not like this: it is direct and requires no intermediary (such as physical eyesight) for its Existence to be made evident to you. Your feeling of being in Existence is the first and last hint for the Existence of the Absolute Self. Do you exist or not?

Q: Yes

B: How do you know? Do you confirm your Existence by going and standing in front of a mirror? Do you require a mirror to establish the fact that you have got eyes? Is not the fact of your vision the proof?

Similarly, your own beingness is proof or persuasive evidence that there is a 'You' which is neither physical nor dependent on anything physical for its sustenance, and this 'You' is the real 'You'. The idea of physicality is mere mental fiction.

All physical matter is made of nothing but mental ideas. If the ideas are abandoned, only Spirit will be the remainder, and that is the Self.

Q: In the same essay, Bhagavan also uses the analogy of an encirclement being laid on a fort. Bhagavan says that as and when the occupants of the fort try to leave, they should be put to death. However, I fail to comprehend how this analogy could be applicable to vichara.

When a distraction in the form of a thought arises, I block the thought with the act of investigating Who am I? But after merely a few minutes, I find the same thought again repeating inside of my mind. But in Bhagavan's example, the army waiting outside the fort would put to death every single person endeavouring to venture outside, and obviously a dead person cannot come back to life.

But in my practice of vichara, *the thoughts do come back even after having been exposed to the axe of* vichara *again and again. So – where am I going wrong in my* vichara*? Why do the thoughts fail to die a definitive death despite having been attacked vociferously by my practice of* vichara*?*

B: The example of soldiers waiting outside a fort, slaying all those who attempt to venture outside, is given in the context of destruction of *vasanas*.

Thoughts do present themselves repetitively whilst the corresponding underlying *vasanas* are still remaining. However, when a *vasana* conclusively dies, it cannot return.

Q: Please explain the difference between thoughts and vasanas. *Until now I was under the impression of* 'vasana' *being the Sanskrit word for 'thought'. It would seem that I have been mistaken.*

B: No, they are not the same. Thoughts are the perceptible manifestations of *vasanas*, and *vasanas* are the underlying inclinations of mind which impel or cause thoughts to arise.

***Vasanas* invariably give rise to thoughts, but thoughts may occur even in the absence of *vasanas*, as happens in the case of the *jnani*. You cannot directly destroy the *vasanas* – it can be done only by tackling thought. As and when thoughts present themselves, return them to the pre-existent 'I'-'I' current. If you exist in this current spontaneously and incessantly, the current will, of its own accord, destroy the *vasanas* and give Liberation.**

But Liberation cannot be had so long as the desire for

Liberation lies latent within the mind. Conquest of desire and weakening of the 'I'-thought happen side-by-side as a result of earnest *sadhana*. As the *sadhaka* introverts his mind more and more, the extent of attention devoted to worldly affairs goes on getting reduced – until the day dawns when there is nothing left in the world that can excite his attention anymore. This is when the mind begins to spontaneously abide in the Heart.

When *vichara* is done with the hidden motive of Realisation in mind, can a successful outcome take place? *Vichara* should be done because of the fascination with 'I' – the curiosity to discover 'I', that is, *Atmajigyasa* [the desire of knowing the Self]. You say 'I am'. Find out 'who is'.

Q: How long is effort needed on the path?
B: So long as there is a 'you' that remains, being capable of making it! There is that state which is beyond our effort or effortlessness. Until that state is Realised, effort is necessary.

Q: I am frequently mentally anguished as a result of paying attention to the goings on of the world. What is the remedy for it?
B: If you go on paying attention to the ego and its misdirections, you will be forced to go the way of your thoughts and find yourself in an entanglement. It is not necessary to think of the concerns raised by the ego as being valid or legitimate. Take no notice of the rowdy ego and its mischievous activities but see only the light which illumines the ego. Decreasing the mind by an effort of the will is never going to make the mind subside.

To bring the mind to surrender, it is necessary to invoke the Higher Power that lies latent behind (or underneath) the mind. This power – call it *Kundalini* [divine energy], *Atmashakti* [power of the Self] or what you will – can be invoked only by plunging the mind (headlong) into the source from which it has arisen, and keeping it merged there until it disappears. One's will, being part and parcel of the mind, is not competent to bring about the mind's destruction. Having surrendered, you are being guided by a Higher Power. Be led

by the same and it will show you the way.

Q: How do I know if I am competent to take up vichara*?*
B: If you feel drawn towards it and if you find that it attracts you, you may take it up. It is not necessary to obtain any proof of competency prior to commencing the quest. Provided it is pursued with complete earnestness, the quest, of its own accord, will draw you deeper and deeper into itself.

Transcend the false idea of the ego's apparent Existence by means of continuously and incessantly pursuing the search for its place to stand, or identity; this search is the essence of the investigation Who am I?

Q: How to get Grace?
B: This question is prompted only by Grace. The desire for Grace is the result of Grace that is already working upon you. Grace is not to be freshly obtained; Grace is the Self. Introversion, perseverance in keeping the mind retained in the Heart, and finally Realisation are all a result of Grace only.

This doubt of whether one is eligible for Grace has arisen because of the expectation to get something external to one Self. Do you expect that Grace is going to drop down on you in a decorated chariot descending from the sky? If you remember to keep the mind retained in the Heart all the time, can there be a surer sign that Grace holds you steadfastly in His relentless grip?

Why the needless anxiety for Grace, or, indeed, for anything at all? In deep sleep did you fret over this want or that? Were you wanting anything in deep sleep?

Q: In sleep the individual soul 'I' was united with the Paramatman *[supreme Self]. On waking the 'I' re-enters the body, because of* prarabdha *[the portion of the* karma *of previous lives that is responsible for the present life].*
B: Oh! Is that so? And where is that *Paramatman* now?

Q: I cannot really say.

B: The *Paramatman* is where you are. In the absence of mind, you are THAT always. Even when mind is active, it is so only in the *vasthu* [substratum] of the Self. Sunder the curtain of thought once and for all and remain peacefully absorbed in the Self. Then there will be no need to devote thought to the fate of the soul in deep sleep and other such things.

16th December 1936

Q: Is effort involved in abiding as the Self?
B: Until the *granthi* [knot between the sentient and the insentient] is ready to be cut asunder, having become denuded of *vasanas*, effort is needed in one form or the other. In the Self itself there is no effort: it is a state of effortless, ever-vigilant *shanti*.

When the stage is reached in your *sadhana* when the mind effortlessly abides as one and identical with the Beingness of the Self, the mind sinks into the Heart and abides there. This is when it can be said that the *sadhaka* is ripe for *jnana*.

Q: How shall I cultivate this effortless self-awareness?
B: By incessant practice. Effortless thoughtlessness while remaining aware is the desired state, and it is the gateway to Realisation.

Q: I find Bhagavan's line of reasoning too abstract. Please give me a practical course of action to follow, from which I can benefit by putting into practice.
B: Yes, theoretical explanations are not required. The Beingness of the Self is always directly experienced by everyone. Only probe yourself and reach its source without fail. You say 'I am'. That means Existence. Remain merged in that beingness.

Sri Gajapathi Aiyer

Narrator and Diarist

Letters to Bhagavan

Sri Gajapathi Leaving the Ashram

Sri Gajapathi Aiyyer
Narrator and Diarist

Whilst compiling this manuscript I can see I have largely ignored the opportunity to question Bhagavan. He watches others raise questions and doubts. He records the conversations. Why does he not himself feel tempted to ask any question of the Sage, except for a handful of occasions? Does he assume his own omniscience? Or perhaps he imagines that Bhagavan might not be able to answer his queries? It is nothing of the kind, gentle reader. Put your anxieties at rest, please.

Many who come to the ashram are raised on a background of *Vedanta*. They are able to tackle Bhagavan on various theories and hypotheses that they have come across in books. I have no such background.

One of my maternal uncles was, at the time I was a teenager, district library superintendent. I could pick up whatever book I liked, provided I either renewed it or returned it on time, and no money need be expended from my pocket.

Being somewhat of an introverted character in those days, I would thus fill all my spare time – of which I had a lot – in reading everything from Geoffrey Chaucer to Robert Louis Stevenson. My background therefore was in English Literature so I knew nothing pertaining to the various doctrines relating to theories of creation, et cetera. My appetite for library books chiefly revolved around fiction.

The Pilgrim's Progress by John Bunyan and *Ramakrishna, the Man-Gods, A study of Mysticism and Action in Living India* by Romain Rolland. The first I chanced upon whilst at school, and the second, the year before college. Whilst reading these two books I would weep without knowing the reason; some strange yearning took possession of my soul and electrified the entirety of my whole. I wanted to...fall in love.

Not with woman or man, for that would be fleeting, transient business. I wanted to replicate what Ramakrishna had done with Bhavatharini – I wanted my love to be accepted by the one who sustained this cosmos by Her will. For then alone would I have the solace of knowing my Love to be Immortal. There is not the least sexual tinge to this Love; this clarification becomes necessary because some minds are quick to interpret all love as being of an amorous nature.

Neither is this Love what one harbours toward family members, friends, and pet animals; that is boring attachment amounting in some cases to, at the most, affection of a long-standing nature. This Love has passion in it. One feels one's chest is going to explode with it any time. One feels like singing and dancing with the Joy of it. Yet what precisely it is – about that one is clueless. The mystery of the matter adds to the ardour of the Love.

Till 5th July 1936 I never succeeded in discovering the object of this Love. On that day when my Lovely Master, who is Love Itself, locked his eyes with mine in a tight embrace that lasted for one moment in Eternity but from which there could really be no disentanglement or disaffiliation, I discovered my Love's Love.

I discovered Bhagavan. Had I read metaphysics I could ask him questions about how the world had come to be; but I had read, by the way, only to kindle this magical Love, which had nothing to ask, expect or anticipate.

Sadhana may be a chore – I have not attempted it. I would not know – but this Enchantress called Love. She is a Divine Privilege. She does not ask your concentration. She gracefully and effortlessly absorbs it into Herself. What is left? Only She-Love. Since she had never any doubts to ask, I never really had anything to say to Bhagavan at all, because, critically, I recognised Her to be the Internal Bhagavan shining from within.

The outer Bhagavan was the banner for the Love that my Heart resonated with. And he proved by his perpetual, rock-like presence that the Love was not some delusional madness, that it was corroborated by physical Reality, by a legitimate source for its sweet fountain-spring of ambrosial nectar. Although being Divine it must needs transcend all physicality.

Therefore, it was indispensable that he should remain outside, because my Love would otherwise become a vain dream once again, with no possible legitimacy for its sustenance or survival. He was there – that was enough!

Letters to Bhagavan

During the Master's lifetime, the practice existed in the ashram for devotees to send in letters asking for all manners and varieties of things. Most begged for Bhagavan's blessings in their endeavours, and specifically would mention that the sheet carrying the reply be sanctified by his hallowed touch.

Many wrote wanting their prayers or wishes to be fulfilled. Others solicited clarification on doctrinal points. Yet other epistles carried doubts raised regarding practice. Sri Bhagavan was not in the habit of answering letters. An intelligent *Brahmin* attached to the ashram was in the habit of attending to the last two varieties of correspondence. Invariably, most letters written in European languages would fall into his hands to be tackled appropriately. He would write and read out his replies to the Master.

When I was maintaining these diaries, I would write them down after a natural, syndicated fashion. Thus, in this manuscript, you behold amalgamated and mingled the content of these letters together with questions asked directly in the Hall. This need not be understood as causing any damage in the authenticity of the content of these diaries. While it is true that the replies were drafted by another, the Master listened to them with great keenness, and if he wanted any modifications, deletions, or additions to be made, he indicated so at once.

He did not mind delivering a rap on the knuckles to the man should Bhagavan in the slightest feel that there was any correction or other alteration required to be made. So, in substance, the answers given in the letters are also His words. Thus, at the time of writing these diaries it never occurred to me to create a split on the basis of what would merely be a theoretical consideration exclusively. Now, whilst compiling this work, it occurs to me suddenly that certain readers might be anxious for such a separation to be available from the text.

Generally, a sizeable portion of long, lecture-like pronouncements found here are from the *Brahmin* who was at the time in charge of the 'doctrinal and foreign correspondence departments' of the ashram. In truth, I am taking so much trouble to make this separation discernible, only to satisfy a chance whim of any Bhagavan devotee who might happen to be able to tell. Actually, it is all thoroughly unnecessary, as far as my opinion goes. Not a single letter could leave the ashram without the Master's express imprimatur; and the Master was not the sort to show neglect in any matter.

The *Brahmin* was quite an educated fellow and had a brilliant insight into Bhagavan's teachings, and frequently acted as his interpreter with Caucasian visitors. Above all, he seems to have been personally selected by the Master himself for the correspondence management task in the doing of which he engaged himself; that ought to say the final word upon the matter.

Sri Gajapathi Leaving Ramana Ashram

At the end of 1936 my family had decided on Vaidehi to be my wife; she was a close relative and known to me. A letter arrived at the ashram addressed to me and I was informed of their decision. My *aththai* [paternal aunt] had decided that if I were not married at the end of my stay at Ramana Ashram, I would become a *sannyasi* [an ascetic], which idea was abhorrent to her. So, she had written to me saying that in February 1937, I was to get married. It was not a question of asking my opinion; they had already finalised it and I was merely to fall in line.

Then Bhagavan folded it and handed it back, extending it towards me, the piece of paper held out between his right index and middle fingers, saying: **"Keep it."** I took it back and anxiously asked, "Should I run away from home to avoid it?"

The Master did not make a response, but somebody in the Hall

had this to say to me: *"When the question of renunciation was being discussed, you yourself, sitting in this very hall, once said that only cowards run away, and that one must, according to Bhagavan's teachings, throw the weight of one's burdens on the Higher Power and carry on with the life of outward action."* Somebody else now subtly made the observation the Master himself had run away from home at the age of sixteen.
B: I did not think, 'I am running away.' That is the difference.

G: So, if I do not think 'I am running away,' I can run away?
B: One who does not think, 'If I do not think, can I do as I please?' One who does not think has ceased to struggle against the apparent will of the Higher Power and has given up his cares and concerns for good, having long ago stepped aside to make way for the intellect to fall into the dictatorship of the numinous intuition that arises in those who have surrendered without reserve.

The actions of the intellect and body of the *jiva* [individual soul] that has unreservedly surrendered itself to the Almighty are guided by him; the mind that is lost as a result of such surrender does not remain to concern itself as to their repercussions or moral propriety. He (the *jiva* who has genuinely surrendered himself) is not responsible for what goes on. Some power takes hold of his body and makes him do things. He is not involved.

G: If I surrender to the Higher Power, can I avoid this impending marriage?
B: One who has surrendered with an ulterior motive has not surrendered at all. Is it possible to deceive God?

G: If I marry, I may not have the mental strength to refrain from sexual activities and they might become unavoidable for that reason. Therefore, Self-realisation will become impossible.
B: That is your opinion.

G: So, running away from home is no good?
B: You may take it from me, that it will make your situation much worse.

G: What is the recourse left for me then?
B: *Ananya sharanagati* [full surrender].

G: If, after that sharanagati, *I get married, entangled in the horrific woes of* samsara *and therefore fail to Realise the Self?*
B: No one remains after *sharanagati* to complain "I have not Realised the Self," or ask, "Even after *sharanagati*, why am I yet to Realise?" or to raise any other doubt or complaint. It is a state of perfect *mounatapas* [silence]. First learn what *sharanagati* is. It is to merge in the source of the ego.

G: So, it seems that I am to surrender once and for all, and not care about what happens afterwards?
B: Yes. Yes, that is it.

Therefore, I had to get married and there was nothing I could do about it. I initially thought why I had to go through such Hell, while others in the ashram were happily settled there forever at Bhagavan's feet.

Then I decided Bhagavan's will was in operation, that whatever happened, happened with his knowledge only, and therefore there was no reason to feel upset. Obedience to his will is my only priority now – my own personal salvation or deliverance from the wheel of births and deaths does not count anymore.

This conviction is the fruit of my intense spiritual training under his watchful eye; the only *sadhana* was Love, and that meant the same as surrender – disappearance of the faculty of personal will, and meek, unquestioning obedience to the Master's will or God's will.

Glossary

Abhyasa
Practice
Adhishtana Swarupa
Substratum of truth
Advaita
Not two, non-duality
Advaita Vedanta
Philosophy of non-duality
Aghori
A group spending time in cremation grounds
Agni-theertham
Holy water place
Aham
I am, Self
Aham Brahmasmi
I am Brahman (I am consciousness)
Aham Spuhrana
'I'-pulsation
Ahamvritti
'I'-thought, the most basic assumption of an 'I'
Ahimsa
Non-violence
Ajata-Advaita
Non-created, unborn; a particular philosophy of non-duality
Ajnana
Ignorance of the nature of reality
Akhandakaravritti
Unbroken experience
Akritopasaka
One who does not have a one-pointed mind
Ananda
Joy, bliss, nature of Brahman-Atman
Anatman
Non-Self
Anna
Old Indian coin
Arul-poerattum
Struggle for Grace
Arunachala
Holy mountain where Sri Ramana Maharshi lived
Asafoetida
Indian spice
Ashtanga
The eight limbs of yoga
Aththai
Paternal aunt
Atma/Atman
The eternal, non-personal Self
Atmajignasa
To enquire about the Absolute Truth
Atmanishtai
True nature
Atmavichara
Self-enquiry
Avarana
Covering, veil of ignorance
Avidya-maya
Illusion caused by ignorance

Bakasanam
A type of yoga posture
Bhakta
A devotee of God
Bhakti
Unselfish love for God, devotion

Brahma
The creator God in Hinduism
Brahman
The eternal Reality, the Absolute Existence
Brahmajnana
Knowledge (realisation) of Brahman
Brahmaloka
Abode of god Brahma and his consort Sarasvati
Brahmin
The priestly, highest case in Hinduism
Buddhi
The subtle intellect, power of discrimination

Chaturyugas
A full time cycle of Hindu cosmology (4,320,000 years)
Chettiar
A Tamil trading caste in South India
Chidakasha
Pure space of consciousness
Chittaikagratha
One-pointedness of mind
Chittam
Mind, memory
Chittavritti
Fluctuations of the mind, thoughts that clutter the mind

Dakshinamurti
Form of Shiva as the supreme teacher
Daridranarayanan
In service to the poor
Darshan
Auspicious sight of a deity or saint
Dehatmabuddhi
I-am-the-body idea
Devas
Divine beings
Drishti-srishti-vada
Creation through perception

Ekatva
Unity
Endaro Mahanubhavala
"Lots of great souls", popular Carnatic song in Telugu
Ezhaikkolam
Traditional decorative art that is drawn by using rice flour

Gopis
Cow-herd girls, devotees of Krishna, bhaktas
Granthi
Knot between the sentient and the insentient
Granthinasam
Destruction of the knot
Gunas
Qualities, attributes
Guru
Teacher

Hanuman
Monkey god, devotee of Ram

Hanuman Chalisa
Hindu devotional hymn in praise of Hanuman
Hathayoga
System of physical yoga techniques
Hridayagranthi
Knot of the heart
Hridaya
Heart, the spiritual center in the body
Hridayapundarikam
Heart – lotus

Idam
Location or position
Indra
The king of heaven and gods in Hinduism
Ishwara
The supreme Being
Ishwara Gururatmaethi
"God, Guru and Self are one"
Irukkai
Source from which thinking emerges, beingness

Jagrat
Waking state (not being asleep)
Jagrat-pramata
Knower of the world, subjective perceiver
Jagrat-sushupti
Experiencing the peacefullness of deep sleep in the waking state
Jagrat-swapna
The mind indulging in fancies, daydreaming
Jamun
Indian black plum
Japam
Meditative repetition of a mantra
Jiva
The indvidual soul
Jivanmukta
Liberated soul, released while living
Jnana
Spiritual knowledge
Jnanaguru
Teacher of true knowledge
Jnanasadhaka
A true spiritual seeker
Jnanasiddha
The one who has accomplished true knowledge (and supernatural powers)
Jnani
The Self-realised sage, one who has perfect knowledge

Kaivalya Navaneetham
Advaita classic in Tamil
Kamandalam
Oblong water pot
Kartritvabuddhi
I-am-the-doer idea, sense of doership
Kevala
Whole, complete, pure

Kevala kumbhaka
Stopping the mind by means of breath retention
Kevala Nirvikalpa Samadhi
Mind temporarily merged in the Supreme Self
Khadarjibba
Indian cotton shirt
Koupeenam
Loin cloth
Kozhakattai
South Indian sweet dumplings
Krishna
Supreme God, eighth avatar of Vishnu
Kritopasaka
One who does have a one-pointed mind
Kuladheivam
Family or village god
Kundalini
Divine Energy located at the base of the spine

Lakh
A hundred thousand
Lakshya
Aim, destination
Loka
Realm in Hindu cosmology
Lokyate iti lokah
"The world is nothing but that which is perceived"

Mahavakyas
The great sayings of the Upanishads
Mahaviksheenaka
The great destroyer
Mahat
Pure subjective awareness
Manana
Stabilised by reflection
Mandapam
A hall within a temple
Manolayam
A state where mind structures are hazily projected
Manonivritti
Mind turned inwards
Mantra-diksha
Mantra initiation
Margas
Paths
Matrubutheshwara
Shrine of Bhagavan's mother
Maya
Illusion, power which manifests the world
Meipporulum prakrirtiyum
Absolute truth and primordial nature
Milagu kootu
South Indian stew
Mouna tapas
Silence, effort to Self-realisation
Mrutyunjaya
Form of Shiva
Mudaliar
A south Indian caste
Mukti
Liberation, freedom from rebirths

Mumukshu
Seeker of liberation

Nan Yar
Who am I?
Naivaedya
Ritual food offering
Nidhidhyasana
Living the truth
Nidra
Sleep
Nirgunopasana
Meditation on the formless Brahman
Nirvikalpa
Without thoughts
Nirvikalpa Samadhi
State of being temporarily absorbed in the Absolute
Nivritti
Mind turned inwards, introverted mind

Pambaram
Spinning top
Panchamabandham
Lowest human class
Pandit
Learned man
Parabrahman
The supreme Self, supreme Brahman
Paramatma
The Absolute Atman, supreme Self
Paripakvi
Fully ripe person
Peerkangkai
Ridge gourd
Periyapuranam
Tamil epic poem
Poorvasamskaras
Old latent mind tendencies, habits
Pooshinikkai-thaan
Pumpkin dish
Prakriti
Principle of matter
Pramata
The subjective knower, knowledge through the mind
Pranava
Cosmic sound
Prarabdha
Past karma that effects our life now, destiny
Prasadam
Sacred food offered to a deity
Puja
Indian worship ritual
Purusha
Principle of pure consciousness

Ragam
Melodic mode in Indian classical music
Rajas
One of the three gunas: passion, activity

Rajayoga
Royal path, system of yoga as taught by Patanjali
Rama
Hindu God and hero of the epic Ramayana, an avatar of Vishnu

Sadhaka
One who engages in spiritual practice
Sadhaka's vairagya
A spiritual practitioner's detachment
Sadhana
Spiritual practice
Sadhsishya
True disciple
Sadhu
One who has renounced worldly life
Sadhvasthu
True substratum
Sahaja
The natural state of being
Sahajajnani
Liberated sage, Self-realised being
Sahajajnanastithi
Established or dwelling in Brahman
Sahajastithi
Natural state
Sahaja Nirvikalpa Samadhi
The mind is dead, resolved into the Self
Sahaja Asamprajnatha Samadhi
Oneness with God
Sahasra avadhani
Excellent poet
Samadhi
Union with Reality
Samsara
Cycle of birth and death caused by karma
Samskaras
Mental impressions, psychological imprints
Sankalpa
Personal will, desire
Sannyasi
Life of renunciation, an ascetic
Sarvadhikari
Ashram manager
Sarvagnar
One who knows everything
Sashwatamanonivritti
Mind always turned inwards
Sat
Truth, absolute existence
Satguru
True Guru
Satsang / Satsangam
Association with truth, spiritual company
Sattva
Clear, light, pure
Savikalpa Samadhi
Mind is forced by effort to hold on to pure being
Shakti
Primordial energy

Shalagramam
Special black stone,
fossil ammonite stones
Shankara
Famous scholar and teacher of Advaita Vedanta (8th Century)
Shankaracharya
Honorary title for Shankara
Shankha bhasma
Ayurvedic medicine,
a gold-based herbal mixture
Shanti
Peace
Sharanagati
Surrender
Shastras
Sacred scriptures, rules
Shiva
One of the supreme Gods in Hinduism (the cosmic destroyer)
Shruti / Sruti
Sacred books
Siddhapurusha
Perfected being,
often supernatural powers
Siddhi
Supernatural power, perfection
Spandabhraja
Absorption in divine bliss
Spandabhraja Samadhi
Absorption in bliss,
union with reality
Sphurana
Pulsation
Sravana
Knowledge from the teacher
Sravana-manana-nidhidhyasana
Hearing-reflecting upon-natural knowing (integration) of the teachings
Summayirutthal (summa iru)
Effortless Consciousness,
natrually being still
Sushupti
Dreamless sleep, deep sleep
Svabhava
Essence, inherent existence
Swami
A Hindu ascetic, a spiritual teacher (used as a title)
Swapna
State of dreaming
Swapnasakshatkara
Falsely imagining oneself to be Self-realised
Swaroopa
Essence, true nature
Swarupa-dhyanatthai vidappidiyai
Relentlessly meditating on the real form

Tabula rasa
Latin: Clean slate
Tamas
Darkness, ignorance
Tamasic
Dark, inertia
Tapas
Austerity, effort to achieve Self-realisation

Tapasvin
One who performs Tapas
Tejas
Radiancy, illumination, effulgence
Thannunarvu
Self-consciousness
Thirupparangundram Murugar Kovil
Colourful temple outside Madurai
Thiruneeru
Sacred ash made of burnt wood and burnt cow dung
Thoel and kudal
Skin and intestines
Thuvaiyyal
South Indian chutney
Trupthi
Satiatedness

Upadesham
Teaching, instruction
Upadhis
Limitation
Upanishads
Sacred scriptures in Hinduism, last part of the Vedas

Vaendudhal
Penance
Vaetti
Cloth wrap for the lower body
Vairagya
Detachment, renunciation
Vasanas
Habits of the mind
Vasthu
Substratum
Vedas
The oldest and most important scriptures in Hinduism
Veda Parayanam
Ancient Vedic chanting, performed twice daily in ashram during Bhagavan's lifetime
Vichara
Self-enquiry
Vichara abhyasa / sadhana
Self-enquiry practice
Vicharamarga
Path of Self-enquiry
Videhamukti
Liberation after death
Vinayakar Chaturthi
Hindu festival for the elephant God Ganesh
Vishayavasanas
Desire after the objects of sense
Vivegam
Prudence, cautiousness
Viveka
Discernment or discrimination
Vritti
Structures of the mind, mental habits
Vrittijnanam
Temporarily merged in the absolute, but the mind's identity still kept unharmed
Yoganidra
Yogic or psychic sleep
Yoganiththirai
Yogic trance

Ramana Book Selection

A Choice of Titles on Sri Bhagavan

Be As You Are – The Teachings of Sri Ramana Maharshi
edited by David Godman, Penguin Books, Tiruvannamalai, 1985

Day by Day with Bhagavan
from the Diary of A. Devaraja Mudaliar, Sri Ramanasramam,Tiruvannamalai, 2002

A Search in Secret India
Paul Brunton, Srishti Publishers and Distributors, New Delhi, 1934

Guru Ramana
S.S. Cohen, Sri Ramanasramam Tiruvannamalai, 1974 edition

The Collected Works of Ramana Maharshi
Sri Ramanasramam,Tiruvannamalai, 6th revised edition, 1996

Sad Darshana Bhashya
translated and compiled by Kapali Sastri, Sri Ramanasramam,Tiruvannamalai, 9th Edition 2006

The Last Days and Maha Nirvana of Bhagavan Sri Ramana
Viswanatha Swami,Arthur Osborne and T.N. Krishnaswamy, Sri Ramanasrama, Tiruvannamalai, 1997

Self-Inquiry (Vicharasangraham) of Sri Ramana Maharshi
translated by Dr T.M.P. Mahadevan, Sri Ramanasramam,Tiruvannamalai, 1994

Talks with Sri Ramana Maharshi
compiled by Sri Munagala Venkataramiah, Sri Ramanasramam,Tiruvannamalai, 1st edition, 1955

A Sadhu's Reminiscences of Ramana Maharshi
By Major Alan Chadwick (Sadhu Arunachala), Sri Ramanasramam, Tiruvannamalai, 2013

Reminiscences of Kunju Swami
Kunjuswami,Translated by P. Ramasamy, Sri Ramanasramam Tiruvannamalai, 1st Edition 2017

Padamalai
Muruganar, edited and translated by David Godman, T.V. Venkatasubramanian and Robert Butler, Avadhuta Foundation, Boulder, 2004

Garland of Guru's Sayings (Guru Vachaka Kovai)
Muruganar, translated by Dr. T.V. Venkatasubramanian, Robert Butler, and David Godman, edited and annotated by David Godman, Avadhuta Foundation, Boulder, 2008

Arunachala Pilgrimage

Arunachala Mountain has been a powerful place of pilgrimage for two thousand years. It attracted the young Ramana after his Self-realisation. Later when Sri Bhagavan Ramana Maharshi became a famous teacher of Advaita Vedanta, an ashram was established around him at the foot of the mountain. It became a popular destination also for Western spiritual seekers and the trend has continued into the present.

Many people visit Ramana Ashram, where the presence and peace of Bhagavan remains omnipresent. It is possible to sit at Bhagavan's samadhi shrine and the shrine of his mother. Vedic chanting is still performed daily. The shrines of Major Chadwick, Annamalai Swami and cow Lakshmi can also be visited.

The editor of this book, John David, has been offering an annual spiritual retreat at the foothill of Arunachala in January yearly for more than twenty years. It is accommodated in a modern ashram with its own retreat kitchen. Satsang meetings, meditation and yoga take place on the ashram roof with a direct view of Arunachala.

www.johndavidsatsang.international/india